COMMUNICODING

COMMUNICODING

Marcia B. Cherney

AND

Susan A. Tynan

WITH

Ruth Duskin Feldman

DONALD I. FINE, INC.

NEW YORK

 Published in the United States of America
by Donald I. Fine, Inc. and in Canada by General Publishing Company Limited.

Library of Congress Cataloging-in-Publication Data

Cherney, Marcia.
Communicoding.

1. Interpersonal communication. 2. Interpersonal
communication—Problems, exercises, etc. I. Tynan,
Susan A. II. Feldman, Ruth Duskin. III. Title.
BF637.C45C48 1989 153.6 88-45848
ISBN 1-55611-122-3

Manufactured in the United States of America

10 9 8 7 6 5 4 3 2 1

Designed by Stanley Drate, Folio Graphics Company, Inc.

To Susan Michels and Kate Blunt,
partners in the Marsten Institute,
without whom there would be no book

CONTENTS

ACKNOWLEDGMENTS

A book like *Communicoding* could not have been written without the advice and support of numerous people. We are indeed fortunate to have had a wide range of business associates and friends share their expertise with us.

We weren't exaggerating in the dedication when we said there would be no book without Susan Michels and Kate Blunt. Their intellectual curiosity and enthusiasm about the world around them was instrumental in shaping many of the core concepts. They understood and worked with the material when it was still in an embryonic stage. Their persistent questioning, keen observations, and insistence on clarity resulted in our greatly refining what we began with. Their practical application of Communicoding* on the job and with our clients enabled us to make this an infinitely more useful book than it might otherwise have been. The last five chapters are the direct product of their work. Susan and Kate kept the faith, pushed us along, and appreciated our efforts. We are deeply grateful.

Kevin B. Tynan, an astute marketing professional, helped us select our writer, find our agent and pick our publisher. Kevin's quick wit and his willingness to listen, even laugh out loud at some of our ramblings, kept us on ground earth.

Frances Peeples is a human resource expert recognized for her ability to clearly tie business objectives to individual and team efforts. Early on, Fran saw that our Team Think strategy had the potential of enhancing team efforts and helping corporations gain a competitive edge.

Ed Crego, Jr. and Ron Armagast, from Laventhol and Horwath, worked with us to develop and validate our first Thinking Style Questionnaire. Their efforts were painstaking and meticulous. Their patience in working with new, raw material was appreciated. The care with which they developed the questionnaire to identify vertical and horizontal thinkers resulted in its providing us with critical information used in writing this book. Ed and Ron also developed a pre- and post-training Results Evaluation Questionnaire to measure training effectiveness for one of

*COMMUNICODING is a registered trade mark of the Marsten Institute.

our first corporate-sponsored Team Think training programs. Their report, "An Evaluation of the Impact of the Team Think Training Program on the Attitudes and Opinions of Employees . . ." told us that our theories really did have practical application.

As anyone knows who has ever written a book, it is a long and tortuous path. We are thankful for the many diverse opinions that helped us shape and hone our thoughts. Many skilled people offered us useful applications, entertaining vignettes, and insightful conversations. These include corporate consultants Susan Sudman, Tom Frey, Carolyn Kenady, Bob Douglas; corporate executives Joel Zemans, Sandi House, Susan Smith, Jack McCarthy, Jennifer Telek; entrepreneurs Gerry Eisenstein, Eileen Eisenstein, Alice Rudolph, Suzanne Hill, Shelly Handman, John Miaso; professionals Marylyn Carleo Grabosky, Mary Krause, Ken Bellah, Larry Clemmons.

People who work in corporations are busy people, and they often would rather not be bothered with the untried and the untested. They want proven products. No kinks to work out, smooth and finished. We were fortunate to have a skilled group of corporate executives and professionals from the Amoco Production Company willing to sit down and work with us even though we were unknown. It was 1984. Our Communicoding products, like the Team Think seminars, were still in an infant stage of development. This talented group of people invited us to sit in on internal committee presentations where we saw vertical and horizontal thinking in action. They let us see first hand the kinds of misunderstandings and conflicts that arise every day in corporate settings. They worked with us to develop hands-on exercises for our seminars. They listened to us. They spread the word among their colleagues. Most important, they used what we developed and told us what worked and what did not. APC was our laboratory, and many individuals there helped show us the way. They were the first to show a real interest in our work; the first to take a chance. We are deeply grateful to all of them: Jim Vanderbeek, Richard Flury, John Campbell, Bill Davis, Michael Rocereta, Chuck Webb, Mike Short, Dan Westbrook, Steve Souders, Karl Arleth, the late Jerry Azman, Karen Stolz, Allan Skorpen, Art Berman, Margot Timbel, Tom Klockenbrink, Lilian Fandriana, Marge Reno, Deanna Petla, Donna Monroe, Bob Wilson, Dave Mankiewicz, Dave Sawicki, Charlie Visser, Tony Nocchiero, David Wight.

As is often the case in the communications field, we, the hired givers of advice, more often than not were the recipients of a great deal of high-level thinking from our clients. We were given the opportunity to observe people and the conflicts that arise among them. We were able to watch Communicoding in action and to have our process critiqued and improved upon. Our clients helped to make the concept real. We are surely indebted to them. We are especially grateful for how graciously our clients put up with our having less time, being too hurried and sometimes too abrupt in our dealings while we were toiling away on this book.

We cannot forget the hundreds of individuals who attended our various Communicoding and Team Think seminars over the past four years. Their questions and anecdotes were nearly always illuminating. Their willingness to try out our methods was encouraging. Special thanks to Nadine Richterman of NR Communication Resources, whose expertise in course writing gave our seminars an added professional touch.

We like to think of ourselves as pioneers, but without the many experts on thinking who went before us, we might still be hitching up our wagons. In particular, Edward de Bono, Isabel Briggs Myers, and Katharine C. Briggs provided us with a framework for the existence of two types of thinking.

Support comes in many forms—some people are good at listening, some at arguing. Some will send you the absolutely right quote or the story that fits perfectly. Some will call to make sure you're okay and some will send a bottle of champagne to make doubly sure you're okay. And some take on the role of actively promoting your ideas. All of our supporters stood by us, believed in us, and never stopped pushing.

Sally Berger and Miles Berger are what support should look like. They listened, they challenged, they cared.

There are many other supporters we could not have done without, including: Leslie Buterin, Elaine Soloway, Marty Kroll, Margo Madonna, Michelle Damico, Barbara Becker, Jim Merriner, Kay Gregg, Lynn Freitag, Dr. Per Freitag, Bob Gaines, Judith Gaines, Brian Finn, Sigmund Eisenschenk, Mary Rouleau, Mary Anne Paradise, Bill Paradise, Renee Tracy, Jim Tracy, Mary Ellen Lieggi, Shirley Cress, Loui Marver, Joyce Bauer, Joy Beaton, Ann Paden.

Children offer a very special kind of support. Christopher and Angie Rose Tynan learned the hard way that books take a long time to write. But they still gave their love and good cheer.

Parents provide support of a very different sort. Marcia's parents, Belle and Harry Cherney, taught her to seek out adventure. They taught her the value of adventure, where to find it, and how to enjoy it. Learning about thinking has been one such adventure.

Susan's parents, Angie and Frank Annunzio, taught her the importance of having principles and living by them. Communicoding is the result.

Lastly, we want to thank Denise Marcil, our agent, who believed in *Communicoding* from day one and taught us how to write a proposal that sells. Susan Schwartz, our editor, deserves our special gratitude for her constant encouragement, for keeping us on track, and for being flexible beyond the call of duty.

And, what can we say that would be enough to express our respect for Ruth Duskin Feldman, co-author of this book? Ruth is the author or co-author of four other books and numerous national magazine and newspaper articles. Working with us, she always raised critical and penetrating questions. She's fast, she's concise, and she's a master of clarity.

- Identify the kind of thinker you are and the kind of thinker you're dealing with.
- Figure out how organizations "think."
- Decipher foreign logic and creativity.
- Influence the foreign mind.
- Talk the way the other half thinks.

By applying these skills, you can alleviate tension, resolve conflict, and convert "personality clashes" into legitimate, manageable, differences of opinion.

THE TWO KINDS OF MINDS

Communicoding reveals two kinds of minds—two natural thinking styles, each distinctly different but equally valuable. One we call vertical, the other horizontal.

There's nothing new about the existence of two kinds of minds, though they've been given various names. In fact, there's a legacy of seventy years of research that helped set the stage for the comprehensive theory and practical methodology of Communicoding.

Among the early explorers of the mind were Isabel Briggs Myers and Katharine Briggs, developers of the Myers-Briggs Type Indicator (MBTI), an instrument for identifying personality types. Their research, based on the theories of the Swiss psychiatrist Carl Jung, dates back to the mid-1920s. They identified sixteen distinct personalities, each of which exhibits some combination of four "preferences," or inclinations. One of the four preferences addresses the way people think.

The MBTI identified two categories of thinkers: those who rely primarily on their senses for information and those who rely primarily on intuition. *Sensing* (S) types, according to Myers-Briggs, are realistic and practical. They pay attention to experience as it is. They are good at taking in, remembering, and working with specific details. *INtuitive* (N) types are imaginative. They go beyond the immediate. They look at the big picture, focusing on meanings and possibilities.

Edward de Bono is another scholar who has advanced a theory that categorizes thinking. His primary interest is in how creative thought occurs. New ideas, to de Bono, result from perceiving links between things normally seen as unrelated. He coined the term "lateral thinking" to describe what happens when the brain breaks out of ingrained patterns. He contrasts lateral thinking with what he calls vertical thinking, which stays in accustomed, traditional channels.

According to de Bono, vertical thinking is analytical; lateral thinking is provocative. Vertical thinking moves in a clearly defined direction; lateral thinking moves in order to generate a direction. Because de Bono sees lateral thinking as critical to innovation, his aim is to help people move beyond vertical thinking and learn to employ lateral thinking.

Starting in the 1960s, research on thinking took off in a new direction. Rather than merely attempting to describe what the brain does by observing people's behavior, neurophysiologists began to peer inside and examine the workings of the brain's machinery.

The early research—much of which was done with brain-damaged patients who had lost specific mental functions—lent support to the belief that each side of the brain controls a different area of functioning. The left hemisphere appeared to perceive details and the way things change from one moment to the next, while the right hemisphere appeared to perceive simultaneous relationships and global patterns. The left side, therefore, came to be seen as logical and verbal, dealing with facts, structure, and planning. The right side came to be seen as creative and visual, dealing with ideas, concepts, and spatial relationships. Popular applications of this research referred to "left-brained" and "right-brained" people as dominated by one or the other of these kinds of thinking.

Brain researchers, however, have cautioned against such premature interpretations of their findings, which are still far from definitive. And, by the 1980s, it was beginning to be recognized that these "half-brained" distinctions were far too simplistic, that thinking is an integrative process, that both creative and logical operations require incredibly complex patterns of neural connections between as well as within the two hemispheres.

Meanwhile, empirical evidence of thinking styles continues to mount. Studies of human behavior continue to find observable differences in the ways people think, even though the organic source of these differences is still unclear. These studies, and the observations of popularizers of their findings, have come up with a variety of systems, terms, and categories. But the consistent, overarching theme has been that people appear to naturally favor contrasting styles of thinking and learning. One style appears more logical, the other more creative.

With each contribution, the snapshot of the thinking styles has become enriched with deeper coloring, sharper tone, subtler shadings. Each of these students of human intellect has increased the growing body of information about how minds work.

Communicoding takes the next step. It uncovers the Master Code that dictates how the two kinds of minds go about gathering, processing, and using information. Communicoding goes further by exposing the logic and creativity of *both* kinds of minds—logic and creativity that takes contrasting forms and thus is frequently not recognizable to the opposite thinker. The unseen creativity of the vertical thinker and the unseen logic of the horizontal thinker are at the very heart of the war that is waged daily between them.

COMMUNICODING: ITS AUTHORS

Communicoding is the product of the Marsten Institute, a Chicago-based consulting firm, which specializes in the "people" side of business. Its founder, Marcia B. Cherney, and her partner, Susan A. Tynan, have more than thirty years of combined experience as communication specialists, in observing, analyzing, and resolving difficulties in relationships. Initially concentrating on marital and family problems, they later applied their knowledge of thinking styles to the corporate environment. They have assisted in closing stalemated deals, settled lawsuits and partnership disputes, and helped businesses better manage their clients and customers. This book reflects those experiences.

Communicoding is the brainchild of Marcia Cherney. Working with clients, she identified the war between opposite thinkers and developed strategies for curtailing it. She took these strategies, which she coined decoding, encoding, recoding, and Team Think, and developed practical seminars and other products now used by Marsten's corporate clients. These new communication tools resulted from Cherney's breaking the Master Code of each kind of mind, revealing the logic and creativity of both.

Susan Tynan helped refine Communicoding by adding some ways to identify and communicate with opposite thinkers. With Cherney, she tested the applicability of the theory with corporate clients. Specifically, she helped to shape the concepts by pointing out the differences between emotional "logic" and thinking and by recognizing how the process of labeling accelerates the war between opposite thinkers. She developed many of the exercises and formats for presentation of the material in this book.

By focusing on mental preferences rather than on other, more nebulous personality differences, the authors have been able to create concrete, workable guidelines to wind down the ongoing war that results from opposite thinking.

THINKING STYLE WARFARE

You'll see throughout this book examples of how vertical and horizontal thinkers, unaware of their fundamental differences, constantly respond to each other in unexpected ways. You'll see that these encounters produce strange and startling results—unanticipated, unwanted, and unpredictable—and wind up consuming time, wasting energy, costing money, wrenching hearts, and baffling minds. The chapters that follow will explain these baffling encounters, showing how and why they begin with suspicion and inexorably lead to hostility.

In the authors' experience, most failed business deals, partnerships, mergers, and management assignments have little to do with lack of talent, skills, or good will. Nine times out of ten, these failures can be traced to misinterpretation on the part of one party or both. Whether the war is within companies or between companies, the costs can be measured in fruitless meetings, frequent redos, employee grievances and absenteeism, high turnover, reduced productivity, lost sales, and customer complaints. Thinking style differences are at the root of many of these problems.

WHAT COMMUNICODING IS AND IS NOT

Communicoding is about brains. It's not about personalities.

Communicoding is about understanding and appreciating opposite thinkers. It illuminates pathways to their logic and creativity and removes barriers to engaging and influencing them. It recognizes that neither kind of thinking is better than the other—just different.

Communicoding is a way to know how your own mind works—vertically or horizontally—and to clearly see the particular contributions of the other kind of thinking. It's not about stereotyping or pigeonholing people. It's not a way to determine who is best suited for which job but a way to determine how best to use each party's natural abilities to get the job done. It's not a way to demonstrate that one type of thinker is better qualified to lead or manage—the most effective leaders and managers have always been those who knew the strengths *and* weaknesses of their own thinking.

IN SHORT

Communicoding dispels myths about each type of thinker—myths that cause unnecessary friction between them.

Communicoding shows a way to limit or stop the war in your daily life and in your organization.

Communicoding is the game plan for smart thinkers.

1 When You Don't See Eye to Eye

People talk about how they can't communicate. If they can't communicate, the least they can do is shut up!

TOM LEHRER

Have you ever:

- Gone into a meeting with THE PERFECT IDEA only to have it bomb?
- Walked away from a discussion in which, no matter how you put it, the other party couldn't understand your point?
- Asked someone to do something and received something that bore no resemblance to what you had in mind?
- Carefully followed someone's directions only to be told that what you produced was not what the other party wanted?
- Avoided asking someone a question because you knew the answer would get you nowhere?

If you answered yes to any of these questions, chances are you've experienced something more than conflict. You've experienced a Communicoding clash—a strange encounter with someone whose words and actions seem mystifying to you.

Communicoding is about getting results from unpredictable people, people about whom the only thing you can predict is that you will have difficulties, but you never can predict when those difficulties will crop up or what will set them off.

When these baffling experiences occur, you have entered the Twilight Zone of Reason, a place where you try to make sense of the nonsensical, yet no matter how hard you try, no matter how logical your explanations for what's going on, you can't change the situation or the likelihood of a repeat performance. In fact, it's very likely in these situations that your logical explanations are *preventing* you from getting the results you want, the solutions you need, and the influence you desire.

ENTERING THE TWILIGHT ZONE

In most communication conflicts, the more facts you have, the more experiences under your belt, the better your understanding of what's happening, the greater the likelihood that the difficulty can be resolved. In Communicoding dilemmas, the results usually are just the opposite. The more information you gather to clear up the situation, the more experience you draw upon, the better understanding you think you have, the greater the likelihood that your problem will remain unresolved and will recur.

How can this be? How can gaining understanding put you on the wrong track? This makes no sense. What possible danger can there be in learning from experience, garnering information, clarifying a request?

Plenty! Let's listen in on an argument that took place between Andrew and Greg, partners in an engineering firm specializing in machine tool products. The partners had developed a breakthrough technology, a high-precision device for dramatically increasing the accuracy of laser cutters used in metal fabrication. The device was to be launched at a machine distributors' convention. Andrew and Greg had high hopes that their new product would revolutionize the industry. If the partners could excite enough distributors to convince customers to fit the device to their existing machinery, the partners would quickly recoup their investment and realize substantial profits.

Andrew and Greg had every reason to try to work smoothly together. Neither anticipated a hassle. Yet, somehow they entered the twilight zone. Their efforts to understand what was happening backfired, and an important discussion that should have taken place never did.

One of Andrew's responsibilities was to prepare the agenda for the meeting. Since he traveled frequently, he and Greg often communicated by mail. Several weeks in advance, Andrew sent Greg a draft agenda with a request to "review and revise as needed." A few items had question marks next to them.

Greg looked over the agenda and saw no problems with it. He did wonder about the reasons for the question marks; but, being busy with his own part of the preparations for the meeting, he put the agenda aside, figuring he'd discuss it with Andrew when they got together for a preliminary run-through.

A few weeks later, Greg received another copy of the draft agenda, this time with the notation, "Please read and revise by our meeting next week. I want your comments!" Reading it over, he was momentarily annoyed when he realized there was nothing new in it. "Andrew must have forgotten that he already sent me this," he decided, and tossed it.

When they met the following week, a confused Andrew questioned Greg. "Didn't you get the draft agenda? I sent it to you twice."

"Yeah, I got it," said Greg.

"Well," said Andrew, growing impatient, "wasn't my note clear?"

"Sure," said Greg. "You asked me to review the agenda and revise it as needed."

"I marked the parts of the agenda that you'd be most familiar with. I wanted to know if you thought we'd run into any problems. I needed your input and I got NOTHING back! I don't get it. Don't you realize how important this meeting is?"

"Hold on!" said Greg. "Of course I do. I did what you asked. I looked over the agenda, and it seemed okay to me. If you wanted something more, you should have said so, instead of cluttering my in-basket with dupes."

"I don't see why I have to draw you a picture," said Andrew, sharply. "It was quite clear that I wanted your opinion on the items I had marked. Especially since those were your areas of expertise. I wanted to ensure a strong presentation."

"And what do you think *I'm* doing?" said Greg, who was riled by now. "I'm swamped working on marketing handouts and the demo arrangements. I don't have time to worry about vague question marks! Why make such a big deal out of the agenda? I still don't see any problems with it. This is just your usual much ado about nothing!"

Each man walked away disgusted. Each felt the other was being totally unreasonable.

Andrew saw Greg as irresponsible. What kind of person would fail to respond to a partner's request for help—especially when the request was repeated, and when it concerned a matter of such obvious significance to the firm? Andrew had asked for Greg's considered judgment on the agenda for a crucially important meeting, and all he had gotten was "It looks okay, no problems." The more Andrew thought about the incident, the angrier he became. It wasn't the first time this kind of thing had happened. If he hadn't been so deeply financially involved in the partnership, he might have been tempted to hang it up right then and there.

Greg, for his part, viewed Andrew as a small-time operator. Why did he constantly insist on wasting Greg's time with unimportant questions? What difference did it make how the agenda was worded so long as all the key points got made and the presentation went well? Furthermore, if Andrew wanted input so badly, why didn't he make that plain instead of sending cryptic messages and then going into a huff? This sort of thing was typical of Andrew, and Greg was sick and tired of it.

This incident may seem petty. The participants might appear to have overreacted, to have become overly emotional. Why (you may be wondering) didn't they just slow down and be more specific about what they had in mind?

But, as often is true in such situations, this was not the first such encounter for Andrew and Greg. Their reactions were the result of an accumulation of such "petty" occurrences over a long period of time, arguments in which efforts to slow down and clarify had proved fruitless.

Why do minor skirmishes like these escalate into major clashes? Why do such "unpredictable" incidents occur with maddening frequency, repeating themselves over and over with the same parties and leading to the same dead ends? Why do efforts to correct the situation often, predictably fail? Weren't Andrew and Greg both speaking English? Weren't they both talking about the same thing? Weren't they both intelligent men? Of course they were. So what explanation could there be? It had to be a personality conflict!

Or did it? Could there be another factor—something that Andrew and Greg were missing? Something that made the ending of this encounter quite predictable? Could it be that disconcerting disputes like this one are rooted in invisible *thinking* differences rather than visible personality differences?

When you're in an exasperating situation like Andrew and Greg's, you may feel like an American diplomat talking to a Soviet diplomat without an interpreter present. And you might very well be on the right track. In such situations, perhaps you actually are dealing with a foreign mind. Someone who doesn't talk your language—whose way of thinking and system of conveying and acting upon thoughts is alien to your own. Someone who seems to be speaking in code: a code you can't crack. Someone to whom you seem just as difficult, just as unpredictable as that party seems to you.

EXPOSING THE WORLD OF OPPOSITE THINKERS

Suppose you, like Lewis Carroll's Alice, suddenly found yourself in a land behind the looking glass, a land in which everything had contours exactly opposite to what you were accustomed. Further suppose that you were unaware of having left your country. How would you feel? How would you cope? How could you explain the strange things you saw, the "backward" people you had to deal with?

When you're in a Communicoding clash—when what happens is the reverse of what you expect—it's a sign that you've entered the land of the opposite thinker, a place where the unpredictable is predictable, where proven communication techniques don't work and the other party's actions defy common sense.

The words *common sense* imply a single, sensible way of thinking that's universally shared. Communicoding reveals that instead of one universal common sense, there are *two.* They arise from two distinct, fundamentally different but equally smart, equally logical styles of thinking. We call these two thinking styles vertical and horizontal. Each has its own domain, foreign to the other.

Thus, confronting someone of the opposite thinking style is like entering a foreign land: a land where the code of thinking and acting—the Communicode—is opposite to what it is in your native one. What makes your "culture shock" even more bewildering is that you don't *realize* you're on alien soil. You keep expecting people to say and do things in a familiar way, and you keep on being surprised and disappointed.

In Chapter 2, we'll describe in detail the topography of the two lands—the characteristic terrains of vertical and horizontal thinking. For now, just visualize two sets of signals that flash in brains, each pointing in different directions—one vertical, one horizontal. Each brainflash triggers a particular action code, a specific strategy for dealing with a situation. Because each brain perceives its own strategy as the only logical route, each party's actions often seem designed to block the other's path.

We're not suggesting that there are only two kinds of people, or that thinking styles account for all interpersonal differences. Obviously, there are many kinds of people, and many kinds of differences between them. Ethnic differences. Educational differences. Socioeconomic differences. Cultural differences. Differences in appearance, in physical condition, in personality, in upbringing, in experience. There are high-strung people and laidback people. There are lazy, incompetent, and impractical people, and, yes, such personality traits often can explain conflicts between people.

Communicoding reveals thinking styles as an important but little-understood difference that is germane to many of the other differences and is at the root of much disharmony and discord. To see why, let's look more closely at what Communicodes are and how they clash.

A CLASH OF CODES

Each thinking style operates through its own Communicode: a code of guiding principles that governs how the thinker processes and acts upon new information. The Communicode therefore is the major determinant of how new situations are handled. When opposite thinkers can't communicate, it's because they are unaware of each other's Communicodes and therefore can't understand each other's behavior.

A Communicoding clash occurs when opposite thinkers are hit by the unexpected: some surprising suggestion, idea or action they can't make sense of. Although they can see and describe what is happening and understand the words used, these actions and words appear nonsensical because the thinking behind them doesn't show. Each party assumes the other's thinking to be obvious ("According to my code, if I did that, the reason would be . . ."). However, since there are two different Communicodes, to assume that the other party's thinking is obvious is obviously misleading.

Because opposite thinkers process information differently, the same words and phrases can have different meanings to the two types of brains. Think back to the quarrel between Andrew and Greg. Because of their differing Communicodes, what was obvious to Andrew certainly was not obvious to Greg.

When Andrew asked Greg to review the agenda, Andrew's horizontal brain was flashing, "Consider desirable impact!" He questioned the section of the agenda where the benefits of the new product were explained. Would the impact be strong enough to convince the distributors of the revolutionary nature of the device? Since Greg was more familiar with the technical aspects, he would know if there was a problem. Obviously, Greg was in a position to assess the danger.

Greg's vertical brain, however, flashed a different signal: "Check feasibility!" The agenda seemed quite workable; he saw no problems with the flow. The pencilled question marks flashed no dangers to him. No wonder he didn't respond to Andrew's "obvious" concerns!

Can you see how the issue between Andrew and Greg became explosive? They didn't realize that they were following different codes, that the behavior of each was perfectly, predictably consistent with his own thinking style. Because they were ignorant of Communicoding, this simple, objective explanation did not—could not—occur to either of them. They didn't realize that the source of their conflict was a hidden difference in thinking: a difference in the signals flashed by each kind of brain. Instead, each was forced to fall back on a subjective explanation, one that focused on personality differences.

Because the conflict took this subjective path, Greg never learned what Andrew's concerns were. Consequently, no discussion or resolution of these issues could take place. The original point that was at the root of the problem got lost.

When you, like Andrew and Greg, are a party to a Communicoding clash, it's as though you're the victim of an optical illusion. You're convinced that what you see is all there is. You believe you have the picture, when in fact there's a second, equally obvious way to look at the situation. You think you know the whole story when all you have is a partial view.

How does your brain get fooled into believing its subjective explanation? Let's see what happens from the moment the brain receives input from an opposite thinker until the moment the clash begins.

THE ANATOMY OF A CLASH

During an interaction, your brain is constantly processing input from the other party: perceiving what this party says and does and then filing that information for ready retrieval. This stored information is what your brain relies upon to make sense of and deal with reality—in this case, the words and actions of the party you're interacting with. Your brain has a processing code: a particular way to sort, store, and retrieve information. You might say that you're either a vertical filer or a horizontal filer.

Now imagine that your brain has received some information it can't process, information that's in the "wrong" format. The brain doesn't know where to put this information in its filing system, its vertical (or horizontal) data bank. An error message flashes. The brain scans for additional information in an attempt to determine where this non-system information should be stored. It searches its old data (past experience, information about the situation or person) and tries to gather new data by listening, clarifying, and restating. The new information only confirms the mismatch. Because the brain has no information about Communicoding, no objective explanation can be found. The brain accurately determines that a code violation has occurred: *Party understood request . . . did not appropriately respond . . . no accident . . . code violated.*

At this point, the emotions take over. Since there is no objective explanation, the explanation must be subjective. ("He's unreliable" . . . "He's overreacting.") When the brain reaches this subjective explanation—usually a negative one—it registers a reaction, and the clash begins.

Note that the brain does not quickly jump to a subjective explanation. On the contrary, it goes through a logical, orderly process that leads to a place where the subjective explanation seems the only alternative. But this logical process has led to a false conclusion. You believe you've gotten to the root of the problem when, in actuality, you're further from it than ever. The subjective explanation gives the brain the illusion that it knows the whole story. The original information that couldn't be processed, the information that is your *only* clue to the source of the problem, has been lost.

To see how serious the consequences can be when important thoughts get lost, let's return to Andrew and Greg.

As it turned out, the presentation didn't receive the enthusiastic response Andrew and Greg had hoped for. It appeared that Andrew's concerns about the distributors' receptivity to the presentation were warranted. The buyers were not sold on the unique benefits of the new product line. The real clincher is that had Andrew's concerns been discussed, Greg might easily have found workable solutions, ways to

ANATOMY OF A CLASH

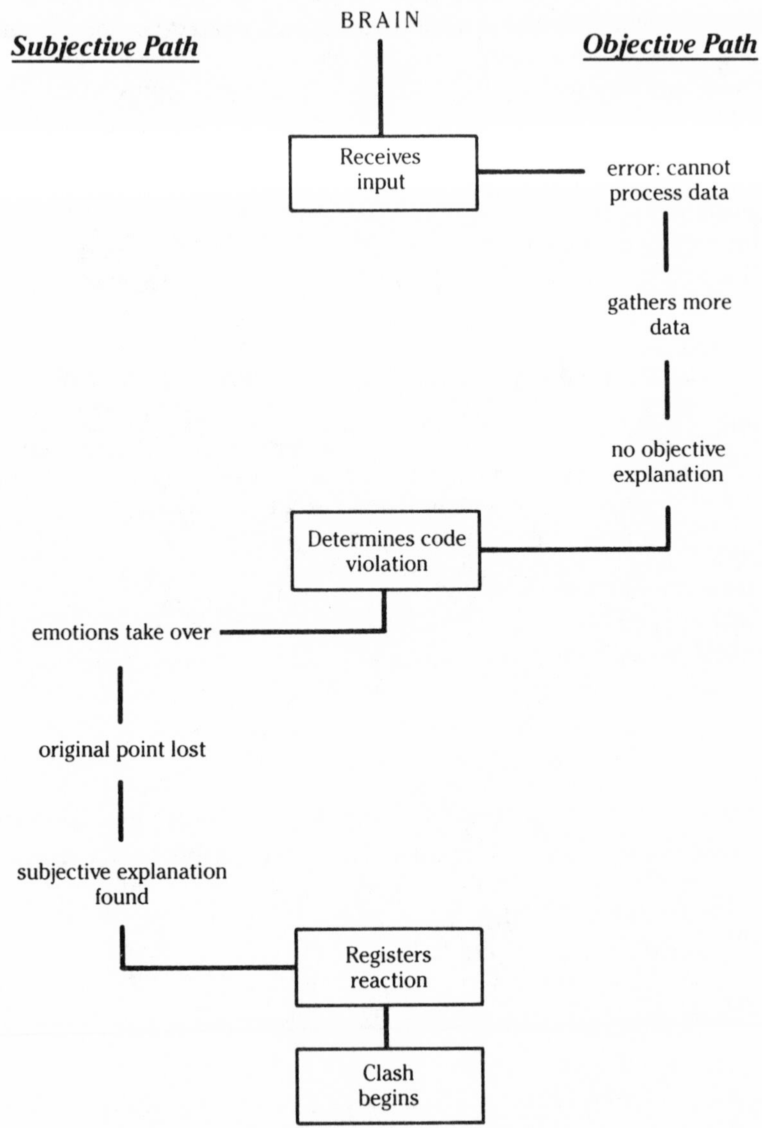

present the product more dramatically. Of course, it's possible that the problems went deeper than the questions Andrew raised or the solutions Greg might have offered, but their subjective explanations stopped them from finding out.

Consequences like these aren't unusual in Communicoding dilemmas. When thinking takes the subjective path, facts are bypassed.

Instead of discussing ideas, concerns, and information, the parties argue the merits of their subjective explanations. Instead of using brainpower from both sides, resolution usually becomes a contest of wills or endurance.

Parties walk away from such an encounter convinced that the outcome was unavoidable. After all, they tried to gather information to find a logical explanation for the occurrence. Each gave the other the benefit of the doubt. If a mutually satisfying solution was reachable, surely these moves would have shown the way! The truth is, when dealing with opposite thinkers, these tactics virtually guarantee that a satisfactory solution will *not* be found.

But why?

HOW COURTESY AND CLARIFICATION BACKFIRE

When you're in a Communicoding dilemma, your subjective conclusions, based on the facts you have, are unassailably logical. What you don't realize is that you're missing the key fact that would enable you to accurately interpret what's going on: information about the other party's Communicode. Why is this missing information so vital? Because without it, you'll be led astray.

Let's look at two more scenarios to see what happens when opposite thinkers attempt to clarify their differences.

SCENARIO 1

Donna and Mel

Donna is senior vice-president of a midsized brokerage firm. Mel, the manager of data processing, seems to be her nemesis.

"Mel, last week when there was a delay in data transmission to various departments, what did you think I wanted you to do?"

"Eliminate the problem," Mel said firmly.

"Great. I thought maybe we had our wires crossed. So, what was the cause of the problem?"

"I don't know—I haven't had time to look into it."

"Wait a minute—I'm confused. I thought you said you knew I wanted you to eliminate the problem, How can you eliminate something if you don't know why it happened?"

If you were Donna, how would you view Mel at this point? How satisfied would you be after clarifying?

S C E N A R I O 2

TED AND PAUL

Ted, supervisor of research at a pharmaceutical plant, approached Paul, his recently-hired research assistant. "I read your report on the new drug we've been testing, and I have to tell you it left me puzzled. Perhaps the problem stems from the instructions I gave you. I'd appreciate it if you'd repeat them for me, and maybe we can clear this up."

To Ted's astonishment, Paul repeated virtually verbatim what Ted had asked him to do.

"Well, then," said Ted, "if you understood that I wanted the background on Chemical X, why did you waste my time with a comparative analysis of fifteen other chemicals I have no interest in?"

"I thought it would give you a broader perspective—"

"I didn't ask for perspective, I asked for background on Chemical X. Now I have to sort through all this information to find what's usable."

If you were Paul's boss, and this was the fourth such incident, what would be your impression of Paul?

When you're hit by the unexpected, the Golden Rule teaches you to do the fair thing, the smart thing: to listen rather than jump to conclusions; to clarify; to restate; and to keep your emotions in check until you make sure that the other party actually received your request and heard what you wanted. Just as you want and expect a fair hearing, you extend the same courtesy to others.

Much of the time, especially when you're dealing with thinkers like yourself, these techniques work well. But these smart, fair methods rarely work with opposite thinkers. Instead they tend to backfire and inflame emotions. In such situations, as in the scenarios, these conventional wisdoms merely misguide you. These proven techniques make matters worse, not better.

The conventional wisdoms are based on a shared "common sense." The assumption behind restatement and clarification is that any sensible person who truly heard the request would respond to it in *the* expected manner. The brain should be able to process the information easily and respond accordingly.

In many cases, when you're at loggerheads with someone—particularly someone of your own thinking style—you may find that the other party did *not* hear what you wanted, or vice versa. In that case, a simple reiteration or rewording of the request usually will do the trick. Clarification clears the way for accord.

But what if (like Donna and Ted, and Andrew as well) you find that your request *was* received? You assumed it was not. In light of the response, how could it have been? To your surprise, it was. Your efforts to gather information to clear up the confusion have produced facts which show that the other party has violated your code. Your request was heard, but your brain can't process the response. How can you explain what happened? Based on the facts at hand, what objective explanation can there be?

Under those circumstances, an attempt to clarify invites rather than heads off a clash. A reasonable person can overlook a misunderstanding, but not a deliberate omission or rejection. It's like waving a red flag in front of a bull. When your request was heard, understood, and still not met, clarification gives you the go-ahead to presume a purposeful violation of your code. A subjective finding about the other party's common sense, character, or motives seems to be the only conceivable explanation.

So, if conventional wisdom doesn't work, what is the answer? What can dramatically reverse the direction of an interaction with an opposite thinker? The application of a New Rule of Communication.

A NEW RULE OF COMMUNICATION

When trying to make sense of the nonsensical, look *first* for a thinking style difference.

In order to understand and resolve a Communicoding dilemma, you must first look not for subjective explanations about the other party's personality but for objective explanations about the other party's brain. Factoring thinking style differences into the equation gives your brain a possible objective explanation for a code violation. Instead of letting your emotions take over, this objective explanation allows you to ask questions to uncover the thinking behind the offending actions.

How do you know when it's time to apply the New Rule? What are the warning signals? Look at the following list:

EARLY WARNING SIGNS OF A COMMUNICODING CLASH

- You can predict that an issue will develop between you and a certain party, but you can't predict when it will arise or what it will be about.
- You are repeatedly surprised by the other party's actions and reactions.
- You find yourself questioning the other party's common sense, character, and/or motives.
- In a particular interaction, only one party appears smart.

We're not saying that Communicoding is the only way to deal with conflict. We are saying that it's the easiest way, and it may be the only way that works when the conflict is with an opposite thinker.

COMMUNICODING GIVES YOU THE EASY WAY

The *simplest* way to resolve conflict is to eliminate the possibility of a Communicoding clash before exploring other explanations. It's the simplest way because there are only two thinking styles, whereas most other differences cover a broad spectrum with infinite degrees of variation.

Certainly personality issues can cause or contribute to conflict. But personality assessments—no matter how logical, no matter how accurate—may not correctly identify the source of the trouble. Personality assessments often mask thinking style clashes that must be recognized and dealt with before conflict can be satisfactorily resolved.

Think about Donna and Mel. Donna, a horizontal thinker, was convinced that Mel could not be eliminating their computer foul-up because he had not located the source of the problem. What if Donna had realized that she and Mel were opposite thinkers? She might have asked him to explain how he was eliminating the problem rather than assume that the only way was to look for the source. Might her reaction have changed if she had discovered that Mel's vertical method, to "clean up the mess," allowed him to quickly restore normal operations and avoid loss of revenue?

What about Ted and Paul? If Ted, a vertical thinker, had been clued in to the existence of another code, he might have tried to understand the logic behind Paul's horizontal response. He might have been surprised to find that the "unnecessary" information in Paul's report was more useful than it appeared. Ted's company was deciding whether or not to put more money into research on Chemical X. By assembling the results of research already done on other, similar chemicals, Paul's report might have saved time and money. But because Ted had no knowledge of Communicoding, he walked away confident that the "background" he was looking for was all he needed.

These stories illustrate that foreign thought must be assessed within the context of its own code. Otherwise, without realizing it, you'll be caught in an optical illusion, unwittingly trusting perceptions that distort your view. You'll see things as going a certain way when, with a longer look and a more tutored eye, you might find that the direction is quite different than it first appears.

Communicoding provides an easy way to uncover the predictability behind the "unpredictable." When you suspect that you've entered a foreign land—a place where the codes of thinking and behavior are

ARE THESE STEPS RIGHTSIDE UP OR UPSIDE DOWN?

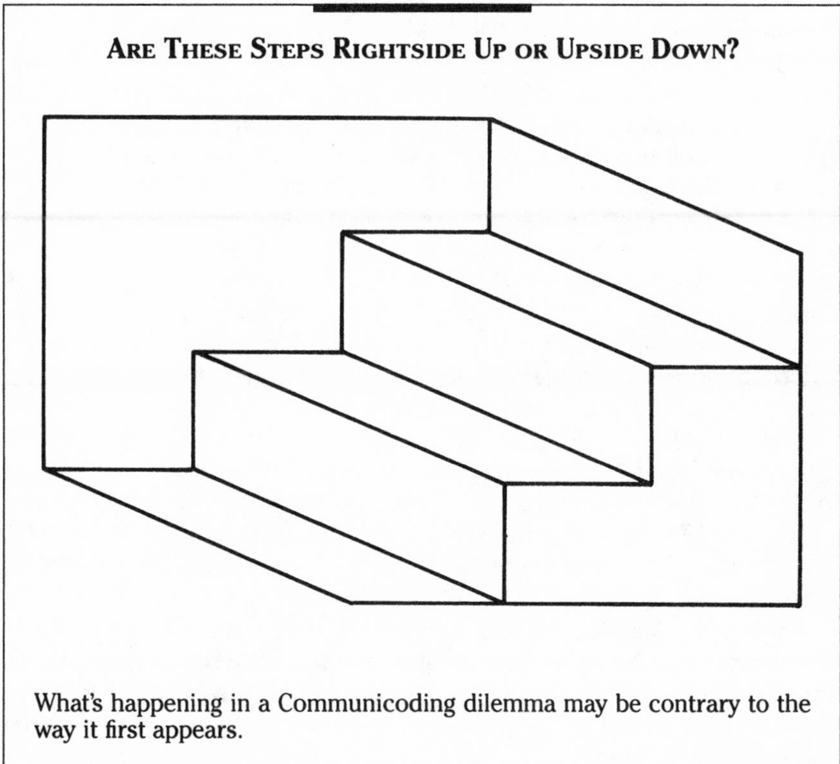

What's happening in a Communicoding dilemma may be contrary to the way it first appears.

startling and strange—don't recoil from that foreignness. Instead, view it as a mystery and an opportunity. Seek clues that foreign thought may be operating and then find the key to crack the foreign code.

WHEN THE STAKES RUN HIGH

What does ignorance of Communicoding cost you? That depends on how deeply invested you are in a relationship with an opposite thinker. How much time, money, and energy have you put into it? What hopes and dreams are riding on it?

If your investment of yourself and/or your resources is marginal, you may be willing to put up with a difficult situation or write it off. Or perhaps, if you wait a while, it will self-correct.

Angela, a vertical thinker, was on a committee to recruit a new marketing director for her company. The chairman of the committee and most of the other members happened to be horizontal thinkers. At the outset, they spent several weeks outlining the job description and debating about the characteristics of the ideal candidate.

Angela became impatient. The process seemed to be taking a long time. Her approach would have been to begin by drawing up a timetable, calling some recruiters and some well-placed people in the industry, locating candidates, and maybe even interviewing a few while refining criteria for selection as she went along.

Eventually, though, she began to see that the method being followed made as much sense as hers. Although the process got off to a slow start, when the committee did get around to interviewing candidates things went more quickly and smoothly because they had a clear picture of what they wanted. Her way would have meant a faster start but perhaps more problems later on, because her view of what she wanted would not have been as clearly defined.

Angela's personal investment in the committee's task was small enough and her initial frustration level low enough that she could afford to give her fellow committee members the benefit of the doubt and wait to see how things turned out. Often, however, that's not the case.

When the personal investment is greater and the stakes are higher, Communicoding clashes tend to occur with disturbing regularity. As you'll see in Chapter 5, their frequent and repetitive nature causes disappointment, mistrust, and eventually hostility to build. You begin to anticipate these trying events before they occur. You begin to feel that they must be deliberately calculated to upset you. By now, you've most likely stopped giving the benefit of the doubt or even attempting to see the other party's point. You've probably built a "case" against him or her, a litany of negative personality traits and ill-begotten motives, a record of past offenses that comes spilling out at the first sign of discord.

Two hours before guests were to arrive, Elaine asked her husband, Dick, to pick up a few last-minute things. She gave him a list of four items. He returned an hour later with twenty-one items and a bouquet of flowers. As he lined up the grocery bags on the kitchen counter, she stared at them in disbelief. "How many items did I ask you to buy?"

"Four. But I thought I'd get a few extra things we needed."

"I don't have time to deal with this," Elaine snapped. Our guests are due momentarily. Why can't you ever do what I ask? You're always making more work for me when I'm in a hurry!"

"Why must you always be so critical?" Dick responded. "I try to be helpful, and this is the thanks I get!"

By the time the guests arrived, Elaine and Dick each had dragged out a laundry list of old grievances and were barely speaking to each other.

Vertical thinkers like Elaine take requests very literally. So when she handed Dick the shopping list, she assumed that he would literally get four items and no more. Dick, a horizontal thinker, saw Elaine as requesting his assistance. So, trying to be helpful and save her a later shopping trip, he anticipated some things they would need during the week. He didn't realize that having to put away extra groceries and arrange the flowers would throw off her schedule of last-minute things to do.

The emotional buildup to such seemingly trivial "misunderstandings" as those described in this chapter has jeopardized many business and personal relationships. All because of a missing piece of information: information about how the other half thinks.

Even health may be at stake. Recent research suggests that hostility, anger, and mistrust may be major contributors to heart attack risk. By lessening hostile reactions, Communicoding can open the door to stronger relationships, new and better ideas, and maybe even longer lives.

THE AGE OF THE BRAIN?

Sometimes we find food for thought in the strangest places. In the April 1989 issue of Cook's magazine, Christopher Kimball, publisher and editorial director, unveiled a theory he calls the Ascending Organ Thesis. The idea has application beyond the kitchen.

"During the '40s," Kimball explains, "you had to have guts." People in those days were judged by their courage and drive. The war hero and the self-made man were the models.

"Then came the '60s, when you had to have heart," Kimball continues. People began to value softness, sensitivity, and self-expression. They looked beneath surface behavior and considered intentions. They sought charisma and sincerity in their leaders.

The '90s, Kimball predicts, will belong to the brain. An evolving self-image is carrying people into an "age of cerebral enlightenment." They're beginning to focus on "smarts," the ability to simplify today's complex problems. They want solutions that are both logical and creative.

Communicoding is the smart thinker's guide for the '90s and beyond. As you explore the lands of vertical and horizontal thinking in Chapter 2, you'll find guideposts to help you find the logic and creativity in both thinking styles. You'll begin to recognize the smart thinking of someone who may have seemed totally illogical and unimaginative to you. When you know how to identify foreign smarts and common sense, you still may not see eye to eye, but you'll be on your way to being able to work with opposite thinkers rather than against them.

2 Two Kinds of Minds

Talking to you is like talking to the wall.

JULIUS SERCHUK

Wrong answers.

Are you fed up with the wrong answers that come across your desk, creep into your family plans, meet you over lunch? Why do people with the right credentials often turn out to be wrong for the job? Why do so many relationships work on paper but not in practice? When did common sense go out of vogue?

Most of us hate wrong answers—someone else's or our own. Whether we receive them or produce them, they divert us from getting where we want to go. Even when they help us by illuminating the path *not* to take, in our heart of hearts we call them stupid.

But what if "wrong" answers aren't as stupid as they appear? Perhaps they're simply unexpected. Perhaps there's something right about those "wrong" answers, something not readily apparent.

Is it possible to figure out what might be right about what's "obviously" wrong? To see what's unseen? To get inside someone's head?

That's exactly what we at the Marsten Institute set out to do.

EXAMINING WRONG ANSWERS

Our particular interest in wrong answers stems from, among other things, our business. The Marsten Institute consults with successful business people. That means we get to listen to lots of clients complain about the wrong answers they get. We also get to complain about how our clients give us wrong answers.

So, the reality of the situation, as we saw it, was that there were large numbers of people who were generally understood to be successful (ourselves included) who appeared to be engulfed by wrong answers. Either (we figured) there were a lot of stupid or lazy people in the world, or there had to be another explanation. We decided to find out.

We talked with chief executives and board members. We interviewed corporate and household managers. We met with lawyers, professors, accountants, and other professionals. We studied hundreds of "wrong" answers.

The first thing we noticed was speed. People move fast. They're in a hurry to get where they're going. No delays. The one who gets the furthest fastest wins. Wrong answers slow people down. Questions slow them down even more.

Right answers speak for themselves. They get people where they want to go. Their merit is self-evident. If the need is for a new direction and someone clearly identifies one that works, that party's creativity is applauded. If the need is for a fast path and someone lights the way, that party's logic is instantly hailed.

Interestingly, no matter how right the answer, we found that people rarely are recognized as *both* creative and logical. It's either one or the other. The converse also is true. Wrong answers are seen as either illogical or unimaginative, rarely both.

How do people make these evaluations? What criteria do they use in judging other people's creativity or logic? The gauge, we observed, is predictably uniform. People evaluate results. Right answers are usable answers. They come in various shapes, sizes, and forms, but if they seem to meet the need, they look right. If not, they look wrong.

People do *not* normally evaluate thinking methods. In our hectic lives, there's rarely time or inclination to examine the rationale behind an answer that appears to miss the mark. In fact, people rarely look into the way *any* answer was developed. From elementary school on, most of us have been conditioned to expect bad grades for wrong answers and no points for asking or explaining how the answers were obtained. Why would we start now, when time is such a precious commodity?

That realization gave us the key to our quest. We began asking people who gave "wrong" answers a question most people are too busy or don't think to ask: "How is your answer on target?" The more questions we asked and the more people we interviewed, the more we saw the "wrong" answers fall into distinct categories. We call these categories vertical and horizontal. Ultimately, our search produced boxes and circles: descriptors of two kinds of minds.

You've undoubtedly seen portraits of these minds before. Although they may have been called by different names, you've read or heard them described by a number of researchers and authors. What we call vertical thinkers typically are seen as practical; what we call horizontal thinkers typically are seen as innovative.

EQUALLY CREATIVE AND LOGICAL

Our investigation, which started with a simple question about the origin of wrong answers, not only confirmed the existence of two kinds of minds but also exposed the creativity and logic of both. We learned that the two kinds of thinkers have a great deal of difficulty appreciating each other. In fact, our interviews revealed that the answers given by vertical thinkers often look dumb to horizontals and vice versa.

As we interviewed people, a pattern of incompatibility emerged:

- Both vertical and horizontal thinkers saw themselves as logical *and* creative.
- Both vertical and horizontal thinkers believed that the other kind of thinker misinterpreted their actions and underestimated them.
- Both vertical and horizontal thinkers did not appreciate compliments given to them by the other kind of thinker.
- Both vertical and horizontal thinkers considered the other kind of thinker's way of doing things wasteful and time-consuming.
- Both vertical and horizontal thinkers thought the other kind of thinker gave wrong answers.

Neither seemed to be aware of how the other kind of mind works in producing *any* kind of answer, right or wrong.

But why? As we further explored the answers each kind of thinker came up with, we uncovered an explanation that was stunning in its simplicity. A way to explain the observable differences in the two kinds of thinkers. A way to make sense of "wrong" answers. A way to understand the tension that exists between the two kinds of minds. A way to expose the creativity and logic of *both* kinds of thinking.

Our explanation boils down to this: Each kind of thinker has a master ability, which molds the terrain of the land each lives in. *Vertical minds detect and manipulate differences. Horizontal minds detect and manipulate commonalities.*

These master abilities determine how each thinker not only shapes answers but perceives the world and makes sense of experience. They are the foundation of each kind of thinker's logic and creativity. Although neither of these tools is intrinsically better than the other, people more often recognize the "obvious" merits of answers developed with their own kind of ability and fail to appreciate the other kind.

In this chapter, we'll give you a brief guided tour of the visible terrain of the lands of vertical and horizontal thinking. We'll reveal the signposts, normally invisible to outsiders, that direct the way the inhabitants think. And we'll expose some myths that contribute to hostilities between the two kinds of minds.

A GUIDED TOUR THROUGH THE LANDS OF VERTICAL AND HORIZONTAL THINKING

THE VERTICAL TERRAIN

When you enter the land of vertical thinking, you are immediately struck by a sense of order, of time and place. Observers of vertical thinkers have concluded that they live in the here and now. They crave action. Their sense of accomplishment comes from doing things that get desired results.

The following attributes are generally acknowledged to be characteristic of the vertical thinker:

- Identifies specific details and the relationship of an issue to practical realities.
- Discerns with ease the immediate (here-and-now) dynamics of problems.
- Works well in structured environments.
- Sees barriers and obstacles to be removed.
- Takes likely paths to reach results.
- Knows what can be accomplished within a given amount of time.

Verticals have been given descriptive designations that reflect these attributes. At best, they are seen as organizers, troubleshooters, producers. At worst, they are seen as shortsighted and tunnel-visioned. They may be accused of not seeing the forest for the trees. In general, though, vertical thinkers, when favorably viewed, are recognized as having common sense, "smarts," and logic.

THE HORIZONTAL TERRAIN

The land of horizontal thinking has contours quite different from those of its vertical counterpart. In this land, you are immediately struck by a sense of direction, purpose, and timelessness. Observers of the horizontal land have concluded that horizontal thinkers are far-sighted and imaginative.

The horizontal thinker is generally acknowledged to have the following attributes:

- Identifies contextual details—the relationship of an issue to a larger perspective.
- Discerns with ease the underlying dynamics of problems.

- Works well in unstructured environments.
- Sees possibilities and benefits to strive for.
- Takes unlikely paths to reach results.
- Knows what impact can be achieved within a given context.

Horizontals have been given designations that reflect these attributes. At best, they are seen as innovators, trend-setters, and planners. At worst, they are seen as wheel spinners, illogical and out of touch with reality. They may be accused of not seeing the trees for the forest. In general, however, horizontals, when positively viewed, are described as creative, intuitive, and conceptual.

THE VERTICAL AND HORIZONTAL CODES: THE DRIVING FORCE

How does each kind of thinker produce answers? What "instructions" does each follow in processing and acting upon information? Researchers have found that all but an infinitesimal portion of incoming information is destined for oblivion. What determines which few pieces of information a particular thinker perceives as important enough to be stored and recalled? What determines how the brain uses that information? Science has yet to tell us. Observation points to some clues. The key is in the vertical and horizontal codes.

THE VERTICAL CODE

The vertical code transmits the master message, FIND DISTINCTIONS. This is a natural and automatic message that plays continuously in the vertical mind. In following this code, the vertical thinker develops the master ability: detecting and manipulating differences.

Perceiving daily a world filled with differences, vertical thinkers can become quite astute about removing obstacles. This is one of a number of natural abilities that vertical thinkers generally can take for granted. These abilities shape and color all they do. Thus the vertical code is the mainspring of their world.

The vertical thinker differentiates situations and happenings into discrete, disconnected events. Specific details are important to the vertical thinker because they are needed to distinguish the essential from the unnecessary. This ability to separate the unnecessary from the necessary is what gives the vertical thinker the edge in identifying obstacles.

Vertical thinkers define a problem by focusing on the aspect that is causing stress—the part that least fits. In shaping answers, vertical thinkers break them down into separate parts. Excluding information is essential to staying on track. Eliminating unnecessary parts permits the selection of appropriate actions.

The master message—FIND DISTINCTIONS—directs the vertical thinker's attention to starts and stops: the points that require clear separations and clean breaks. Thus, vertical thinkers see and draw lines. Because they see starts and stops, beginnings and ends, vertical thinkers are very aware of time. They know how long a task will take and how to schedule tasks within a given time period.

The vertical ability to manipulate differences allows these thinkers to maneuver various parts of a situation or problem. They can speed things up or slow things down. They can put pieces in any order. They are masters of changing the here and now. They collect patterns of differences: a variety of ways of doing, ordering, anticipating, reviewing, and so forth.

Knowledge of the vertical code gives us a new way to illuminate the criticisms sometimes made of vertical thinking. At worst, vertical thinkers are viewed as too rigid—possibly an overuse of their natural ability to draw lines. At times, vertical thinkers are seen as willing to move only one step at a time—as overcautious, playing it safe, refusing to take risks. But, from a vertical perspective, taking one step at a time allows them to continually adjust to a changing environment, to respond to differences. To the vertical mind, to overstep or overguess is foolhardy and dangerous. There are simply too many distinctions to anticipate and find.

Vertical thinkers have at times been viewed as having tunnel vision and one-track minds. Sometimes they are scornfully referred to as "bean counters." But when counting many beans, someone is cultivating the ability to perceive subtle differences among beans. Could this affair with detail be the vertical vehicle for developing depth?

THE HORIZONTAL CODE

Like the vertical thinker, the horizontal follows a code, a master message: FIND CONSTANTS. This message is transmitted naturally and automatically and plays continuously in the horizontal mind. In following this code, the horizontal thinker develops the master ability: detecting and manipulating commonalities.

And, like vertical thinkers, horizontal thinkers derive from their master message and master ability a number of other natural abilities that these thinkers generally can take for granted. Operating within a world of commonalities, horizontal thinkers can become quite astute about perceiving benefits—one of the natural abilities that shape and color all they do. Thus the horizontal code is the mainspring of their world.

Horizontal thinkers see situations and happenings as interrelated—everything is connected. What's important to horizontal thinkers is the general principle, or constant, which allows them to see the association among apparently unrelated events—what is sometimes called the underlying theme. This ability to associate the unrelated is what gives the horizontal thinker the edge in identifying benefits.

In defining problems, horizontal thinkers look at what's most frequently repeated: the common mistake, the link between present and past. In shaping answers, essential information includes a circle of all the seemingly unrelated variables that will most likely have an impact upon the situation. The horizontal answer anticipates how these variables will affect the chosen course. By identifying the common thread among these variables, the horizontal thinker perceives what must be protected if the desired result is to be realized. The common thread, therefore, determines the plan.

The master message—FIND CONSTANTS—directs the horizontal thinker's attention to ebbs and flows, the points at which situations or happenings mesh and blend. Horizontals see events as continuous cycles, which, like the seasons, simply flow into each other, with no clear line where one ends and the next begins. Thus the horizontal thinker is intensely aware of the broad changes that occur within the passage of a period of time.

The horizontal ability to manipulate commonalities allows these thinkers to see the unity in seemingly disparate events. By overlapping or interweaving events, things can be speeded up or slowed down, and directions can be altered.

Knowledge of the horizontal code gives us a fresh way to look at criticisms of the horizontal thinker. At worst, horizontal thinkers are viewed as wheel spinners—possibly an overuse of the ability to see circles and connect everything?

Although horizontals at best are seen as risk-takers, at worst they may appear out of touch with reality. The horizontal code reveals that both impressions describe the same behavior. The ability to associate seemingly unrelated things allows horizontal thinkers to envision possibilities. If a possibility leads to a successful result, the thinker is lauded as daring; if not, the thinker is dismissed as unrealistic.

Horizontal thinkers have at times been viewed as unfocused, sloppy, and imprecise; they are sometimes scornfully referred to as scatterbrained. But when spotting many unrecognized relationships, someone is cultivating the ability to perceive subtle similarities among numerous apparently unrelated happenings, thoughts, or events. Could this affair with relationships be the horizontal vehicle for developing breadth?

THE CODES: NATURAL OR ACQUIRED?

We have referred to the vertical and horizontal master messages as natural and automatic. People appear to naturally and easily follow either the vertical or the horizontal code.

By no means, however, does this shut the door on use of the other code and the abilities that derive from it. As we'll discuss in detail in Chapter 3, experience and respect for what each kind of thinker sees the other doing encourages each to acquire abilities of the other thinking style. Although we personally have never met anyone who was equally skilled in both sets of abilities, we have met many people who thought they were or tried to be. In fact, it is possible to overdevelop the acquired abilities at the expense of natural abilities.

Like an athlete, the most effective player on the intellectual field is the one who is aware of his or her natural talents and develops and uses them to the fullest. As an athlete picks up some of the particular skills other players demonstrate in tough spots, a thinker acquires "foreign" skills that life teaches are needed. In the next section, we'll be giving several examples of vertical and horizontal logic and creativity, examples taken from news reports and biographies of real people.* We're not necessarily saying that the *people* involved are vertical or horizontal. We haven't met them, and we can't tell whether the skills displayed in these incidents are natural or acquired. We are simply citing these examples to help you understand the way each kind of thinking operates.

FAST PATHS AND NEW DIRECTIONS

One of the questions that intrigued us during the course of our investigations was: Why is it that, when horizontal thinkers *do* see vertical thinkers as smart, they almost invariably applaud vertical logic while rarely acknowledging vertical creativity? And why are verticals, on the other hand, more likely to applaud horizontal creativity while rarely acknowledging horizontal logic?

We knew that in this world of hurry, worry, and work, results are what count. We noticed that when the purpose is to find fast paths (logical solutions), vertical thinkers more often seem to do the trick. When the purpose is to establish new directions (creative solutions), horizontal thinkers more often seem to fill the bill. We wondered why.

Here's what we discovered about the special abilities of the two kinds of thinkers.

VERTICAL LOGIC

To find the fastest path, vertical thinkers eliminate obstacles in their way. They look at the end point, identify the route, eliminate the unnecessary, and then break up the trip into small, discrete, doable

*Several of the examples in this chapter are adapted from Joseph J. Fucini and Suzy Fucini, *Entrepreneurs.* Boston: G. K. Hall & Co., 1985.

steps. In examining what makes one problem different from another, the vertical brain follows its code—FIND DISTINCTIONS—by dividing each problem into its parts: When did it begin? Who was involved? What took place?

Vertical logic is the vertical brain's ability to methodically make separations—to see the disconnections between connections, to climb from one rung to the next. Ironically, this process of disconnection gives vertical logic a stabilizing force. It confers a sense of boundaries, of order, of power, of discipline, which provides a modicum of control.

Picture vertical logic as a box. As the vertical mind begins to move into an action mode, the box stretches into a ladder. The ladder reaches out to find the fastest path. Each rung represents a different segment that must be traversed in order to get where the thinker wants to go—like lining up all the ducks in a row. A complex task like running a department may involve a series of ladders on each side of the box, which fall into place to form a three-dimensional grid.

VERTICAL CREATIVITY

Why, as we've noted, is vertical creativity often unrecognized? Probably because of the particular form it takes. Creativity is applauded when it visibly provides a new direction. But instead of setting out in a totally new direction, verticals begin the process by first creating a mess! They build by taking apart. They start connecting by disconnecting. They agree with the famed artist Pablo Picasso, who broke three dimensions into two and explained that "Every act of creation is first of all an act of destruction."

Vertical creativity, therefore, initially looks much like vertical logic in slow motion. Indeed, the two go hand in hand. Someone who has the logical ability to separate the pieces of a puzzle also has the flexibility to manipulate them: put them in a different order, create a new pattern, perhaps eliminate some pieces, and do it again and again. Each reconfiguration becomes something new, as when the elements in a chemical reaction recombine into compounds with totally different characteristics.

Thus, *vertical creativity is the ability to explode something that already exists and design something new from the fragments.* Why do that? Often the purpose of breaking an association is to break into uncharted territory, enter a new frontier. Sometimes the purpose is to achieve a particular effect. In writing a story, for example, a vertical thinker can move around elements of the plot. If the aim is an orderly chronology, the pieces may be arranged differently than if the aim is to build suspense, and the resulting story will be quite different.

Now that we've described how vertical logic and creativity work, let's look at some examples—first of how vertical creativity provides new directions, then of how vertical logic provides fast paths. Again, we're not necessarily saying that the people being described are naturally vertical thinkers, but that these are examples of vertical thinking at work.

NEW DIRECTIONS VIA VERTICAL CREATIVITY

What kinds of new directions can vertical creativity provide? Let's count some ways:

- How can you see in the dark? Thanks to Conrad Hubert, we have the flashlight. Hubert bought the rights to another man's invention, an "electric flowerpot" fitted with a tube that had a battery on one end and a tiny light bulb on the other. The idea was to light up the plant, but there were few buyers. So Hubert detached the tubes and sold them on their own, as the Eveready Flashlight.
- Larry Bridges, producer of music videos such as Michael Jackson's "Beat It," also produces offbeat commercials in which he uses video techniques like flash pans and quick cuts. By breaking up people's sense of time, he captures audience attention. In commercials, he explains, people expect something new at certain definite intervals—say, five seconds, ten seconds, fifteen seconds. By altering this expectation through a rapid juxtaposition of images and a driving beat, Bridges heightens the impact.
- Joseph Bulova, a turn-of-the-century jewelry manufacturer, was bent on keeping up with fast-changing American lifestyles. He changed the look of rings by patenting the first signet ring with interchangeable initials. And he established the first line of watches with standard, interchangeable parts. His business prospered through a constant attention to changing and updating features of his product line.
- Gabrielle "Coco" Chanel's fashions are timeless. In the early 1920s, she made a revolutionary fashion statement that freed women from Victorian constraints. Her "New Look" emphasized comfort and elegant simplicity, discarding the then-fashionable look of elaborate ornamentation. Later she introduced a perfume, Chanel No. 5, the first not to use a floral scent.
- So you think a chair is a comfortable thing to sit in? Imagine a chair that is a "manipulation of posture," challenging you to get in or out of it! Or a wooden stool called Chair-Nobel and shaped like a nuclear power plant! Paul Ludick is a modern furniture designer who uses materials like chain-link fencing, stones, and cap pistols. Desirable to anyone, you ask? A collector paid $4,200 for one of his chairs.
- How to take an airline carrier that lost $75.7 million in a single year to the number one spot in the industry eight years later, with profits of $476.8 million for the parent company? One of the first things

Robert Crandall did in 1980, when he became chairman of American Airlines, was to persuade the airline's unions to drastically cut wage scales for new hires in exchange for guaranteed lifetime employment. This then-novel wage structure resulted in huge savings in labor costs and enabled American to double its workforce in just six years.

What do all these stories have in common? They are stories of dismantling in order to create, constructing new directions by breaking up established associations. Vertical creativity at play.

FAST PATHS VIA VERTICAL LOGIC

Now for some examples of the efficiency of vertical logic:

- In 1917, Edwin W. Cox, a door-to-door salesman of aluminum cookware, had the problem of how to get into households to demonstrate the advantages of his then-unfamiliar product. His solution was to offer a free introductory gift, something that answered every homemaker's complaint: food sticking to pans. Cox developed a steel wool pad saturated with dried soap—the S.O.S. ("Save Our Saucepans") pad. Ironically, the pads, which did open doors, soon became more popular than the pans.
- At the turn of the century, George Safford Parker, a teacher who sold pens on the side, found he was spending more time fixing leaky pens than either selling new ones or preparing lessons. He resolved to build a better pen. His invention of a rubber feed bar that prevented ink from leaking was one of the innovations that made Parker pens international best-sellers by the end of the 1920s.
- Orel Hershiser, pitcher of the Los Angeles Dodgers, knows why the no-windup pitch works for him. As he explains it, it's a more compact motion than the traditional one. It's smoother, more accurate, just as fast, has fewer moving parts, and—best of all—because his hands come up no higher than his chest, it doesn't block his view of the plate.
- Christoph Eschenbach, the new conductor of the Houston Symphony Orchestra, hopes to elevate the organization to the world-class category. Eschenbach faces an orchestra whose star has dimmed, whose deficit has risen, and whose funding sources have shriveled. In a community hit by the oil bust, the Houston Ballet and Houston Grand Opera are offering stiff competition for scarce cultural resources. Eschenbach's strategy: narrow the field. Identify and court the segment of potential patrons least affected by the bust. Already his efforts are paying off; ticket sales rose about 30 percent in his maiden season.
- In the early 1900s, pineapple was virtually unknown to Americans outside the territory of Hawaii because it spoiled too quickly to ship.

James Dole, an ambitious young Harvard graduate, solved the problem by canning the fruit—and created an industry that became Hawaii's second largest.

- Need to replace a piece of broken china? Thanks to Josiah Wedgwood, you can. In the 1760s, Wedgwood became the first potter to be able to produce consistent, standardized patterns and hues. How did he do it? By keeping meticulous records of the materials and processes he used, so that when he obtained an effect he wanted to duplicate, he had the exact formula.

Each of these men, from Cox to Wedgwood, identified an obstacle to be eliminated. They knew what they wanted to accomplish. Their forte was saving time and minimizing effort by breaking down a process and finding a way to eliminate unnecessary actions—the need to repair a pen, the need to wind up for a pitch, the need to reproduce a color from scratch. Each of these examples illustrates vertical logic in action. A logic that is able to separate parts to achieve the fastest forward motion—the fastest path.

HORIZONTAL CREATIVITY

We share Edward de Bono's sentiments (as expressed in *Lateral Thinking,* one of his more than a dozen books on the subject): "In order to be able to use creativity we must rid it of this aura of mystique and regard it as a way of using the mind—a way of handling information." In that spirit, we further peel back the secret of horizontal "magic."

Horizontal creativity is the horizontal brain's ability to make new associations among unrelated items, ideas, or events. The ability to envision novel, unpredictable connections is a hallmark of horizontal thinking. The more unusual the associations, the more clever or inspired the thinking appears to be.

Picture horizontal creativity as a circle. As the horizontal mind begins to move into an action mode, the circle stretches and enmeshes to become a net. The net reaches out to find a new direction. It does this by trapping apparently unrelated information that has to be sifted down to its essence and assimilated in order to find a new association, a new trend. A complex task like running a department may involve a series of circles, a three-ring circus of intersecting curves and overlapping areas.

HORIZONTAL LOGIC

Although horizontal thinkers generally are considered weak in the logic department, horizontal logic actually is an important application of the horizontal code: FIND CONSTANTS. The horizontal brain does this by casting a wider and wider net, taking in more and more information until it can find coherent connections among apparent disconnections. Then, tightening around the constant—the coherent, salient ingredient—it weaves together an action plan geared to find the fastest path.

Thus, *horizontal logic is the ability to methodically find the common thread, the most firmly connected piece.* Like vertical logic, it creates order from chaos. As vertical logic uses the principle of exclusion, horizontal logic uses the principle of inclusion to find the right move.

At this juncture, the horizontal mind may look very slow. Ironically, it is rapidly reviewing its file of past associations. Caution and correctness in identifying the constant are critical. The right constant controls or encircles all relevant variables. Move or manipulate the constant, and all the variables are pulled easily and automatically in that direction. Move in the same direction and you achieve the largest benefit. Find the constant and you find the fastest path.

To a vertical mind, which pictures logic as a row of dominos falling in line, this wouldn't sound like a very fast path. But to a horizontal mind, the shortest distance between two points may not be a straight line. Horizontal logic is more like the path of a billiard ball, careening with controlled purpose until it drops in the side pocket.

Contrary to the prevalent notion of the horizontal thinker as intuitive, horizontal creativity often goes hand in hand with horizontal logic. Charles Darwin, for example, didn't suddenly dream up his theory of evolution. He spent years collecting meticulous data on plants, animals, and fossils, searching for an underlying theme (the constant). Then he came across an essay by Thomas Malthus, an English economist, describing how natural disasters and wars keep population growth in check. Applying Malthus's ideas to his own data evoked a new association in Darwin's mind, which he eventually developed into his principle of natural selection.

Now that we've described how horizontal creativity and logic work, let's look at more examples—first of how horizontal logic provides fast paths, then of how horizontal creativity provides new directions. Remember, we're not necessarily saying that the people in these examples are naturally horizontal thinkers, but that these are examples of horizontal thinking.

FAST PATHS VIA HORIZONTAL LOGIC

What can horizontal logic do? Just watch:

- Hassler Whitney, an innovator in the field of geometry, was curious about why schoolchildren shied away from math. Preschoolers, he observed, showed a natural ability to learn complex numerical principles. Somehow this natural tendency of youngsters to think through problems on their own got turned off during the early school years. Whitney saw a connection between rote memorization, a commonly used teaching technique, and the stifling of children's ability to see and apply mathematical principles in their everyday lives. By making this connection, he came up with a simple theory to explain and prevent "math anxiety."

- Fred Maytag was concerned about the slow seasons in his farm machinery business. What he needed was a product with year-round demand. The realization that "dirty clothes know no season" led him to introduce the first washing machine.
- Heinrich Steinweg, a German piano maker, and his five sons, who had been in business with him, came to America in 1850 and changed their name to Steinway. They asked themselves what was the fastest way to learn about the piano industry in their adopted country before trying to break in. To obtain a wide spectrum of experience as quickly as possible, all six of them took jobs at different piano factories. Within three years, the Steinways—using the combined knowledge they had gained about how pianos were made, marketed, and sold in the United States—opened the House of Steinway & Sons in Manhattan. Within little more than a year, Steinway pianos were attracting national attention.
- Ed Fredkin, a self-taught physics professor at Massachusetts Institute of Technology, has a fast path to explaining the universe: It's a computer. Fredkin believes that its essence is information—more basic than matter or energy. He believes that everything consists of bits of information, which behave in accordance with a single programming rule—"the cause and prime mover of everything." When asked how he came to this conclusion, he replied, "I find the supporting evidence for my beliefs in ten thousand different places. And to me it's just totally overwhelming . . . What I see is so compelling that it can't be a creature of my imagination."*
- Billy Scholl's main interest in life was the human foot. As a teenager, he vowed to become the "foot doctor to the world." In the early years of the twentieth century, Dr. Scholl began developing a full line of foot care products, set up a correspondence course for shoe salesmen, and employed consultants to lecture on proper foot care. His 1916 Cinderella foot contest for the "best pair of feet in America" exemplified his steadfast conviction that raising the nation's foot-consciousness was essential to the sale of therapeutic foot products.
- In the late 1920s, Dan Gerber and his father Frank, co-owners of a cannery, developed a product for which they anticipated great demand: commercially strained baby food. A preliminary canvass con-

*Robert Wright, *Three Scientists and Their Gods.* New York: Times Books, 1988.

vinced them that the market was there, but how to reach it? Dan Gerber ran an ad in Good Housekeeping offering mothers six jars of the new product if they sent in one dollar and the name and address of their local grocer. Thus he was able to approach dubious wholesale buyers with a readymade list of customers for the new product. Within three months, Gerber Strained Foods were distributed nationwide. Indeed, he caught the flow!

All these men clearly saw interconnections and made links to find the fastest path. Their focus: to examine all the variables related to a problem so as to produce the largest benefit. Once having pinpointed the constant, they easily arrived at the least number of actions to take. By seeing such constants as "Dirty clothes know no season," "People want strained baby food," and "Raising foot-consciousness sells foot products," the horizontal mind was able to identify actions that logically followed. Horizontal logic in action.

NEW DIRECTIONS VIA HORIZONTAL CREATIVITY

What do blue jeans, evaporated milk, signed baseballs, and more have in common? Horizontal creativity!

- It's hard to believe that one of the most popular pants today, the blue jean, began as unsold tent canvas. During the 1850 California gold rush, Levi Strauss tried to peddle the canvas to prospectors. Unsuccessful, he realized that the material could be used to make sturdy pants for the miners. The pants went over big, and Levis (later made from indigo-dyed denim) soon were being worn by the general public.
- After a long series of commercial failures, Gail Borden finally achieved success in the dairy business at the age of fifty-six. After seeing four children die from drinking contaminated milk, he was determined to find a way to make milk safe to drink. He knew from experience with one of his earlier inventions, dehydrated meat biscuits, that food could be kept fresh longer by reducing its moisture content. But boiling milk in open pans, the only way he knew to evaporate the water in it, left a burnt taste. A visit to a Shaker colony, where vacuum-sealed pans were used to condense maple sugar, gave him the answer. Why couldn't the same process be applied to milk? It could. The vacuum-condensation process removed the water more efficiently, with less heat and no unpleasant flavor.
- In the 1890s, Albert Spalding hit upon a novel idea that, today, looks obvious. To market his sporting goods, Spalding persuaded prominent sports figures, in return for a fee, to let him use their signatures

on his equipment. Thus was born a new marketing device—association of a brand name with star endorsements—which is still used one hundred years later.

- While out West convalescing from an illness during the 1860s, John Batterson Stetson of New Jersey saw cowboys wearing wide-brimmed ten-gallon hats. Sensitive to the East coast's growing interest in the wild West, he decided to make and sell the big hats back home. His handmade Stetson hats were so popular that he had to open a factory to keep up with the demand.
- What is it? Betty James saw her engineer husband Richard's failed invention—a spiral spring intended to counteract the effect of ships' vibrations on nautical instruments—fall off a laboratory shelf. Watching the coiled spring's snake-like movements, she quickly realized that it would make a great toy—the Slinky.
- How does one gain a woman's fancy? Georges Matchabelli, an expatriate Russian prince, did it by being the first to blend perfumes to match ladies' personalities. Soon Prince Matchabelli perfumes, packaged in crown-shaped bottles and named after royalty like Catherine the Great, became internationally famous.

How to find a new direction? These pioneers did it by connecting things that hadn't been connected before: tent canvas and pants, sugar condensation and evaporated milk, sports stars and amateur sporting equipment, cowboy hats and Eastern gents, a nautical spring and a toy, perfume and personalities. Their minds grasped new associations and spun out new products, new markets, new strategies. Horizontal creativity at work.

QUESTIONING THE ANSWERS

Now that you have a better understanding of how vertical and horizontal minds work, let's take a closer look at why each kind of thinker's answers often look wrong to the other and why these misconceptions about foreign thought can produce communication difficulties. It's because, to each thinker, the other often appears to be asking unexpected, unnecessary questions—or not asking the important questions at all.

If you entered the land of vertical thinking and asked the first party you met how to find a hotel of a certain class, that party most likely would direct you to one close at hand. In the land of horizontal thinking, that's not what would happen. Instead, your question would be met with another question. You'd probably be asked what kinds of activities you had planned. You might be given a list of hotels to consider. Or you might be asked whether a small inn might be more congenial.

Which answer is more logical? That depends on your point of view.

When someone is looking for a fast path, the usual assumption is that the destination is clear and obvious. The vertical answer may seem more logical because vertical thinking immediately heads for the stated destination. But the horizontal thinker, before proceeding, must first be sure that the destination *is* clear and obvious. Otherwise, time will be wasted. To the vertical, the destination is known; to the horizontal, it needs to be determined. So the horizontal begins by asking questions: "Is this where we really want to go? Why do we want to go there? What else is or should be included or connected? What linkages will provide fastest movement?"

To the vertical, speed is gained by dividing and subtracting; to the horizontal, speed is gained by multiplying and adding, taking in more variables in search of the underlying objective.

Suppose your boss says, "We need to generate more business. I want to see more reports, more client visits." If you're vertical, your next questions will probably be, "How many more reports? How many more visits? By what date?" You have accepted the destination as a given; your logic proceeds by breaking down the task.

If you're horizontal and your boss gives you the same instruction, your next questions are likely to be, "Why do you want more reports and more visits? Where will they get us? Why aren't our quotas being met now?" A vertical boss won't see the horizontal logic at work. Instead, the vertical will feel sidetracked, blocked, slowed down. To the vertical, the question should be "How do we get from here to there?" not "Where should we be going?"

Thus, to a vertical, horizontal logic seems peculiar and counterproductive—a detour, an irrelevant academic exercise. The vertical feels impatient, tense, and uncomfortable with this kind of logic. Similarly, the horizonal often is impatient, tense, and uncomfortable with vertical logic. The vertical path is undeniably fast, but is it going to the right place? If not, won't it end up being slow?

The vertical perceives the horizontal as asking too many unnecessary questions. The horizontal perceives the vertical as not asking enough questions, or not asking the right questions.

A similar tension exists when the two kinds of thinkers search for new directions. To a vertical, finding new directions means that something established must be changed. So the vertical thinker begins a creative effort by disassembling something that's already there—asking what existing pieces should be broken apart or left out.

This business of rearranging old pieces looks strange and destructive to the horizontal. It appears to be backtracking, slowing things down. It seems overly simplistic. Horizontals feel impatient, tense, and uncomfortable with this kind of creativity. Their intricate network of associations is being tampered with, dismantled.

The vertical, on the other hand, often feels impatient, tense, and uncomfortable with horizontal creativity. The direction is undeniably new, but are all the necessary pieces in place? If not, won't the new direction turn out to be a blind alley?

In short, instead of providing immediate, clear answers, vertical creativity and horizontal logic become turn-offs. They appear to merely raise unnecessary, unexpected, distracting, time-consuming questions. In our fast-paced world, "unnecessary" questions are perceived as wrong answers. Conversely, horizontal creativity and vertical logic also are disturbing to the other kind of thinker because they don't appear to ask the questions that need to be asked.

Both kinds of questions, in actuality, anticipate dangers that the other kind of thinker is unlikely to see. Throughout this book, you'll see many specific examples of vertical and horizontal abilities to anticipate dangers. The notion that the dangers you anticipate are the only ones to be concerned about may be a dangerous delusion.

UNMASKING THE MYTHS

Because of the lack of understanding of the foreign code, opposite thinkers often misunderstand and misinterpret each other's behavior. The charts on the next page unmask five common myths about vertical thinking and five common myths about horizontal thinking. For each myth, the charts expose the misunderstanding by explaining the proper interpretation of the behavior—how it would be read within its own code.

TO SUM UP

The main thing we hope you've gained from this chapter is an increased ability to evaluate smartness. The next time you get a "wrong" answer, ask yourself, "Is this answer really stupid, or could it be a smart reply from an opposite thinker?"

Are we saying everyone is equally smart? Of course not. Obviously, some people, even within the same "land," are brighter than others—better able to apply the code and use the master ability. There may even be some airheads in your life, but perhaps not as many as you thought.

We're all rushing to the right answers—the ones that appear to get us where we want to go. Maybe sometimes the right answers are the "wrong" ones.

A LOOK AHEAD

Are we trying to typecast your thinking? YES. Are we trying to stereotype your personality? NO. Although, as you'll see, there are

Five Myths About Vertical Thinkers

The Myth	*The Reality*
Vertical thinkers . . .	*Vertical thinkers . . .*
Lack flexibility	Have great flexibility in rearranging parts; may appear inflexible because eliminated options are usually not discussed
Lack creativity—offer step by step solutions	Show creativity in figuring out what steps to include in what order
Are shortsighted	Ensure future travel by eliminating present obstacles
Lack spontaneity	Can spontaneously rearrange parts, plans, or steps, even at last minute
Enjoy repetitious activity	See variety in similar-appearing activities

Five Myths About Horizontal Thinkers

The Myth	*The Reality*
Horizontal thinkers . . .	*Horizontal thinkers . . .*
Wander from point to point—can't focus	Focus on the common thread each point shares, which may not be obvious to listeners
Are slow to act—take too long to develop plans	Save time by spending enough time developing plans to avoid wrong paths
Are visionary	Go through a logical process of linking present and past to future—no magic
Can't organize their thoughts—skip parts of story	Organize thoughts according to significance to underlying theme, not chronological order
Are indecisive	Examine potential fallout before proceeding, to avoid wasting time, energy, and resources

many "cultural variations" within the vertical and horizonal lands, the bottom line is that you are a "citizen" of one land or the other. When confronted with new information or problems, you'll normally use your master ability and follow your native code.

On the other hand, through contact with the "outside world," you've undoubtedly acquired some "customs" (abilities) of the foreign land. In the next chapter, we'll explore how people acquire foreign skills. We'll also demonstrate the costs of one of America's preoccupations: trying to DO IT ALL, to be both vertical and horizontal.

3 Doing What Comes Naturally

No man ever made an ill figure who understood his own talents, nor a good one, who mistook them.

—JONATHAN SWIFT

As you were reading the first two chapters of this book, you may have wondered *why* some people think and behave vertically and others horizontally. We at the Marsten Institute wondered, too. After observing, testing, and counseling thousands of people from many walks of life, we concluded that each person has a natural predisposition to a certain thinking style. Although the precise mechanism by which this comes about is unclear, human beings seem to be born with a tendency to channel their mental processes in one or the other direction: a talent for either vertical or horizontal thinking.

We're not saying, however, that a vertical person can't anticipate far-reaching consequences, or that a horizontal person can't meet a budget or a deadline. The boundaries between the two kinds of thinking aren't that rigid. Almost no one is purely horizontal or vertical; most people possess a range of both kinds of skills. Through experience, they've picked up clues to how the other half thinks.

LEARNING FROM MISTAKES

Life has a way of teaching us what abilities we're missing. If we keep on doing the same thing over and over with the same unsatisfactory results, most of us eventually come to realize that there may be another, better way of accomplishing what we want to do.

Sandra (vertical) loved giving parties, and she gave lots of them. She loved thinking about the party beforehand, selecting the decorations, deciding on a menu, picturing the whole event from start to finish. But after a while, she noticed that she didn't much enjoy the party itself. She was so anxious and tired that she couldn't relax and have fun.

It finally dawned on Sandra that almost invariably, the day before the party and especially in the few hours before her guests arrived, she was playing catch-up. Inevitably she had forgotten something, like polishing the silver fruit bowl or buying film for the camera or tape to hang the balloons.

Thinking over her party-preparation routine, Sandra began to realize that she would tackle a variety of tasks as they came up, with little advance planning. She would make a "To-Do" list each day, plunge in, and get things done. And she did very well—for about 80 to 90 percent of what she had to do. It was that last 10 or 20 percent that did her in.

Sandra decided that it might be a good idea to think further ahead. Taking a tip from a friend who happened to be horizontal, she began the preparations for her next party by writing down a number of categories, such as "Food," "Decorations," "Dishes and Utensils," "Paper Goods," "Entertainment," and so on. Under each category, she tried to anticipate and list all the tasks that would have to be done, so she wouldn't forget anything. Then she set up a schedule that would help her do as much as possible in advance.

The new technique worked. Although she occasionally backslid into her old ways, Sandra was able to eliminate most of the last-minute frenzy and greet her guests with aplomb.

NATURAL AND ACQUIRED ABILITIES

What Sandra did, as most of us do from time to time, was to add to her repertoire of *natural* mental abilities some *acquired* abilities that appeared to be needed in the situation. Acquired abilities—which can be called upon to seek an answer, solve a problem, or make a decision—are learned, usually quite consciously and deliberately, through observation and experimentation, as a result of perceived necessity.

As a vertical thinker, Sandra was accustomed to fitting tasks within a time frame; but her customary time frame was very short. Once life taught her the necessity to learn the horizontal skills of longer-range planning and categorizing, she was able to apply her ability to get things done within a broader time frame.

Still, it was a lot harder and more time-consuming for Sandra, a vertical thinker, to sit down and make those comprehensive lists, visualizing the finished party as a whole and anticipating every kind of need that would have to be taken care of, than to handle things as they occurred to her. Because natural abilities are inborn, they take little effort. Acquired abilities require much more time, work, and concentration, especially at first. And, although acquired abilities often improve with practice, they're never as effortless and seldom as effective as natural abilities. Yet, as you'll see later, the very effortlessness of natural abilities can discourage attention to these talents while encouraging attention to acquiring abilities that don't come naturally.

We, at Marsten, have observed that people who achieve the highest degree of success with the least amount of discomfort operate under the leadership of their natural abilities. They have a keen sense of what skills come naturally to them and what skills do not.

LIFE UNDER THE LEADERSHIP OF NATURAL ABILITIES

It's easy! It's paced, focused, and balanced. It's what we think satisfied people's lives should be like: sure-footed, calm, energized, with a variety of interests and time to pursue them.

At times, we all find these qualities in our lives. But it's unusual to maintain them consistently. Many people succeed in giving the appearance of leading the paced, focused, balanced life of a naturally-driven person, but when some aspect of their lives goes awry and pressure mounts, the facade falls away.

Naturally-driven people can maintain their cool under pressure. They aren't necessarily stronger than other people, or harder workers. In fact, they often make more mistakes. The key difference is that they act as coaches rather than taskmasters to themselves. As coaches, they can more accurately tell when they're off track and can adjust accordingly. They can more accurately pinpoint what assistance they need and when they need it. They are often keen observers. When a mishap occurs, or something other than what they expected, they view it as an indication of the next step that needs to be taken, rather than as a mistake.

These people have a realistic picture of how long something should take them to do. If it takes longer, that becomes an important clue for them to stop. *Stop* is an important word to them, because they know that if they don't stop, they will overdo and overpush themselves and others. This stop mechanism allows them to nurture and monitor the use of their natural abilities. To put it simply, they view themselves fairly: objectively, accurately, and benevolently. They can afford to, because they are continually building on a solid foundation: a base of natural abilities.

New learnings are easy for them. They know how to teach themselves. They can anticipate what will be difficult to grasp and assist themselves accordingly. Their natural abilities are their instrument, and as their own coaches, they understand the importance of observing themselves in action.

Naturally-driven people are excellent managers. In the same way that they manage themselves, they are interested in spotting, tapping, and developing the natural abilities of others. They are confident that they can cultivate natural abilities in others, as others have done for them.

They coach others in the same fashion that they coach themselves: objectively. Over the years, they have learned to accurately read themselves. They, therefore, are patient; they expect that it will take some time to learn to accurately read other people. Working with them is relaxing and pleasant rather than frantic and trying. When there's a screw-up, they are truly interested in finding out what wasn't grasped or understood.

Does this portrait seem idealized? If you're lucky enough to have been parented, mentored, or managed by a naturally-driven person, or to have associated with such a person, the picture should be a recognizable one. You not only know that such people exist but most likely have learned from, and been impressed with, their facility to achieve—and to achieve enjoyably.

If life is so great under natural leadership, why don't we encounter naturally-driven people more frequently? The answer is that it's often not obvious which are our natural and acquired abilities. The fact is, many of us have difficulty sorting them out.

Because natural abilities are easier to use, people would normally lean most heavily on their natural thinking style—unless something interfered with its normal development. That "something" is called *values.*

CAN VERSUS *SHOULD:* THE ROLE OF VALUES

Acquired abilities reflect values: they are abilities we value enough to learn even though they are alien to us. We train ourselves in behavior that's characteristic of the other thinking style because someone or something (usually a parent or some other important person in our lives) teaches us to value that kind of behavior.

Abilities are what we *can* do; values are what we believe we *should* be able to do. We may not initially be able to do what our values dictate. But with enough time and effort, we can acquire those valued abilities to some degree.

NATURAL ABILITIES	ACQUIRED ABILITIES
■ Natural abilities reflect talents	■ Acquired abilities reflect values
■ Talents are innate	■ Values are learned

LEARNING FROM MODELS AND MENTORS

How do "mixed" thinkers get that way? The values they cherish and the abilities they develop stem largely from observation of admired models and encouragement by parents, teachers, and mentors. Values and abilities are learned from both words and actions, both directly and indirectly.

AT HOME

The first and most important training ground is, of course, the home. Children tend to emulate their parents' values. If a parent and child have the same thinking style, there's a high likelihood that the values the child learns will reinforce his or her natural style. But if parent and child have different styles, the parent—by both precept and example—will most likely encourge the child to learn the parent's skills.

Ellie is horizontal by nature but has a vertical mother, whom she admires greatly. As a child, Ellie took on her mother's vertical values and worked very hard to model herself after her mother, both because the girl respected her mother's vertical competence and because she wanted her mother's approval. For example, Ellie learned a number of shortcuts her mother used in the kitchen, like measuring all the liquids for a recipe in the same cup instead of separately. Ellie's desire to please and to be like her mother was so strong that she valued these acquired vertical abilities more than her natural horizontal ones. She began talking like her mother, too, using such characteristically vertical expressions as "right now" and "Let's get down to brass tacks."

Another example: Tom (vertical) and his father, Richard (horizontal), loved to discuss current events at the family dinner table. Tom, as a schoolboy, would come to the table armed with stories about the day's events. Richard would challenge his son by asking questions to stimulate his thinking. The questions he asked were broad ones that dealt with why things happened the way they did. He would push Tom to compare events and draw out implicit, underlying themes. He would help his son to recognize what these daily events could tell him about the nature of the society in which he lived. Tom loved these discussions with his dad. They became so much a part of his childhood that when he became a father, he found himself doing the same sort of thing with his own children. And, despite his own naturally vertical thinking style, he took a similar questioning tack, tying together themes from a series of incidents, as he remembered his father doing.

Thus both Ellie and Tom, having absorbed their parents' values, acquired abilities contrary to their own natural thinking styles.

Often, as with Ellie and Tom, a girl grows to think like her mother and

long-shot deals because she's stuck with tying up loose ends on current ones. Juggling all the details that have to be managed to put a deal to bed is wearing her down. "After all," she says, "it's not as if I or my staff are new at this. I'm spending more and more time closing old deals, and there isn't as much time left to chase as many as I'd like. What was once exciting and different is becoming routine and mundane. I wonder if it isn't just time for me to move on."

■

In reading about Kathleen, it's clear that her natural horizontal abilities—anticipating industry trends and coming up with different angles to sweeten deals—are the ones in which she excels. Her acquired vertical abilities—internal management of projects and personnel, including anticipating time and task management for herself and her staff—give her a lot more trouble. Although her work performance has indisputable benefits, those benefits are achieved at a stiff cost. Her manner of handling the vertical aspects of the job is taking a high toll.

EXERCISE: KATHLEEN—WHAT'S THE COST?

Let's take a closer look at the benefits and costs of Kathleen's overvaluing her vertical abilities. Remember, sometimes taking the time to focus on someone else can give you valuable insight into your own situation. In the exercise on the next page, we would like you to try to determine the costs of Kathleen's behavior, not only to Kathleen herself but to her staff and her company as well. We have listed some of the benefits. After doing the exercise, you can compare the two columns and decide for yourself whether the benefits are worth the costs.

Your task: In the blanks provided, fill in the costs you see in Kathleen's behavior. Then look at the answer sheet and compare your answers with ours.

DOING THINGS THE HARD WAY

In denying the difference between natural and acquired abilities, people like Kathleen do things the hard way. They needlessly take on functions that someone else could do better and more easily. Seeking to get ahead, they get further behind. They waste a great deal of time on these "difficult" tasks, unwilling to "give in" and get help. As a result, projects take three times as long as necessary and often have to be redone, and the quantity or quality of output suffers. The consequences both for the individual and for the enterprise can be distressing and costly, and the final outcome is likely to be less than optimal.

EXERCISE:

Kathleen

What's the Benefit?	*What's the Cost?*
To Kathleen? ■ Being perceived as a star performer ■ Viewing self as playing a critical role—holding everything together ■ Financial rewards	To Kathleen?
To her staff? ■ Appreciation for hard work and long hours ■ Bonuses, parties, extended vacations for all members of group ■ Being associated with a star performer	To her staff?
To the company? ■ Great deals done on time ■ Good public relations ■ Day-to-day hassles handled within department, without involving superiors	To the company?

ANSWER SHEET:

Kathleen

What's the Benefit?	*What's the Cost?*
To Kathleen? ■ Being perceived as a star performer ■ Viewing self as playing a critical role—holding everything together ■ Financial rewards	To Kathleen? ■ Feeling trapped, worn-out, bored; excitement waning ■ Disappointment, dissatisfaction with inability to rely on others ■ Overworking—other aspects of her life suffering
To her staff? ■ Appreciation for hard work and long hours ■ Bonuses, parties, extended vacations for all members of group ■ Being associated with a star performer	To her staff? ■ Wasted time, many redos, unpredictable hours ■ Lack of reward for initiative and individual contribution ■ Stress, tension, repetitious work
To the company? ■ Great deals done on time ■ Good public relations ■ Day-to-day hassles handled within department, without involving superiors	To the company? ■ Fewer deals, missed opportunities ■ Overdependence on Kathleen; inability to maintain current level of performance without her ■ Underdevelopment of up-and-coming players

Wouldn't it be more sensible and more productive for Kathleen to recognize and concentrate on doing what she does best—smoking out and setting up deals—and to delegate some of her internal management responsibilities or team up with someone who could handle them more easily?

If Kathleen were vertical instead of horizontal, the facts of her story would be somewhat different, but the point would remain the same. In overvaluing acquired abilities, she would have to struggle harder to anticipate trends and turn up "sleepers." Internal operations would be smoother—contracts prepared in a less hectic environment, with fewer hitches and omissions—but the deals themselves might well lack luster.

There are emotional costs as well. People who overvalue acquired abilities, like Kathleen, suffer from a great deal of inner tension. The more they tell themselves they can do the job, the more anxious, frustrated, bogged down, stressed-out, and just plain tired they become. They find themselves enjoying their work and their lives less and less. Eventually they may begin to lose self-confidence.

Yet, instead of facing the fact that they're fighting a losing battle, they tend to redouble their efforts. They end up trying to DO IT ALL. After all, when following one's values, how can one go wrong? They push themselves and their subordinates harder and harder in the same direction—put in more hours, take work home, draw up yet another plan to improve the process—until one day, like Kathleen, they decide they've had it, they're burned out and ready to quit.

TRYING TO DO IT ALL

Naturally-driven people know their strengths and weaknesses. They acquire abilities of the opposite thinking style but realize that these abilities are their weaker suit. When a job calls for high-level thinking in these areas, they rely on others.

People who overvalue their acquired abilities don't readily differentiate between their strengths and weaknesses. They believe themselves to be equally talented in both areas and, consequently, try to DO IT ALL.

The wish to DO IT ALL—to be equally horizontal and vertical—can be a powerful one. It derives from a pervasive societal delusion: the idea that everyone should be able to *be* everything and *do* everything.

From childhood on, we read and hear inspiring stories about people who accomplish remarkable feats: scaling Mt. Everest, painting a masterpiece, discovering a polio vaccine. We marvel at examples of people overcoming disabilities through hard work, strong desire, and inspiration: a one-legged Vietnam veteran walking across the United States to raise money for cancer; Don Krebs, who—when a waterskiing accident left him a quadriplegic—refused to give up but instead built an award-winning business providing sports equipment to the handicapped. Even as we admire these extraordinary examples of motivation, effort, and achievement, we feel an inner tug: "If they can do it, why not I?" Well-meaning advice about the power of positive thinking encourages us to believe that we can be and do anything we truly set our minds on. One of the most popular children's stories of all time is that of a little engine who found out he could pull a long, heavy train over a mountain by telling himself, "I think I can, I think I can!"

In addition, despite lip service to the value of cooperation, society encourages us to be lone rangers rather than team players. We talk team spirit, but we reward individual stars. We feel we should be able to do all aspects of an assigned task. It would be a sign of weakness (and a sure route off the fast track) to admit that someone else could handle any part of it better than we can.

This prevalent misconception creates resistance to current scientific findings that people differ in brain organization and function. "The idea of different brains is tricky," Dr. Daniel Hier, chief of neurology at Michael Reese Hospital in Chicago, has been quoted as saying. "It goes directly against one of the fondest notions in our culture: that anyone can do, or be, anything he wants, so long as he is willing to work hard enough."*

Thus many people continually strive to be more and more, believing that their shortcomings, limitations, and errors are merely due to insufficient motivation and effort. If they're number two, they try harder. If at first they don't succeed, they try, try again. If they can't pull their load, it's because they don't try hard enough.

There's a significant problem here. People who believe that they are, or should be, both horizontal and vertical demand the impossible of themselves and others. They expect and try to operate as if they can DO IT ALL—and do it all equally well. In actuality, they overvalue their weaknesses—their acquired abilities—thus lowering their functional results while increasing the amount of time, energy, and frustration incurred by themselves and others. No matter how significant the accomplishment, they feel drained and dissatisfied.

The dissatisfaction haunts them. Somehow they know that the results obtained, the products developed, the sales won, take too much out of them. Somehow they feel the task should have been doable in less time with fewer mistakes. They blame the situation, the department, their staff, their superiors, and, at times, even their own motivations. But rarely do they pinpoint the real culprit—the overuse of acquired abilities and the underuse of natural ones.

*Peter Gorner, "Meeting of Minds," Chicago *Tribune,* May 4, 1988, Section 5, pp. 1, 6.

UNDERUTILIZING NATURAL ABILITIES

One of the most serious consequences of trying to DO IT ALL is a waste of natural abilities. In highlighting values at the expense of natural abilities, people like Kathleen fail to recognize, let alone cultivate, their native potential.

Our society contributes by forcing us to pay the most attention to what we do least well and play down what we do best. As we grow up, experience often teaches us to highlight weaknesses rather than strengths, to focus on eliminating the negative rather than accentuating the positive. A bright teenager who brings home a report card with A's in English, French, and history, is apt to find that his father's first question is "Why the B-minus in algebra?" Employees are more often admonished for making mistakes than praised for superior performance. A promotion generally hinges on keeping one's nose clean and not goofing up.

Geared to do the difficult, we become suspicious of the easy. Accomplishment is supposed to require purposeful activity; success seldom happens by accident; achievement is a reward for obstacles surmounted. Thus many people fail to recognize their natural thinking abilities and the effortlessness they require.

Cutting through that cultural overlay to differentiate between natural and acquired abilities can be difficult. The following exercise may help you begin that important task.

EXERCISE: SORTING ACQUIRED FROM NATURAL ABILITIES

This exercise will give you practice in recognizing which of your abilities are natural and which are acquired. The exercise has three parts. In the first part, we've listed some common abilities that many people use to some degree. We'll ask you to try to determine which of these abilities are natural to you and which are acquired. The second and third parts of the exercise will focus on abilities that are of special interest to *you.*

As we've explained, values may confuse the way you currently manage yourself. To cut through this confusion, you need to return to the original scene of your learnings. Try to recall when and where you first developed an ability: at home, at school, on the job, or elsewhere.

The key factor to keep in mind in distinguishing between acquired and natural abilities is the degree of instruction and practice you originally required in order to use the ability. Acquired abilities most likely required specific instruction and deliberate practice—probably repeated practice—before they could be utilized at a satisfactory level. Natural abilities, too, may have required some teaching, but these skills were undoubtedly picked up quickly and easily; indeed, you may not even remember how you learned them. You may have surprised yourself as well as others with your ability to duplicate what you were instructed to do.

EXERCISE:

Your Acquired and Natural Abilities—Part I

Your task: Look at the following list of abilities. For each ability, check the appropriate column, depending on whether you believe it is, for you, acquired or natural.

Ability	*Acquired*	*Natural*
Reading a map		
Assembling a mechanism or toy		
Selecting stocks		
Telling a story		
Planning a move, trip, or party		
Finding shortcuts in doing a task		
Organizing a committee		
Prioritizing work		
Balancing a checkbook		
Remembering names		
Being on time		
Giving clear, concise directions		
Organizing your desk, closet, or garage for maximum utility		
Finding multiple uses for things		
Developing filing systems for your important papers and tax records		
Telling jokes		
Finding humor in situations		
Setting parameters		
Reading poetry		
Solving jigsaw puzzles		
Making an outline for a report		
Designing landscape plans for your home		
Writing letters		

The abilities listed above may or may not be ones that you use very much. Now that you're warmed up and are getting the hang of recognizing whether abilities are natural or acquired, let's move on to the second part of the exercise. Think of some abilities that you use a great deal in your daily life: abilities that people praise or compliment you for, abilities that you're particularly proud of, or things that you think *anyone* could do. Then try to decide whether these abilities are acquired or natural: again, by thinking back to the amount of instruction and practice they originally required.

If you still have trouble deciding whether an ability is natural or acquired, ask yourself the following questions: Do you dread doing some of these things even though you think you're good at them? Do you put them off until the last minute? Do you become impatient with yourself because you don't do them as quickly as you think you should? A *yes* answer to any of these questions may indicate an acquired ability. A *no* may indicate a natural ability.

EXERCISE:

Your Acquired and Natural Abilities—Part II

Your task: List some abilities that you use frequently. Again, check the appropriate column to indicate whether you believe each ability is acquired or natural.

Ability	*Acquired*	*Natural*

Now go back and tally the abilities you've listed under each category in Part II:

Acquired ______ Natural ______

Are the two lists in Part II approximately equal in number? If not, which list is longer? Chances are that it's your list of acquired abilities. After all, these abilities took more effort to learn, and the effort extended is long remembered.

Remembering acquired abilities more readily also may be a clue that you're overvaluing these abilities. The final part of this exercise may help you decide whether that's the case.

EXERCISE:

Your Acquired and Natural Abilities—Part III

Your task: From the lists in Parts I and II, select three abilities that are *most* important to *you.*

Ability	*Acquired*	*Natural*
1		
2		
3		

Again, do your choices indicate a leaning in either direction?

In this exercise, was it easy or hard for you to distinguish between your acquired and natural abilities? If you seem to lean toward your acquired abilities, do you think you might be overvaluing them? Are you possibly a person who's trying to DO IT ALL? Maybe at times feeling it just isn't worth it? Do you sometimes feel overworked, muddled, or frazzled? Perhaps it's time to lean more heavily on your natural abilities and seek more balance and clarity in your life.

OBTAINING BALANCE AND CLARITY

What we've tried to demonstrate in this chapter is the advantage of *consciously* recognizing your natural abilities and leading with what comes naturally. The reason we've made such a point of it is that many people don't do this. They have difficulty discriminating between natural and acquired abilities. They underutilize their natural abilities. They overvalue their acquired abilities. They do things the hard way. They often mismanage themselves and others. They try to DO IT ALL. The result is increasing imbalance and confusion in their lives.

You can achieve balance and clarity if you:

- Recognize which are your natural abilities and which are your acquired abilities.
- Use acquired abilities to supplement your natural abilities where you feel the need, but not at the expense of your natural abilities.
- Seek help from someone of the other thinking style—an "expert" in the area of your acquired abilities—when appropriate.

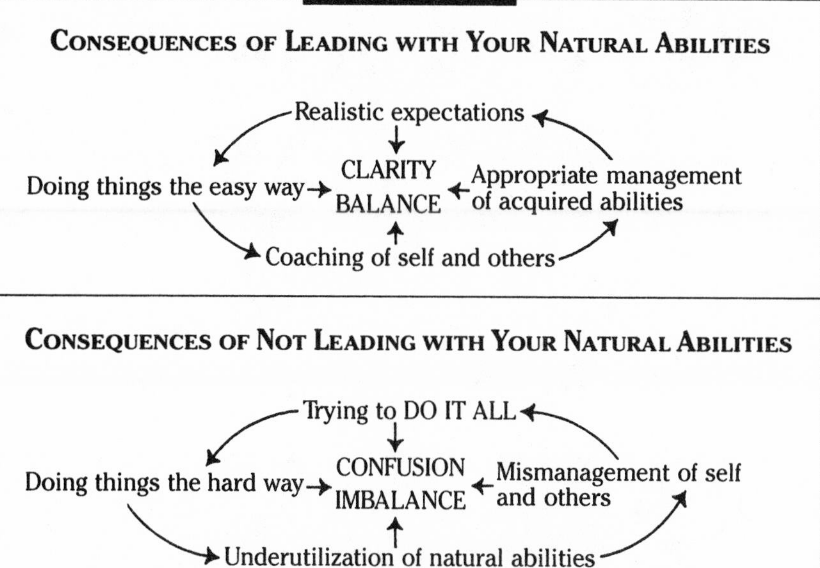

TO SUM UP

The image you present to the world is a mosaic of your natural thinking style—the innate abilities you use to handle situations, solve problems, and process information—plus abilities acquired on the basis of learned values that tell you how you *should* handle situations, solve problems, and process information. The more your values depart from your natural thinking style, the more unclear the image you project to yourself as well as to others, and the more unaware you may be of your natural abilities.

Acquired abilities are welcome additions to natural abilities. However, if you overvalue these abilities, you're likely to incur high costs—both to you and to those who associate with you. DOING IT ALL means inefficiency, frustration, and the stifling of effortless natural abilities. Doing what comes naturally is not only the *easiest* way but the most *productive* way for all concerned.

Now that you see the importance of doing what comes naturally, you're probably eager to figure out which kind of thinker you are. The next chapter will give you several tools to identify your own thinking style.

4 Find Your Own Mind

The first step is to see your strokes as they are.

—W. TIMOTHY GALLWEY, *The Inner Game of Tennis*

To identify your own kind of mind requires you to observe what you actually do, not what you want to be able to do or feel you should do. This can be a difficult task. Athletes, with the help of their coaches, consciously develop and practice the art of self-observation. W. Timothy Gallwey, in *The Inner Game of Tennis,* describes how one of his students dramatically improved his backhand by watching his reflection in a large window. But many of us, when we try to observe ourselves, get in our own way. Our emotional reactions—fear of making a mistake, of looking foolish; the wish to be more competent than we actually are—prevent us from clearly perceiving ourselves. If we could step out of our way and see ourselves clearly, our specific strengths and weaknesses would become obvious to us.

This is as true of mental abilities as it is of physical ones. Many people need conscious practice and experience before they can truly observe their own intellectual behavior. Because of the wish to DO IT ALL and the tendency to overvalue the natural abilities of the opposite thinking style, they tend to confuse what they *actually* do with what they would *like* to be able to do, what they *say* they do.

If you try to describe your thinking on the basis of the image you want to convey rather than on the basis of what's real, you'll only get in your own way. How your brain functions will become obvious if you can get out of your own way and observe yourself in action.

So, let's begin.

WHICH KIND OF THINKER ARE YOU?

As you read the previous chapters, you may have begun to form an idea of what your natural thinking style is. In fact, you may even be fairly certain at this point that you're either vertical or horizontal. The description in Chapter 2 of the patterns of thought that typify the two kinds of brains—the distinctive way in which each perceives, organizes, stores, and retrieves information so as to make sense of the world—may have triggered your recognition of the characteristic manner in which *your* brain tends to operate.

On the other hand, you may be uncertain as to which is your thinking style. As we stated in Chapter 3, nobody's brain is completely horizontal or completely vertical. You may believe that you do some things in a horizontal way and others in a vertical way. Or you may believe that you're equally good at both kinds of thinking. Such reactions are perfectly understandable. Nothing about human beings is purely black or white. Everyone is made up of shades of gray.

Remember, we're not talking about two kinds of *people.* People are complex. Their uniqueness and specialness derive from a wide range and combination of personality traits—traits like tenacity, aggressiveness, kindness, and so forth. We're talking about two kinds of *brains.*

WINDOWS INTO YOUR MIND

This chapter will provide a series of "windows" into your brain. They are windows of opportunity, which will give you a chance to guide and sharpen your observation of yourself. Each "window" gives you a different perspective on how you behave in common, everyday situations. The more clearly you can observe yourself through these "windows," the more easily you'll be able to tell when you're dealing with a foreign thinker and to recognize a Communicoding conflict in the making.

Each of the "windows" is designed to indicate something about the way your mind works. Of course, none of them will give you absolute answers. *You* know yourself best. Only you can determine for sure which kind of thinker you are. But, taken together, the clues you'll gain by looking through these "windows" will help you to see more objectively how your brain naturally operates. (In Chapter 6, we'll give you another set of indicators to help you decipher the Communicodes of the people you deal with and figure out their thinking styles.)

The "windows" are presented in two groups. Even if you think you already know your thinking style, try to approach them with an open mind, without preconceptions. After going through each group, you'll have a chance to stop and take stock of the clues you're obtained up to that point and what they tell you about your thinking.

DON'T OUTSMART YOURSELF

A word of caution before you peek into the first "window."

You've undoubtedly taken countless tests in your lifetime. You may have become quite adept at "psyching out" the quiz, guessing what answers the testmaker had in mind. You may find it fun and often advantageous to "beat the system."

In this game of "windows," you can probably figure out which answers would make you look like a vertical thinker, which like a horizontal. But the only person you'll be outsmarting is yourself. You'll be losing out on the opportunity to find your own mind—a discovery that will set you on the road toward ending your Communicoding dilemmas.

WINDOW 1: TRACK YOUR TENDENCIES

By observing the way you tend to handle certain life situations, you'll gain valuable clues to your brain's main tendency.

Your task: Check the choice (either *a* or *b*) that comes closest to describing what you typically do in each of the following situations. If you do both *a* and *b*, check whichever you tend to do first.

1. In conversation, when making your point, do you more often:
_____a. Start at the beginning, then fill in the middle, and work toward your conclusion?
_____b. State your conclusion first?

2. When tackling a problem, do you tend to:
_____a. Isolate the incident?
_____b. Connect the incident with previous ones?

3. Are you more likely to illustrate points with:
_____a. Analogies?
_____b. Stories?

4. When analyzing ideas, are you more likely to:
_____a. Quickly see potential problems?
_____b. Quickly see potential opportunities?

5. Do you usually find statistical material in a report most useful in:
_____a. Checking the accuracy of the conclusions?
_____b. Establishing the inferences made?

6. Upon first learning new information, are you more likely to remember:

_____a. Why and how something occurred?
_____b. What happened and what was done?

7. If you lose your audience, is it usually because you:
_____a. Got bogged down in specific details?
_____b. Went off on tangents?

8. At worst, when people poke holes in your logic, do they tend to call your thinking:
_____a. Too cut and dried?
_____b. Too obtuse and hard to follow?

9. Generally speaking, do you favor theory that:
_____a. Explains information in new ways?
_____b. Has potential applications?

10. When trying to persuade someone to your point of view, do you tend to think it's more important to:
_____a. Demonstrate why you want to do something and the impact it will produce
_____b. Demonstrate what you want to do and the savings that will result?

11. Do you generally get most impatient with people whose focus seems:
_____a. Too narrow?
_____b. Too broad?

12. When describing a movie, do you more often relate:
_____a. The theme, message, or moral?
_____b. The plot, chronology of events, or character descriptions?

13. When reviewing and cleaning out your files, do you tend to think first about:
_____a. What you want to get rid of?
_____b. What you want to keep?

14. When you have a difficult decision to make and you think you have enough facts, do you believe your time would be most productively spent:
_____a. Eliminating choices that won't work?
_____b. Reviewing various possible interpretations of the facts?

15. When asked a question, do you usually:
_____a. Answer the question as raised?
_____b. Clarify the assumptions underlying the question?

16. When working on a group project, do you get more frustrated when a lot of time is spent discussing:
_____a. The purpose of the project?
_____b. How to go about doing the project?

17. When reading the recommendations in a report, do you look primarily for:
_____a. How the recommendations can be implemented?
_____b. How the recommendations support the overall goal?

ANSWER KEY: TRACK YOUR TENDENCIES

This key (and the others in this chapter) tells you whether your answers exhibit a vertical or horizontal tendency. As you add up your answers to this and the other "windows" in this chapter, you'll be accumulating either a positive or a negative score. The greater the positive score, the greater your tendency toward vertical thinking; the higher the negative score, the greater your tendency toward horizontal thinking. (It's important to note that the use of positive and negative numbers is purely a scoring technique and in no way reflects the relative merits of either thinking style!)

To score: Circle the score that corresponds to your answer to each question (*a* or *b*). For example, if your answer to Question 1 was *a*, your score is −1; if your answer to Question 1 was *b*, your score is +1.

To tally your total score:

1. Total your positive scores.
2. Total your negative scores.
3. Combine your positive and negative totals. You will come out with either a positive or negative number for your final tally. There are 23 possible positive or negative points. If, for example, your positive total is 16 and your negative total is 7, your final tally is +9. If, on the other hand, your *negative* total is 16 and your *positive* total is 7, your final tally is −9.

1. a. −1
   b. +1
2. a. +2
   b. −2
3. a. −1
   b. +1
4. a. +1
   b. −1
5. a. +2
   b. −2
6. a. −1
   b. +1
7. a. +2
   b. −2
8. a. +2
   b. −2
9. a. −1
   b. +1
10. a. −1
    b. +1
11. a. +1
    b. −1
12. a. −2
    b. +2
13. a. +1
    b. −1
14. a. +1
    b. −1
15. a. +1
    b. −1
16. a. −1
    b. +1
17. a. +2
    b. −2

WINDOW 1 TALLY
\+ total = ______
− total = ______
Tally #1 = ______

WINDOW 2: WISDOMS

Throughout time, people have passed down wisdoms: sayings meant to be helpful guides in life. You can probably remember wise adages you were taught at home or in school. In business and industry, wall plaques or employee orientation packets frequently contain reminders of the wisdoms cherished by the particular organization.

Your task: Check the one saying in each randomly selected pair to which you most easily relate.

CHECK ONE:

1a.____ Better to slip with the foot than the tongue.	or	1b.____ When two people in business always agree, one is unnecessary.
2a.____ The pen is mightier than the sword.	or	2b.____ No use crying over spilled milk.
3a.____ Look before you leap.	or	3b.____ Use it or lose it.
4a.____ Strike while the iron is hot.	or	4b.____ Make no small plans.
5a.____ The early bird catches the worm.	or	5b.____ Every cloud has a silver lining.
6a.____ Be careful what you wish for—you may get it.	or	6b.____ You can't have your cake and eat it too.
7a.____ An ounce of prevention is worth a pound of cure.	or	7b.____ Actions speak louder than words.
8a.____ What goes around comes around.	or	8b.____ A bird in the hand is worth two in the bush.
9a.____ What you see is what you get.	or	9b.____ Absence makes the heart grow fonder.

10a._____ Better late than never.	or	10b._____ Just do it.
11a._____ Take care of the details and the big things will take care of themselves.	or	11b._____ Failure is the halfway point on the road to success.

ANSWER KEY: WISDOMS

As before, circle the score for each of your answers in the key below. Then combine your positive and negative scores. Possible points: +11 or −11. Remember, the higher your positive tally, the stronger the likelihood that you're a vertical thinker; the higher your negative tally, the stronger the likelihood that you're a horizontal thinker.

1. a. +1
   b. −1
2. a. −1
   b. +1
3. a. −1
   b. +1
4. a. +1
   b. −1
5. a. +1
   b. −1
6. a. −1
   b. +1
7. a. −1
   b. +1
8. a. −1
   b. +1
9. a. +1
   b. −1
10. a. −1
    b. +1
11. a. +1
    b. −1

WINDOW 2 TALLY
\+ total =______
− total =______
Tally #2 =______

WINDOW 3: ACTION STEPS

In our work with companies in a variety of industries, we have found that, when the technical verbiage is stripped away, there are two generic patterns of action that people typically take when asked to come up with certain kinds of results.

Your task: For each item in the left-hand column, select the series of action steps (A or B) that most closely parallels the steps *you would take to produce it.* Circle the appropriate letter (A or B).

	Steps A	*Steps* B
Strategy	1. Define the specific objective and what is necessary to do now. 2. Evaluate different ways to accomplish objective. 3. Choose the most workable route.	1. Decide what impact is sought. 2. Identify arenas that will be affected. 3. List factors that need to be in place.
		Steps selected: A or B
Data	1. Delineate the particulars on said subject. 2. Identify missing ingredients.	1. Delineate the variables associated with said subject. 2. Identify commonalities.
		Steps selected: A or B
Done Deal	1. Identify all loopholes—ways that increase loss. 2. Initiate vehicles to safeguard against loss.	1. Identify all loopholes—ways that decrease gain. 2. Put in place vehicles to ensure gains.
		Steps selected: A or B
Idea	1. Write down any and all thoughts that occur to you. 2. Develop a mental picture of your idea and its implications.	1. Isolate, from array of thoughts available, one that has particular merit. 2. Test it against data already available to see whether it is valid.
		Steps selected: A or B
Reviewing Recommendation	1. Is the conclusion feasible? 2. Are all the to-dos necessary? 3. Does the plan address the downside it will create?	1. Does the conclusion support the goal? 2. Are all the affected arenas and players delineated? 3. Do the benefits outweigh the costs?
		Steps selected: A or B

ANSWER KEY: ACTION STEPS

As before, circle the score below that corresponds to the series of action steps (A or B) you selected for each item on the chart. (For example, if you selected Series A for "strategy," your score is +1.) Combine your positive and negative scores. Possible points: +5 or −5. Positive tally indicates vertical thinking; negative tally indicates horizontal thinking.

Strategy	A. +1
	B. −1
Data	A. +1
	B. −1
Done Deal	A. +1
	B. −1
Idea	A. −1
	B. +1
Reviewing Recommendation	A. +1
	B. −1

WINDOW 3 TALLY
\+ total = ______
− total = ______
Tally #3 = ______

HALFTIME

Let's stop and take stock. After looking through three "windows," how clear is your view? Add up your tallies so far to find out. First total your positive tallies, if any. Then total your negative tallies, if any. Finally, combine your negative and positive totals to get your halftime score. Possible points: +39 or −39. If your halftime score is positive, check off "vertical" for your halftime indication. If your halftime score is negative, check off "horizontal" for your tentative indication. The higher your positive or negative halftime score, the stronger the vertical or horizontal indication.

Window	*Tally*		*Halftime Totals*	
1. Tendencies	______		+Total =	______
2. Wisdoms	______		−Total =	______
3. Action Steps	______		**Halftime score** =	______

Halftime indication ______ Vertical (if +) or ______ Horizontal (if −)

If you initially had an inkling of your thinking style, do the indicators so far support that impression? Or do you feel more doubtful, more confused, in need of more information? Vertical thinkers are likely to be acutely aware of any inconsistencies in the scoring. Horizontal thinkers, on the other hand, are likely to be wondering about the pieces that are missing or don't quite fit together at this point. If you're having these reactions, the next set of "windows" may clear up the picture.

WINDOW 4: WORD PAIRS

Most people tend to use some words or expressions more than others. This "window" will show you something about your affinity for certain common words and expressions.

Your task: Look at each of the following pairs of words or expressions. Circle *a* or *b,* depending on which of the two words or expressions appeals to you the most. Think about what the words mean, not how they look or sound.

1. a. surrounding — b. territory
2. a. certainty — b. probability
3. a. matching — b. overlapping
4. a. purpose — b. priorities
5. a. slice — b. splice
6. a. intact — b. up and down
7. a. doing — b. questioning
8. a. creativity laced with logic — b. logic laced with creativity
9. a. angle — b. curve
10. a. interpret — b. experience
11. a. preparation — b. implementation
12. a. rivers running — b. waves leaping
13. a. premise — b. conclusion
14. a. separate — b. blend
15. a. round — b. straight

ANSWER KEY: WORD PAIRS

Once again, circle the positive or negative score that corresponds to each of your answers (*a* or *b*). Then combine your positive and negative scores. Possible points: +22 or −22. Remember, the higher your positive tally, the stronger the likelihood that you're a vertical thinker. The higher your negative tally, the stronger the likelihood that you're a horizontal thinker.

1. a. −1	4. a. −1	7. a. +1	10. a. −1
b. +1	b. +1	b. −1	b. +1
2. a. +2	5. a. +2	8. a. −1	11. a. −2
b. −2	b. −2	b. +1	b. +2
3. a. +2	6. a. −1	9. a. +1	12. a. +2
b. −2	b. +1	b. −1	b. −2

13. a. −1
    b. +1
14. a. +2
    b. −2
15. a. −2
    b. +2

WINDOW 4 TALLY
+ total = ______
− total = ______
Tally #4 = ______

WINDOW 5: DESCRIBING A MOVIE OR BOOK

The way you tell about a movie or book can be a clue to your thinking style. *Your task:* Think of the last movie you saw or the last fictional book you read. Write down, in two sentences or less, what it was about.

____

____

____

Now look over what you've written. Is it primarily a summary of the plot (what happened in the story) and/or a description of the main characters? Or is it primarily a statement of the moral or theme—why the story was told, what it teaches? For example, if you were telling about Ernest Hemingway's *The Old Man and the Sea,* you might say that it's about an aging fisherman's desperate struggle to pull in a giant fish. That would be a statement about plot and characters. Or you might say that it's a story about the nobility of human striving against the forces of nature. That would be a statement about the moral or theme.

Scoring:

If your statement is primarily about plot or characters, your score is +5, a vertical indication. If your statement is primarily about the moral or theme, your score is −5, a horizontal indication. If your statement is about both, what did you say first?

WINDOW 5 TALLY
+ total = ______
− total = ______
Tally #5 = ______

WINDOW 6: DEFINITIONS

Following is a list of five common, everyday words: words we all use frequently. Most people take it for granted that the meanings of these words are clearly and universally understood. Actually, their meanings are quite different to horizontal and vertical thinkers. So the way you define these words may be a clue to the type of thinker you are.

Your task: First, look at each word and define it in your own words. Do not use a dictionary. Simply write down the FIRST definition that comes to mind upon seeing the word. If someone asked you what the word means, what would you say?

Word	*Definition*
Detail	
Fact	
Plan	
Goal	
Idea	

Scoring:

Look at each of your definitions and compare it with the one on the accompanying chart, "Vertical and Horizontal Definitions." Is your definition more like the vertical or the horizontal one? (Of course, your wording won't be the same as ours; look for the essence.)

If your definition is closer to the horizontal one, circle *−1* below; if it's closer to the vertical one, circle *+1*. Then combine the pluses and minuses, as before, and enter your tally below. Possible score: +5 or −5.

Detail	+1 or −1
Fact	+1 or −1
Plan	+1 or −1
Goal	+1 or −1
Idea	+1 or −1

WINDOW 6 TALLY
+ total = ______
− total = ______
Tally #6 = ______

Vertical and Horizontal Definitions

Word	*Vertical Definition (Points: +1 for each)*	*Horizontal Definition (Points: −1 for each)*
Detail	Specific part of an idea or plan necessary to achieve the goal; if not attended to, idea or plan won't be implemented.	Small point; part of a total picture or larger whole; the most minute element.
Fact	Something known to be indisputably true.	Truth as it relates to a situation.
Plan	*(Noun)* Step-by-step outline of how to get something done or achieve a result. *(Verb)* To outline steps necessary to achieve desired result.	*(Noun)* Set of related ideas that will, in the end, help achieve a goal. *(Verb)* To organize related ideas for systematic completion.
Goal	Specified or intended end result of a course of action.	Objective or purpose of achievements.
Idea	Thought for solving a problem or changing or initiating a course of action.	Concept or general stream of thinking.

COUNT THE CLUES

Now it's time to total the indicators from all six windows and see how clear a view they give you of your natural thinking style. Record all your tallies below and combine the positive and negative totals to get your final score.

Window	*Tally*		*Final Totals*
1. Tendencies	_______		
2. Wisdoms	_______		
3. Action Steps	_______	+ Total =	_______
4. Word Pairs	_______	− Total =	_______
5. Movie or Book	_______	**Final score** =	_______
6. Definitions	_______		
Final indication	_______ Vertical (+)	or	_______ Horizontal (−)

Is your final score positive? If so, you're most likely a vertical thinker. Is your final score negative? If so, you're most likely a horizontal thinker. (Remember, the positive or negative numbers are used for scoring convenience and are not meant to imply any judgment about either kind of thinking!)

The higher your final score, whether positive or negative, the more certain you can be about your identification of your thinking style. Look at the following key and see what your final score tells you about how clearly you see yourself:

If your score is:

±35 or more **CLEAR VIEW.** You know your own mind. You lead with your natural abilities and can differentiate them from your acquired abilities. With the information provided throughout this book, and especially in Chapter 6, you should be able to easily identify opposite thinkers.

±15–25 **CLOUDED VIEW.** You know your own mind most of the time, but in some instances you have trouble differentiating between your natural and acquired skills. Since you have some difficulty distinguishing your natural abilities, you'll most likely have some difficulty recognizing opposite thinkers. The more exaggerated or obvious the other party's behavior, the more easily you'll be able to identify his or her thinking style. When an opposite thinker displays mixed signals, you'll probably have a hard time making the identification. So, when observing an opposite thinker, be sure to get at least three pieces of evidence before drawing a conclusion.

At this point, you should move on to the Self-Observation Inventory on page 77. It should help you to more clearly distinguish between your natural and acquired abilities and see more clearly what kinds of actions you take in a given situation and in what order. Remember, the more clearly you see yourself, the easier it will be for you to identify others.

±0–15 **OBSTRUCTED VIEW.** You have difficulty deciding what kind of thinker you are. When observing yourself, you are fighting your natural tendencies. More than likely, your values are obstructing your view of your actual behavior. You need more information to achieve clarity about yourself.

The next two sections of this chapter—Ask a Friend and the Self-Observation Inventory—will help clear the view. Since you're fighting your natural abilities, it would be helpful to have a friend give you some input. More than likely, the friend can see you more clearly than you see yourself. Since your friend has no preconceived idea of how you should act, he or she will be better able to observe what you actually do most often in a given situation. In addition, self-observation over a longer period of time will help crystallize your view of which of your abilities are natural and which are acquired.

ASK A FRIEND: TRACK YOUR TENDENCIES

If your final score indicated an obstructed view, you need a more objective opinion at this point. Of course, only *you* really know what goes on inside your head. But seeing yourself as others see you may help you sort out your own thinking. So have a friend answer the questions below about you, and then compare the friend's answers with the ones you gave to the similar questions at the beginning of this chapter.

Have your friend check the choice (either *a* or *b*) that comes closest to describing what you typically do, or do first, in each of the following situations. Your friend may not be able to answer some of the questions about you. If so, move on to the next question.

1. In conversation, when making a point, does he/she more often:

_____a. Start at the beginning, then fill in the middle, and work toward the conclusion?

_____b. State the conclusion first?

2. When tackling a problem, does he/she tend to:
   ______a. Isolate the incident?
   ______b. Connect the incident with previous ones?

3. Is he/she more likely to illustrate points with:
   ______a. Analogies?
   ______b. Stories?

4. When analyzing ideas, is he/she more likely to:
   ______a. Quickly see potential problems?
   ______b. Quickly see potential opportunities?

5. When reviewing statistical material in a report, does he/she point out:
   ______a. The accuracy or inaccuracy of the conclusions?
   ______b. The inferences that can be made?

6. In retelling an incident, is he/she more likely to emphasize:
   ______a. Why and how it occurred?
   ______b. What happened and what he/she did?

7. When he/she loses your interest, is it usually because he/she:
   ______a. Got bogged down in specific details?
   ______b. Went off on tangents?

8. At worst, does his/her logic tend to be:
   ______a. Too cut and dried?
   ______b. Too obtuse and hard to follow?

9. Generally speaking, when discussing theory or theoretical concepts, does he/she focus on:
   ______a. How information is explained in new ways?
   ______b. The potential applications?

10. When trying to persuade someone to his/her point of view, does he/she tend to emphasize:
    ______a. Why he/she wants to do something and the impact it will produce?
    ______b. What he/she wants to do and the savings that will result?

11. Does he/she generally get most impatient with people whose focus seems:
    ______a. Too narrow?
    ______b. Too broad?

12. When describing a movie, does he/she more often relate:
_____a. The theme, message, or moral?
_____b. The plot, chronology of events, or character descriptions?

13. When reviewing and cleaning out files, does he/she tend to focus first on:
_____a. What to get rid of?
_____b. What to keep?

14. When making a difficult decision, once enough facts are in hand, does he/she tend to spend the most time:
_____a. Eliminating choices that won't work?
_____b. Reviewing various interpretations of the facts?

15. When asked a question, does he/she usually:
_____a. Answer the question as raised?
_____b. Clarify the assumptions underlying the question?

16. When working on a group project, does he/she generally get more frustrated when discussing:
_____a. The purpose of the project?
_____b. How to go about doing the project?

17. When reviewing the recommendations in a report, does he/she look primarily for:
_____a. How the recommendations can be implemented?
_____b. How the recommendations support the overall goal?

SELF-OBSERVATION INVENTORY

For those of you with clouded or obstructed views, this checklist will help you get a clearer view of yourself. Duplicate it and use it to observe yourself each day for two weeks. Watching yourself during an extended period of time is the best indicator of all.

Since you have difficulty differentiating between your natural and acquired abilities, the checklist will help you turn your attention to specific situations you encounter each day and observe what you actually do rather than what you think you should do. The checklist focuses on four types of situations in which you will most likely find yourself during a given day: working on a project, solving a problem, being commended, and being criticized.

Daily Self-Observation Inventory

In each of the four categories of this checklist, select *one* item out of the pair on each line that best describes what you actually did or what actually happened. If you did both, select the one you did first. Circle the score next to the item you selected (+1 or −1). Then total your scores for each category. Possible points for each category: +3 or −3. (If you didn't have an experience in a particular category on a given day, just skip it and go on to the rest.)

1. When working on ____________________ project today, I:

+1	Picked a route and went with it	*or*	Examined alternative routes	−1
+1	Primarily stuck to subject at hand	*or*	Integrated related subjects	−1
+1	Focused on deadline	*or*	Focused on ways to improve	−1

Tally: ________

2. When solving ____________________ problem today, I:

+1	Cleaned up the mess	*or*	Found the source	−1
+1	Zeroed in on specific problem	*or*	Connected it with other problems occurring	−1
+1	Worried about what was still broken	*or*	Worried about what still had to be uncovered	−1

Tally: ________

3. I was commended today for:

+1	Responding quickly to a crisis	*or*	Preventing a crisis	−1
+1	Meeting a deadline	*or*	Polishing a product	−1
+1	Eliminating unnecessary ingredients	*or*	Adding essential ingredients	−1

Tally: ________

4. I was criticized today for:

+1	Rushing to complete something	*or*	Taking too long to start something	−1
+1	Getting bogged down in specific details—not getting to the point	*or*	Going off on tangents—not sticking to the point	−1
+1	Being too narrow	*or*	Being too broad	−1

Tally: ________

Daily Tally

List tallies for today. Circle V (if +) or H (if −) to show whether each tally indicates a vertical or horizontal tendency. Then combine tallies to get your score for the day and transfer it to the two-week tally sheet. Possible points each day: +12 or −12.

1.	________	V (if +) *or* H (if −)
2.	________	V (if +) *or* H (if −)
3.	________	V (if +) *or* H (if −)
4.	________	V (if +) *or* H (if −)
SCORE FOR THE DAY	________	V (if +) *or* H (if −)

Two-Week Tally Sheet

List your score for each day. At the end of two weeks, combine all your daily scores and write your cumulative score at the bottom of this sheet. The higher your positive cumulative score, the greater the likelihood that you're a vertical thinker. The higher your negative cumulative score the greater the likelihood that you're a horizontal thinker.

	DAY 1	*DAY 2*	*DAY 3*	*DAY 4*	*DAY 5*	*DAY 6*	*DAY 7*
SCORE FOR THE DAY	______	______	______	______	______	______	______

	DAY 8	*DAY 9*	*DAY 10*	*DAY 11*	*DAY 12*	*DAY 13*	*DAY 14*
SCORE FOR THE DAY	______	______	______	______	______	______	______

CUMULATIVE SCORE: ______ H or V (circle one)

TO SUM UP

If, by now, you have a fairly clear picture of your own thinking style, you've taken the first crucial step toward resolving Communicoding difficulties with opposite thinkers. (If you have any lingering doubts about your thinking style, continued use of the Self-Observation Inventory should resolve them.)

When you know your own mind, you'll begin to see a pattern in the kinds of people and information you're attracted to—and the kinds of people you have trouble with, the kinds of actions that seem odd or unexpected. Once you know what kind of thinker you are, it becomes easy to understand why you become impatient or upset when greeted by these unexpected thoughts or actions.

The next chapter will give you insight into what you do when faced with foreign behavior. You may be surprised to recognize that you are reacting out of prejudice. Your horizontal or vertical mindset is causing you to misjudge and mislabel opposite thinkers.

There's nothing new about prejudice. Communicoding reveals a new explanation for it. Once you see how your thinking style prejudices come into play and what they cost you, you'll be ready to use your reactions as a clue to identify foreign thinking and deal with it more constructively.

5 Dumb, Devious, Indifferent— or Just Different

New opinions are always suspected, and usually opposed, without any other reason but because they are not already common.

—JOHN LOCKE, *An Essay Concerning Human Understanding*

Throughout history, trailblazers have met with ridicule and rejection because their ideas challenged the conventional wisdom. Socrates, who sought to teach his fellow-Athenians the difference between opinion and knowledge, was tried for "corrupting the youth" and condemned to death. Galileo, who demonstrated that the earth revolved around the sun, was convicted of heresy and forced to recant. The French Impressionists' tradition-shattering paintings were banned from the Louvre. Orville and Wilbur Wright were told that their contraption would never fly. Great works of literature and music, ahead of their time, have languished in obscurity for years, decades, or centuries.

We may shake our heads at our benighted forebears who blindly dismissed such departures from established truth and taste. We may deplore the persecution of pioneers whose innovations ultimately proved their worth. Yet how often does history repeat itself, on a much subtler level, in our daily lives? Are we open to ideas that are new to us, or do we scoff and squirm because these unconventional ideas disturb our equilibrium and challenge our cherished assumptions? Do we take the time to examine these unfamiliar ideas, or do we find it easier to explain them away?

To spurn the unaccustomed—like babies pushing out their tongues upon tasting strange foods—is a virtually instinctive human response. Thus, when confronted with the opposite thinking style, we tend to greet this alien pattern of thought with skepticism or scorn—reactions that are generally matched on the other side. Eventually an undeclared war of ideas breaks out: each side upholding the banner of truth and logic, each side unwittingly repeating the mistakes of history.

Let's look more closely at how this hostility develops and what we lose by it.

HOSTILITIES BEGIN WITH THE UNEXPECTED

Whether you're a vertical thinker dealing with a horizontal or vice-versa, more often than not you've probably experienced disappointment, frustration, and anger.

Take, for example, what happened between Hank and Fred. The two of them were to go into partnership on an oil-drilling venture. As they waited for their attorney to arrive to put the finishing touches on the terms of the agreement, Fred (vertical) asked Hank (horizontal), "Have you seen Barnes [the lawyer] recently?"

"Oh, on and off for the past couple of months," Hank replied.

When the attorney came in, he shook Hank's hand and said, "I enjoyed our meeting Friday."

Fred immediately turned to Hank and said, "Why didn't you want me to know about your meeting last week? Are you keeping something from me? What is it you don't want me to know about this deal?" With that, he tore up the papers and stormed out.

What made Fred so irate? Being vertical, he had expected a specific answer to his question about Hank's having met with the lawyer. Certainly he expected to be informed of any meeting that had occurred as recently as the previous week. But Hank, being horizontal, saw time as a continuum. He normally didn't pay attention to specific instances, or even remember them, unless they were important. The Friday meeting, to him, wasn't worth mentioning. It was but a minor step in the process of arriving at the partnership agreement—an insignificant meeting to confirm the finishing touches on a done deal.

The key to the breakdown of relations between Fred and Hank was the element of surprise. Each man behaved in a way that the other did not—could not—expect, given his own thinking style.

HOW ANTAGONISM BUILDS

Transactions between vertical and horizontal thinkers frequently produce unanticipated results. It's obvious why these unhappy surprises kindle irritation. What's not so obvious is why these flickers of irritation don't just die—why they smolder and flare again and again.

If these unnerving encounters were just isolated occurrences, they might be quickly forgotten. But with opposite thinkers—although they don't realize it—these "unpredictable" incidents are actually quite *predictable* and therefore annoyingly repetitive. Each additional entanglement confirms the initial suspicion and heightens the hostility. Eventually the combatants may find themselves in a full-scale feud.

Let's watch how antagonism can build between a vertical mother and her horizontal child.

Jane decided to get after her thirteen-year-old son, Jeff, about the state of his room. "Clear up that clutter!" she demanded. "I want all that stuff on the floor put away—RIGHT NOW!!!"

When Jane came back an hour later, she was amazed to find that the pile in the center of the floor seemed to have grown. Jane freaked out. "Why haven't you done as I told you?" she shrieked. "It looks like you've taken out even more stuff! Are you trying to defy me?"

"You want everything done yesterday," Jeff yelled back. "If you don't like my room the way it is, don't come in!"

Typical case of generation gap? No, what we have here is a perfect example of a thinking style gap. When Jane issued her ultimatum, she, being vertical, assumed that clearing up the room would take no more than half an hour. It was a simple matter of walking around the room, picking up each object one at a time, and either putting it in a drawer or throwing it in the wastebasket.

Jeff, being horizontal, had a very different way of approaching the task. First, he needed to *organize* the clutter on the floor. That meant putting it into categories (books, games, clothing, and so on) and then subdividing the categories into subcategories (for example, "clothing" into pants, shirts, underwear, and so on). He planned to put each subcategory in a separate drawer. Of course, first the drawers would have to be empty. So, for the past hour he had been rearranging the things on the floor into piles and then adding to each pile from the contents of his drawers.

Jeff was stunned at Jane's outburst. He had just spent a whole hour doing what he thought she wanted him to do. If she didn't appreciate his efforts, she could just shove it!

LATER THAT EVENING. . .

When opposite thinkers have an ongoing relationship, they generally try to come up with ways to iron out their differences—procedures for working or living together. Unfortunately, these procedures generally break down.

When Jeff had cooled off, the boy went to his mother to try to explain. He told her that he really had been cleaning his room, that he had been devising a system to make sure it would stay orderly—that he just needed more time. Jane apologized for jumping to conclusions. She agreed to give him one more day. Both walked away feeling better.

The next day Jeff worked hard on developing his system. He thought of every possible category and subcategory he would ever need. He couldn't wait to show his mother. When she came home, he rushed into the living room and excitedly asked her to come into his room.

Jane could hardly believe her ears. "He's finally done it!" she thought. "He's finally got that room in order!"

But when Jane walked into the room, it looked twice as bad as the day before. Before Jeff could open his mouth, she flew into a rage: "Is this some kind of sick joke? How could you ask me to come into this pigsty?"

Jeff, bewildered, couldn't figure out why his mother was so mad. He tried to ask her, but she stormed out of the room and slammed the door, shouting, "Is this the way you keep your promises?"

Jeff threw a shoe against the door. "You're nuts!" he yelled. Then, crushed, he sat down on the bed. "What's she talking about?" he muttered. "I said I'd have my system finished today, and I did. She didn't even listen to me. I swear that woman's crazy!"

Of course, Jane wasn't crazy, nor had Jeff welshed on his promise. Both had agreed that the task would be completed in one day. But Jeff thought the task they had agreed on was the completion of the *system,* while Jane thought it was the clearing of the room.

Both felt deceived and indignant. The solution that had been meant to lessen the friction between them had only increased it.

NOT AGAIN!

Like stubborn weeds, misunderstandings rooted in thinking style differences seem to sprout in new spots, in slightly different shapes, no matter what measures are taken to keep them under control. Each attempt at resolution raises new expectations that are destined to be dashed again. We're deluded into believing that the "mistake" has been eliminated and won't recur. We walk away feeling successful, confident, and secure that the time and effort expended have saved future time and effort. And then the same sort of thing happens all over again. We perpetually hope for the best but obtain less than the best results.

Joe (vertical) was manager of the order department at a toy manufacturing plant. When a new computer program was installed at the plant, Joe explained the program's capabilities to his staff and warned them of bugs that might come up.

After the program had been in operation for several weeks, it became clear that Joe's staff were having trouble getting adjusted to it. Alan, his supervisor, called Joe to his office. "It has come to my attention that your employees are making a great many errors with the new computer program," Alan said. "Has it been fully explained to them?"

"Of course," said Joe. "I took them through it step by step." Being vertical, he didn't see how any further explanation would be necessary.

"That's all you did?" said Alan (horizontal), frowning. "Maybe they don't understand the objective of the program, what we're trying to accomplish with it." So, following his boss' suggestion. Joe reluctantly called another staff meeting. As Alan had coached him to do, he reintroduced the program, telling the employees why the company had purchased it, what it could do for the firm, and how it would eventually lessen their work load. Only then did he ask what problems they were having. Finally, by again taking them through the steps of the program, he showed them how to avoid or solve those problems.

Alan's idea worked beautifully. After a few weekly meetings to check on how things were going, he and Joe agreed that the program was fully in place and results were excellent.

Two months later, Joe again had to introduce a new process—this time, for filling out order forms. Again it was brought to Alan's attention that an unusual number of mistakes were coming out of Joe's department. Again he called Joe to his office.

"Did you implement the procedure we agreed upon?" Alan asked.

Joe paused, mystified. "Agreed upon? I don't recall our discussing any procedure regarding these forms."

"I mean the procedure we adopted when your department was introducing the new computer program—explaining the purpose to the employees before describing the mechanics of it."

"No, I saw no reason to do that," said Joe. "This is just a simple process for filling out order forms. It's nothing like learning a new computer program. Sure, my people are making some errors. They've only been using this new form for a couple of days. Give them time—they'll get the hang of it."

Alan was aghast. Couldn't Joe see that whether the new information had to do with computers or order forms, the same principles for motivating the staff would apply? Curtly, he told Joe to call a meeting and follow the procedure as before.

Joe walked away, shaking his head: "Alan makes such a production of everything! Sure, his idea helped with the computers. But there's no reason to overcomplicate something as simple as filling out a form. All my people need is a reminder of what to do and when."

Clearly, Alan and Joe were on a collision course. It was just a matter of time.

EXPECTING THE UNEXPECTED

Why do vertical and horizontal thinkers—with the best of intentions—find it so difficult to permanently resolve their differences? After each disheartening encounter, the parties think they've eliminated the problem. Then, when they least expect it, another unpleasant surprise pops up. Each time it's slightly different: a shift here, a nuance there. Each clash necessitates more discussion, more effort to come to agreement, more time—followed by renewed demoralization.

Eventually vexation grows into resentment. The aggravating confrontations now occur routinely. Yet their timing is unpredictable and their emergence uncontrollable. Only one thing is sure: the knowledge that they *will* happen sooner or later. The parties reach the point where they dread their next run-in. An invisible wall of anticipated antagonism has come between them. The unexpected has become expected.

MISLABELING: HOW WE EXPLAIN SURPRISES

We've all had experiences like Hank's and Fred's, Jane's and Jeff's, Alan's and Joe's—experiences in which someone let us down by doing or saying something upsetting, even outrageous. Most of us have had such disconcerting experiences not once or twice but frequently and continually.

Befuddled, bothered, and bewildered, we scramble to explain the strange behavior to ourselves and to others. But no matter how we search our minds for an explanation, the other party's words and actions seem to come out of left field. And since we can't make sense of his behavior, there must be something wrong with him! He must be stupid, malicious, or insane!

We attach negative labels like these in an attempt to explain behavior that otherwise seems inexplicable. The "explanation," however, comes from the logic of our own thinking style; and, seen from this distorted perspective, foreign thinking inevitably looks flawed. "I wouldn't do that if I were in his shoes—no rational person would," our thoughts run. "He must be trying to pull a fast one." Or, "She must have a screw loose to come up with such an off-the-wall idea!"

Rarely does it occur to us that our explanations might be mistaken. "Common sense" tells us that there's a universal logic to human behavior. Knowing only one way of thinking (our own), we naturally assume it's the only reasonable one. Anyone observing the other party would agree that our labels are justified! Little do we know that we lack the critical piece of information needed to solve the puzzle: awareness of two different thinking styles. Without that vital information, the labels of which we're so certain, so confident, are actually *mis*labels.

Remember Hank and Fred, the would-be partners who were taken by surprise—Fred because Hank didn't tell him of the Friday meeting, and Hank because Fred ripped up the partnership papers? Let's pick up the action where we left off and see how each man explained (labeled) the other's unexpected behavior.

"Liar!" cried Fried (vertical), as he left the room. It was obvious to him that Hank was cooking up something underhanded with the lawyer. If Hank had omitted telling him about the Friday meeting in answer to a perfectly clear and simple question, he could only have done it purposely.

"Paranoid!" muttered Hank (horizontal). Fred must be crazy—why else would he tear up the papers over nothing? Hank knew he wasn't withholding any information from Fred. How could anyone in his right mind break up a deal over something so trivial as the failure to mention a meeting at which nothing important had occurred?

So the mislabeling begins—each side expecting the other to think the same way, each expecting the other to act in a readily comprehensible manner, and each taken aback by the unforeseen result. Surprised by the unexpected, we misinterpret. Misinterpretation breeds conflict and mislabeling. The true meaning of the occurrence is lost; the label remains.

Of course, if Hank had *purposely* omitted telling Fred about the Friday meeting, he *would* have been withholding information and proving himself untrustworthy. But Hank was not Fred; because of their opposite thinking styles, they viewed the significance of a particular meeting differently. So, "If I were in his shoes . . ." could only prove deadly to the relationship.

Here's another illustration that makes the same point. Joan, a junior partner in a major law firm, was offended by the way Sam, the senior partner in charge of her department, fussed over money issues. Every time he received her expense account forms or budget requests, he called her to his office and asked at least a dozen questions about what, to Joan, were the most minor points: Why had she bought a book of parking tickets? Didn't another department in the firm already have the computer program she was proposing to purchase? Why had she taken Client X and his associates to dinner? "It's as if he doesn't trust my judgment," she complained to a colleague in the department. "I'd never given anyone I respected the third degree like that."

Actually, Sam had a great deal of respect for Joan's legal judgment, as she did for his. He considered her work promising and was quietly shepherding her rise in the firm. Because Joan was vertical, she thought he was literally challenging each specific item in her budget requests and expense forms, whereas Sam, being horizontal (and having been around for twenty years) saw these items in a broader context, as potentially suspect to the key players in the organization. He wanted to make sure that Joan could readily explain them so that they wouldn't raise red flags with the powers that be.

However, Sam never explained his thinking to Joan. To him, it was obvious. Nor did Joan ever tell Sam how she felt about these periodic grillings—she imagined it was obvious. "What an untrusting, nitpicking tightwad!" she thought. "If I were in his shoes, I wouldn't insult my subordinates by making them account for every penny!"

One day Joan notified Sam that she was accepting a position with another firm. Sam was surprised at what he saw as Joan's ingratitude but said nothing. "If I were in her shoes," he thought, "I'd never be so disloyal."

And so, misunderstanding and mislabeling brought an end to what started out to be a mutually rewarding relationship.

QUESTIONING COMPETENCE OR MOTIVES

To reiterate: We affix negative labels to behavior that's unexpected, that doesn't fit in with our thinking style. What *makes* the behavior unexpected, creating the perceived need for labeling, is unawareness of Communicodes and thinking style differences. We try to make sense of the behavior, consistent with our own logic. We feel confident of our explanations. But translating foreign thinking into the language of our logic won't work: the foreign thought is almost bound to appear inferior—in terms of competence, motives, or both.

John was president of City Community Hospital. Peter was chairman of the board. Like most hospitals, CCH was experiencing tremendous financial strain due to rising medical costs and increasing demand for services.

John (horizontal) was constantly approaching the board with proposals for new purchases such as advanced laser surgery equipment, which he felt were important so as to stay ahead of the competition. Although these projects offered no immediate financial relief and some required a substantial up-front investment, John argued that they'd pay off in the long run. "These techniques are the wave of the future," he told Peter. "If we start putting them in place now, we'll be a jump ahead of everyone else. We'll outlast them all!"

Peter (vertical) listened in amazement. "You must have your head in the clouds. We're having trouble making ends meet right now. How can you even *think* of spending money we don't have? And what if a better technique comes along next year?" To himself, Peter thought, "I'll have to talk to the board about replacing John. We need a president who'll straighten out the financial mess we're in. Anyone who's so focused on tomorrow that he can't manage today is the wrong man for the job."

John, in turn, saw Peter as foolish and shortsighted: "Can't he see that if we don't look ahead we're courting disaster? Perhaps I'd better get my resumes out. There's not much future here."

Did you catch the negative labels? "Head in the clouds" . . . "Focused on tomorrow" . . . "Foolish" . . . "Shortsighted." Each man doubted the other's judgment. What a waste! Two intelligent people, each with a legitimate point of view, were thinking of parting company because mislabeling was closing their eyes to each other's value.

Now let's look at a situation in which motives rather than competence were at issue. Two companies were negotiating a $10 million dollar aircraft equipment sale. Company A, the seller, had the wares that Company B wanted at the right price and could deliver on time. Yet the deal, which had been in the works for several months, was falling apart.

Company B's representatives were beginning to perceive the seller's representatives as "hustlers" because they were pressing for an immediate answer. Company A's representatives, on the other hand, couldn't figure out what was taking the buyer's representatives so long to make up their minds: "They're a bunch of crooks. They must be using our bid as leverage with our competitors. What other explanation could there be for such a long delay?"

The explanation, of course, was a difference in thinking styles. Company A's representatives (vertical) kept calling Company B because they believed that by staying on top of the situation they'd show that they were Johnny-on-the-spot, ready and able to answer any question or concern. Company B's people (horizontal) were deliberating slowly because they wanted to make sure they had anticipated every contingency.

And so, because of a misinterpretation of motives, a deal beneficial to both sides might have gone down the drain. Both companies might have walked away saying "Good riddance!" when the deal might easily have been saved—and in fact, was. Fortunately, Company A consulted us. We explained that Company B's behavior was typically horizontal. We advised Company A to stop calling and wait for Company B to dot all the *i*'s and cross all the *t*'s. They did, and got the contract.

IN THE EYE OF THE BEHOLDER

Because of thinking style differences, the same behavior can be labeled quite differently, depending on who's doing the viewing.

An insurance company received a complaint: a policyholder was getting her monthly statements after the due date and consequently was being charged for late payments. The employee to whom the complaint was routed happened to be vertical. He immediately called the complainant back and assured her that he would locate the problem. In the course of the conversation, he asked her to verify her address and found that her area had been assigned a new postal zip code. Because the company's computer still showed the old zip code, the statements were being delayed in the mail. Within an hour, the employee corrected the error—got the zip code changed on the computer and the late charges dropped. His vertical boss praised him as efficient, thorough, and attentive to detail.

If the boss had been horizontal rather than vertical, the reaction to the employee's behavior might have been quite different. The horizontal boss, concerned that the complaint could be symptomatic of a larger problem, might have considered the employee sloppy, lazy, and *in*attentive to detail. "Why didn't you do a check to see whether other customers are having this problem?" the boss might have rebuked him. "How many of our customers are in areas with new zip codes? Are we set up to correct such changes, or do we merely react when we discover an error by accident?

Which assessment of the employee's behavior—the positive one or the negative one—was accurate? The answer is, both and neither. The employee simply met the expectations of the vertical boss but failed to meet the expectations of the horizontal boss. In reality, in many instances, *the thinking behind people's words and actions isn't positive or negative; it's vertical or horizontal.*

Because labeling is in the eye of the beholder, many common labels are mislabels: Communicode words for thinking style differences. Depending on who's doing the viewing, horizontal behavior may be lauded as "global," "thorough," and "farsighted," or the same behavior may be ridiculed as "grandiose," "academic," and "unrealistic." Vertical behavior may be praised as "down-to-earth," "efficient," and "pragmatic" or decried as "shallow," "opportunistic," and "tunnel-visioned." (See box.) Sometimes people label opposite thinkers positively, when the

In the Eye of the Beholder

The same behavior may be viewed either positively or negatively through the eyes of different kinds of thinkers. The left-hand column describes some characteristic vertical and horizontal behaviors. The other two columns list some positive and negative labels, or Communicode words, that are often attached to people exhibiting these patterns of behavior.

	Characteristic Behaviors	*Positive Labels*	*Negative Labels*
V	Examining particulars	Down to earth	Shallow
	Alleviating problems	Productive	Steamroller
	Stressing necessities	Pragmatic	Opportunistic
	Getting things done	Innovative	Tunnel-visioned
	Meeting deadlines	Efficient	Shortsighted
H	Envisioning the big picture	Global	Grandiose
	Seeking root causes	Insightful	Academic
	Stressing possibilities	Thorough	Dreamer
	Looking ahead	Farsighted	Impractical
	Covering all bases	Innovative	Unrealistic

unexpected words or deeds strike the beholder as useful; but generally, as we've shown, foreign behavior is misunderstood and negatively labeled.

Unfortunately, because labels characterize *people*—not just specific behavior—they tend to stick. The labels become self-fulfilling prophecies. The horizontal boss who considers the vertical employee sloppy and lazy will expect trouble from that employee's department and will be quick to blame him for future errors whether they're his fault or not.

The following exercise may bring home how misleading it can be to prematurely label people on the basis of quick, initial impressions.

EXERCISE: DON'T CLOSE THE BOOK!

What if, every time we came upon something unexpected in a literary work, we stopped reading, closed the book, and refused to finish the story? How silly that would be! Yet that's exactly what many people do in their everyday dealings. They close the book before the full story can be told. By mislabeling, they cut off vital information about the other party's thinking. They label, walk away, and stop the facts from unfolding.

In this exercise, we'll retell three familiar fictional stories. We'll stop the story after an unexpected event and ask you to describe a character's behavior as you would see it if you stopped reading at that point. Perhaps doing this exercise, and seeing how different your view of these well-known characters might be if you didn't know how the stories came out, will dramatize the need to get more facts the next time life confronts you with the unexpected.

Your task: Read each story and answer the following question: HOW WOULD YOU EXPLAIN THE CHARACTER'S STRANGE BEHAVIOR? Then read our synopsis of what was missed by closing the book.

STORY #1

The Wizard of Oz

We meet the Wizard of Oz when Dorothy and her friends come to ask him to grant their most cherished wishes: the Scarecrow for brains, the Tin Woodman for a heart, the Cowardly Lion for courage, and Dorothy to go home to Kansas. The great and terrible Wizard tells them that first they must kill the Wicked Witch of the West. But when they return after accomplishing that seemingly impossible task, the Wizard, in the form of a disembodied voice, tries to put them off. Suddenly Dorothy's dog, Toto, trips on a screen, which crashes to the floor, revealing an ordinary, little, old, bald man, adept at stage effects and ventriloquism. The unmasked Wizard confesses that he isn't a Wizard at all but a circus performer who was carried to Oz by a runaway balloon.

How surprising to our troops that the man on whom they had placed such high hopes was not what he claimed to be! HOW WOULD YOU EXPLAIN THE WIZARD'S STRANGE BEHAVIOR?

■

At best, at this point, we see the Wizard as a pathetic clown, trying to puff up his importance. At worst, we see him as a charlatan, deceiving and endangering those who put their trust in him. How could he have asked Dorothy and the others to take the terrible risk of attempting to kill a powerful witch when he knew he couldn't follow through on his promises? Was he just trying to get rid of them to avoid exposure? Was he "a very bad man," as Dorothy said?

What we don't see, by stopping the story, is that although the Wizard had no magic, he was a kind and caring man who possessed a special wisdom that enabled him to grant the travelers' wishes. The Scarecrow, Tin Woodman, and Lion *thought* they needed brains, a heart, and courage. But the Wizard saw that they actually needed external reassurance of those qualities, which (as they had amply demonstrated) they already possessed. So the Wizard stuffed the Scarecrow's head with pins and needles to make him sharp; inserted a silken heart into the Tin Woodman's metal chest; and had the Lion drink an elixir to give him courage. All three were overjoyed. He had given them just what they thought they wanted. He even tried to take Dorothy back to Kansas in a hot-air balloon, giving up his royal reign as the "Great and Terrible" Wizard of Oz.

So, we find when we read beyond the surprise, the Wizard was, as he told Dorothy, "a very good man"—though "a very bad Wizard."

S T O R Y # 2

My Fair Lady

Professor Henry Higgins, a speech specialist, meets Eliza Doolittle, a poor flower girl peddling posies in front of the Royal Opera House. He alarms her by taking notes on her low-class dialect, and she makes a scene. Higgins laughingly boasts to a friend that with six months of speech training he could pass her off as a duchess at an Embassy ball.

The next day, this dirty wench surprises the erudite professor by appearing at his door. She insists she isn't looking for a handout; she offers to pay a shilling for lessons so she can learn to speak well enough to be "a lady in a flower shop."

What could be more unexpected than this guttersnipe's showing up on the great professor's doorstep? Did she really believe that a man of his reputation would take her for a student—and for a shilling, no less? HOW WOULD YOU EXPLAIN THIS STRANGE BEHAVIOR?

■

At best, we see Eliza as a pitiful dreamer, seizing on Higgin's offhand boast in hopes of accomplishing what anyone with an ounce of sense would realize was impossible. At worst, we see her as an impudent upstart: How could she dare to bother the great professor with her silly request?

By stopping the story, we don't see how deeply committed Eliza was to her dream—how intelligent, strong-minded, and hard-working she turned out to be. Not only was she able to absorb the professor's crash course in speech and conduct befitting a lady, but "proper" speech revealed her as a far wiser, more insightful human being than her brilliant but self-centered mentor.

S T O R Y # 3

Robinson Crusoe

Robinson Crusoe, the sole survivor of a seventeenth century shipwreck, is cast ashore on a desert island. As soon as the tide recedes, bringing the wrecked ship closer to shore, he swims out to the vessel. Pulling himself up by a low-hanging rope, he finds the ship's food and other supplies dry and unspoiled. He constructs a makeshift raft by tying together masts and spars.

Looking ashore, he notices that the now incoming tide has washed away his shirt and jacket, which he had left on the beach. He finds some clothes on the ship, as well as carpenter's tools, guns and ammunition. Only then does he begin to think about how he can get to shore with his finds, "having neither sail, oar, nor rudder . . ."

How could Crusoe have gone to all that trouble assembling provisions and making a raft without figuring out how he could steer it to safety? HOW WOULD YOU EXPLAIN THIS STRANGE BEHAVIOR?

■

At best, we may feel sorry for Crusoe because of all he had been through, and we may understand his failure to act in the most logical manner under the strain of his circumstances. At worst, we may see him as shortsighted and foolish. How could anybody build a raft and not think about how to move it?

By stopping the story at this point, we don't appreciate Robinson Crusoe's resourcefulness: his ability to handle any and all adversity as it presented itself to him. Of course, he did find some broken oars and was able to guide the raft into an inlet. With much difficulty, for the water was rough and his cargo kept shifting, he managed to land—demonstrating, as he continued to do again and again during his many years alone on the island, how adept he was at meeting the challenge of survival.

In real life, people often "stop the story," believing they have the whole picture. They jump so quickly to mislabeling that they seldom even ask themselves or the other party what might explain his or her "strange" behavior.

We hope that closing the book on these familiar characters may have helped convince you to keep the door open the next time the unexpected occurs in your life. Not only may you find out that the surprising action or thought isn't as suspect as you first thought, but you also may learn that your mislabeling is causing you to lose the valuable contributions a foreign thinker can make.

STICKS AND STONES. . .

Contrary to the old adage, mislabeling *does* hurt—and not only the party who's labeled. One of its greatest and least understood costs is that it shuts off the unique contributions opposite thinkers are capable of. When you look at labels rather than at the ideas other people are trying to get across, they don't get the chance to show what they can do, and you don't get the benefit of their abilities.

Let's look first at a very simple example. Hal and his wife, Sally, both horizontal, frequently go out to dinner. Sally keeps a file of restaurant reviews. She puts them into folders according to categories: trendy, nice ambience, quick service, and so forth. When Hal and Sally want to go out to eat, they decide what kind of place they're in the mood for, look through the appropriate folder, and try out the restaurant that sounds best. Hal boasts that his wife is very efficient and well-organized.

Now suppose that Sally is married to Mike (vertical). Mike might see her system as inefficient and time-consuming: "Why do we need to go to all this trouble just to pick a place to eat? There are several good restaurants that we know we like. I don't feel like doing research every time we go out to dinner."

Of course, Mike and Sally can have an enjoyable evening without "doing research." But they'll be losing the contribution Sally could make: identifying new and different places that both of them might enjoy even more.

In our second example, there's more at stake. Mary Beth and Max, who had been married for ten years, decided it was time to build a house. They set a target date of March 15 to start construction so that they could move in before the children's new school opened in September.

Max (horizontal) was the "possibility person." Every weekend he went out to look at new houses, and every night he pored over architectural magazines, looking for ways to perfect their dream house. Mary Beth (vertical) saw her role as "feasibility foreman." She kept track of what had to be done each week in order to ensure timely completion.

In the early stages of the planning, they stayed pretty much on track. But as time went on, Mary Beth's deadlines got pushed further and further back. By March 30, excavation hadn't yet begun—in fact, the plans and specifications hadn't even been completed.

The problem was that Max kept finding new touches he wanted to add. One day, for example, he came home and described a new type of window with built-in shades that were not only strikingly attractive and dust-free but would help maintain room temperatures more efficiently. "Sounds great," Mary Beth agreed, "but if we keep making these changes we're never going to get the project out to bid, and we won't be able to move in before the kids start school."

"You can't see beyond the end of your nose," Max retorted. "What difference does a few weeks make? We're going to live in this house for the rest of our lives!"

So Mary Beth backed down—again. "I guess I can drive the kids to their new school for a while," she said. Meanwhile, she was thinking, "I just hope we can get construction started by the end of summer. If we aren't done with the outside work by November, we may have to hold it over the winter, and then we'll be delayed almost a year. Should I start the kids in the new school or not?"

Mary Beth's managerial abilities were important to the project, and her concerns about deadlines were valid. Unfortunately, Max's negative mislabeling of her behavior, and her willingness to accept the label, deprived both of the benefit of her vertical ideas. Clearly, the best use of their talents would have been a combination: Mary Beth assisting Max in limiting the possibilities . . . Max expanding Mary Beth's vision of doability.

BOTH KINDS OF THINKING ARE INCOMPLETE

Vertical and horizontal thinkers have different kinds of contributions to make in any situation—be it as information providers, inquirers, or problem solvers. But each contribution, no matter how valuable, is *incomplete.* And, as the examples throughout this chapter have shown, incompleteness leaves both kinds of thinkers open to criticism, blame, and labeling. For instance, Peter, the chairman of the hospital board, saw the need for keeping current costs down but failed to consider the longer-range costs of failing to keep abreast of new techniques. Jeff, the horizontal teenager with the messy room, came up with a solution so complicated as to be virtually incapable of timely completion.

We've shown how negative labeling results in the loss of valuable contributions. But positively labeling the other thinking style also can do harm if it causes you to lose sight of the incompleteness of the other person's contribution and the value of your own. In the example about building a house, Mary Beth's and Max's positive labeling of Max reinforced their negative labeling of her. She was so much in awe of his ideas that she deferred to him, and her own needed contribution was lost by default. She recognized the incompleteness of her own thinking ("We're going to live there for the rest of our lives") but failed to acknowledge the incompleteness of *his* thinking ("If we don't stop adding new ideas at some point, we'll never live there at all").

DOUBLE NEGATIVE

In this final example, negative labeling flows both ways, and contributions from both sides are lost.

Steve (horizontal), the manager of a fast-food restaurant, was troubled. The fast-food place across the street, which was similar in menu and ambiance, always seemed to draw a bigger crowd. Yet Steve felt the food at his place was fresher and tastier. Why did people prefer the other place?

Steve spent several days at both places carefully comparing such variables as waiting time, food quality, and service. His observations bore out his original impression: the food at his place had the edge. He concluded that the critical problem was customer service. The staff at the other place had a better attitude. They were friendlier, more polite, and, all in all, gave the place a warmer feeling.

So Steve developed an incentive program that he felt would improve customer service and increase business. His idea was to put a sign at the cash register next to an empty fish bowl marked "Staff" and another fish bowl full of quarters. The sign would read:

DID OUR STAFF:
- Serve you promptly?
- Treat you courteously?
- Give you what you ordered?

If the answer was yes, the customer was to take a quarter out of the fish bowl and put it into the fish bowl marked "Staff." If the answer was no, the customer could take a quarter and keep it.

Steve could hardly wait to tell Mark, the owner, about his great idea. But to his surprise, Mark, being vertical, immediately pointed out some execution problems: "How do you know people won't just walk away with the quarters regardless? Also, people may have different interpretations of 'prompt' and 'courteous.' And what if the answer to one question is no but the others are yes?"

Steve was flabbergasted. He couldn't understand why Mark didn't see the beauty of his plan. If the boss was so unappreciative and overcritical, he'd just drop the whole idea. To his horizontal mind, pointing out the negatives without acknowledging the overall value of the idea was tantamount to rejection.

Actually, Mark thought Steve's suggestion was useful—it just needed some fixing. But Mark, being vertical, had difficulty acknowledging the soundness of an idea until he saw that the obstacles to implementation could be overcome. He was surprised when Steve didn't follow through. "He must be too lazy to work out the kinks," Mark thought.

Here again, the labels each man used ("Unappreciative, overcritical" and "lazy") represented misinterpretations of the other's unexpected behavior. The result? Both contributions were lost, and a program that might have been highly effective was scuttled. How many deals are lost, partnerships terminated, marriages broken up, and lawsuits initiated because of such misunderstandings? Wouldn't it be easier and more productive to take the time to clarify the differences?

SUMMARY EXERCISE: MISLABELING AND ITS EFFECTS

The purpose of this summary exercise is to give you practice in analyzing situations in which unexpected behavior results in mislabeling and lost contributions. We've purposely selected common, everyday situations that result in minor skirmishes. In situations like these, the parties typically get all riled up and later can hardly remember what the argument was all about, yet the label often lasts. It's important to recognize how little it takes for a person to be negatively mislabeled and how much is lost as a result.

Each horizontal row of the chart below is a vignette about an interaction between two people of different thinking styles. The left-hand column briefly describes the initiating action. The second column describes the unexpected response. The third column is the negative label: how the initiator views the person giving the unexpected response.

Your task: For each story, read the first three columns. Think about why the response was unexpected and thus was negatively mislabeled. Then shift gears. Fill in the last two columns, putting yourself in the shoes of the person who was negatively mislabeled (a position we've all no doubt been in many times!). In the next-to-last column, identify the contribution that could be lost by the negative label. Ask yourself: What might be the usefulness of the unexpected response? In the last column, select a positive label for the unexpected response. How would you view yourself if you had made that response?

EXERCISE:

Mislabeling and Its Effects

Initial Action	*The Unexpected*	*Negative Label: How doer of the unexpected is viewed*	*Contribution Lost*	*Positive Label: How doer of unexpected views self*
V boss tells H employee what specifics to include in report.	H employee keeps interrupting, embellishing scope of boss' ideas.	Upstart ("Has to do it his way . . . doesn't know who's boss")		
H husband tells V wife to investigate landscapers to cut grass.	V wife hires neighbor's landscaper: "They have a beautifully manicured lawn."	Lazy, sloppy ("Always takes easy way . . . didn't bother to compare prices")		
H parent gives V daughter list of sources she could review to get unusual facts for term paper.	V daughter tells parent that teacher said they only had to use sources he listed.	Lazy, unimaginative ("Won't push herself")		
H boss tells V employee of new program he has created to improve morale.	V employee finds fault with all the particulars.	Fuddy-duddy ("Loves the status quo . . . blocks change")		
V boss tells H employee to make a phone call and report results immediately.	H employee repeats conversation verbatim rather than telling bottom line.	Idiot ("Can't separate what's important from what's not")		

ANSWER SHEET:

Mislabeling and Its Effects

Initial Action	*The Unexpected*	*Negative Label: How doer of the unexpected is viewed*	*Contribution Lost*	*Positive Label: How doer of unexpected views self*
V boss tells H employee what specifics to include in report.	H employee keeps interrupting, embellishing scope of boss' ideas.	Upstart ("Has to do it his way . . . doesn't know who's boss")	Adding variables boss may not have considered	Creative Intelligent Analytical
H husband tells V wife to investigate landscapers to cut grass.	V wife hires neighbor's landscaper: "They have a beautifully manicured lawn."	Lazy, sloppy ("Always takes easy way . . . didn't bother to compare prices")	Appreciation of getting landscaper who does a good job in short time with little hassle	Efficient
H parent gives V daughter list of sources she could review to get unusual facts for term paper.	V daughter tells parent that teacher said they only had to use sources he listed.	Lazy, unimaginative ("Won't push herself")	Ability to follow specific instructions, stay within parameters of assignment	Obedient Responsive
H boss tells V employee of new program he has created to improve morale.	V employee finds fault with all the particulars.	Fuddy-duddy ("loves the status quo . . . blocks change")	Identification of problems that have to be solved to implement idea	Realist
V boss tells H employee to make a phone call and report results immediately.	H employee repeats conversation verbatim rather than telling bottom line.	Idiot ("Can't separate what's important from what's not")	Recognition of possible importance of information other than result	Thorough Detailed

In these vignettes, did you see how easy it is to attach negative labels to behavior that might seem quite reasonable if given more thought? Did you see how much can get lost, and how quickly? Can you imagine how the hostility between these thinkers might grow? Chances are this wasn't the first and won't be the last such encounter.

Can you remember a similar conflict you've been in? Did you negatively label the other party? If so, what contribution did you lose as a result?

TO SUM UP

In this chapter, we've described how antagonism develops between vertical and horizontal thinkers. What starts out as unexpected behavior causes disappointment and mistrust. The continual, repetitive nature of these encounters excites suspicion, combativeness, and eventually, hostility.

When people who don't understand Communicoding try to make sense of these unexpected occurrences, their interpretations generally are based on their own logic rather than the logic of the person being described. As a result, they mislabel and misjudge, questioning the competency and/or the motives of the foreign thinker. Once the label is in place, any contribution the other party may have to offer gets lost.

To prevent mislabeling, it's necessary, first of all, to be aware that all people do not think the same. Viewing another person through the lens of your own logic will usually cause the other to look inferior.

Secondly, it's important to realize that the unexpected *will* occur, and, rather than being disgruntled by it, to welcome it as a clue that you may have entered a foreign land rich in wealth that you can share if you don't walk away prematurely.

In the next chapter, we'll give you various techniques for spotting and identifying foreign thinkers. Once you start trying to understand foreign behavior on its own terms, you may be surprised that it isn't as strange as it first appears.

6 How the Other Half Thinks

Oh is it true
There's no Ground Common enough for me and you

—LOU REED, "Good Evening Mr. Waldheim"

If certain parties continually drive you up the wall, if the strategies you work out to smooth your relations with them perpetually fail, could the culprit be a thinking style difference? How can you tell? When you experience a mystifying clash, take the other party's "bizarre" behavior as a tipoff—a clue that the origin of the conflict may not be as mysterious as it seems.

Think like an anthropologist: look for patterns. Is your strange encounter an isolated occurrence, or do such "unpredictable" incidents occur with predictable frequency in your life? Is this particular party your nemesis, or might you have a more general problem—a problem with opposite thinking?

WINDOWS TO FOREIGN THOUGHT

This chapter will give you the investigative tools you need to detect patterns of foreign thought that may be causing your communication disturbances. Using these tools, you'll be able to draw back the curtains of subjective judgment and open some "windows" on how the other half thinks. Through this series of "windows," you can observe—closely, calmly, and dispassionately—the people who cause you the most grief. The people who interfere with where you want to get.

The special "glass" in these windows will filter out your emotional reactions and give you an eye-opening view. It will allow you to see through the surface image these parties project and penetrate to the codes that govern their behavior.

Each window will add to the breadth and depth of your perspective. Taken together, they'll give you a series of indicators, or clues, that you can analyze to learn whether opposite thinking is the explanation for your mysterious clashes.

Of course, as we pointed out in Chapter 4, the better able you are to observe *yourself*—to gaze into the "windows" of your own brain—the more clearly and accurately you'll be able to observe others. You'll be better able to focus on what they are *actually saying or doing*.

"TIPPING" THE SCALES

As you go through the "windows," you'll be detecting clues to foreign thought. Looking at someone's behavior through the "windows" allows you to isolate it from its real-world environment and study it like a scientist in a laboratory. After you've made your observations and arrived at a hypothesis about the other party's thinking style, you'll need to go out "in the field" and look for hard evidence to support your hypothesis.

Following each "window" is a practical tip—a way to field test the accuracy of your laboratory findings. Each tip gives you a way to confirm the existence of foreign thought. If opposite thinking is confirmed, the tension between you and the other party will quickly ease.

As you use the tips, you'll start to talk the way the other half thinks. You'll probably find yourself heading off clashes before they occur. As you continue to read this book and add to your repertoire of Communicoding strategies, you'll be able to tip the scales toward productive dealings with people who have previously mystified you.

THE PRELIMS: SCREENING CANDIDATES

Start by screening candidates for observation. The best candidates are the ones who frustrate you the most, who drive you crazy, who get in your way. The ones you want to avoid but can't. Look again at the box, "Early Warning Signs of a Communicoding Clash." If these signs are showing up in your relations with a certain party, there's reason to suspect opposite thinking.

EARLY WARNING SIGNS OF A COMMUNICODING CLASH

- You can predict that an issue will develop between you and a certain party, but you can't predict when it will arise or what it will be about.
- You are repeatedly surprised by the other party's actions and reactions.
- You find yourself questioning the other party's common sense, character, and/or motives.
- In a particular interaction, only one party appears smart.

After reviewing the list of signs, you probably have more than one candidate in mind. Since you're looking for patterns in your communication problems, it will be wise to go through the series of windows with two or three of these candidates. To start with, pick the one to whom the signs point most strongly. The harder a person is to deal with, the easier it should be to recognize foreign thinking.

Got your party in mind? Then let's begin. Where to start looking for clues? Where you are right now: in your own head.

WINDOW 1: LOOK AT YOUR LABELS

This first window opens inward rather than outward. The clue is in your own mind. As you saw in Chapter 5, your tendency to misinterpret and mislabel "bizarre" behavior can be an important indication that you're dealing with foreign thinking.

Let's look at the labels you attach to others and use them as an indication of which kind of thinking you're dealing with.

Your task: Look at the following pairs of contrasting thoughts. Choose the one thought in each pair that you've more often had about the other party. Circle *a* or *b*.

1. a. "Thinking too shallow"
b. "Can't get to the point"

2. a. "Overcomplicates the situation"
b. "Oversimplifies the situation"

3. a. "Doomsayer"
b. "Pie-in-the-sky mentality"

4. a. "Too cut and dried"
b. "Too obtuse and hard to follow"

5. a. "Can't see the forest for the trees"
b. "Can't see the trees for the forest"

6. a. "Takes forever to start"
b. "Jumps in without a clear idea of where he/she is going"

7. a. "Ideas are great in theory but have little practical application"
b. "Ideas suggested are not new—just the same thing in different words"

8. a. "Can't make a decision—goes round and round"
b. "Makes snap decisions—not well thought out"

9. a. "Can't answer a simple question"
b. "Answers without thinking"

10. a. "Forgetful—can't remember what happened and what was done"
b. "Forgetful—can't remember why and how something occurred"

ANSWER KEY: LOOK AT YOUR LABELS

Compare your answers with the key below. Total the positive and negative scores and combine the totals. Possible points: +10 or −10. The greater the positive tally, the greater the indication of vertical thinking; the greater the negative tally, the greater the indication of horizontal thinking. (Remember, as we explained in Chapter 4, the use of positive and negative scoring is purely for convenience and does not reflect on the value of either thinking style.)

1. a. +1
   b. −1
2. a. −1
   b. +1
3. a. +1
   b. −1
4. a. +1
   b. −1
5. a. +1
   b. −1
6. a. −1
   b. +1
7. a. −1
   b. +1
8. a. −1
   b. +1
9. a. −1
   b. +1
10. a. −1
    b. +1

WINDOW 1 TALLY
+ total = ______
− total = ______
Tally #1 = ______

Now that you have your first indication of vertical or horizontal thinking, it's time to apply that information. How can you use your negative thoughts to confirm when foreign thinking is at play?

Here's your first tip:

Tip #1
Turning "Fiction" Into Fact

Since people of one thinking style tend to have predictably negative thoughts about people of the other thinking style, wouldn't it be convenient if there were an easy way to use those negative thoughts as a reference guide to verify the presence of foreign thinking?

There is. The accompanying "Fact and Fiction" charts provide a dictionary—or rather, a "fictionary"—of vertical and horizontal behavior. Here's how to use it:

On the chart for *your thinking style,* look up in the first column ("The Situation") what the other party is doing. In the second column ("The Fiction"), you'll find the label, or subjective explanation, that this party's behavior probably brings to your mind. The third column ("The Fact") tells you how to read the same behavior according to the opposite thinker's code.

If you find yourself in one of the situations described in Column 1 and your thoughts about the other party resemble "the fiction," check out the facts. Say to yourself, "What is this party actually doing? Is it what's described in Column 3?" If the answer is yes, the other party is probably a foreign thinker. If the answer is no, your original conclusion may be right!

Use your "fictionary" often; familiarize yourself with its contents. You'll be surprised at how many potential blow-ups you'll avoid by turning fiction into fact!

FOR HORIZONTALS ONLY:

The Fact and Fiction About Vertical Behavior

The Situation: When other party . . .	*The Fiction: How you react . . .*	*The Fact: According to V-code . . .*
Makes a point	"Thinking so shallow"	States conclusions first
Tackles a problem	"Oversimplifies the situation"	Isolates the incident
Analyzes new ideas	"Doomsayer"	Quickly sees potential problems
Expresses thoughts	"Too cut and dried"	Speaks in specific terms and sticks to subject
Tries to persuade	"Can't see forest for the trees"	Stresses what he/she wants to do and savings that will result
Starts a project	"Jumps in without a clear picture of where he/she is going"	Expects picture to change as he/she proceeds; uses beginning to shape finish—goes from A to B, B to C, etc.
Makes a decision	"Snap decision—not well thought out"	Quickly eliminates what won't work
Is asked a question	"Puts no thought into answer"	Answers question as raised
Is asked to recall information	"Never remembers details" (the context)	Remembers details surrounding what happened and how it was carried out (the events)
Discusses theory	"Can't see how it adds to what we already know"	Sees usefulness as practical application

FOR VERTICALS ONLY:

The Fact and Fiction About Horizontal Behavior

The Situation: When other party . . .	*The Fiction: How you react . . .*	*The Fact: According to H-code . . .*
Makes a point	"Can't get to the point"	Starts at beginning, fills in middle, works toward conclusion
Tackles a problem	"Overcomplicates the situation"	Connects to previous problems
Analyzes new ideas	"Pie-in-the-sky mentality"	Quickly sees potential opportunities
Expresses thoughts	"Too obtuse and hard to follow"	Speaks in general terms and brings in related subjects
Tries to persuade	"Can't see trees for the forest"	Stresses why he/she wants to do something and impact it will produce
Starts a project	"Takes forever to start"	Determines picture of finish before starting—goes from Z to A.
Makes a decision	"Can't make a decision—goes round and round"	Reviews various interpretations of facts
Is asked a question	"Can't answer a simple question"	Clarifies assumptions underlying question
Is asked to recall information	"Never remembers details" (the events)	Remembers contextual details—why and how something came about
Discusses theory	"Can't show usefulness, potential application"	Sees usefulness as explanation of information in new way

WINDOW 2: TELLTALE PHRASES

Sherlock Holmes frequently astounded his friend, Dr. Watson, by deducing the occupation, place of origin, educational background, and other information about a perfect stranger from keen observation of (among other things) the person's manner of speech. You, too, may have found that you can make educated guesses about other people by paying attention to the expressions they use in everyday conversation. You may be able to spot a lawyer, for example, by the use of such expressions as "It's my position that. . . ." You may be able to recognize a Southerner by the use of dialect ("you-all"). What you may not have realized before is that you may be able to get clues to someone's thinking style from certain characteristic Communicode expressions.

In this "window," you'll see a list of typical vertical and horizontal phrases, which you can use as clues to your party's thinking style. Careful, though: Language doesn't tell the whole story. Just as a Chicagoan who moves to Texas may take on local colloquialisms like "Howdy," many people adopt idioms of the other thinking style. Their choice of words may reflect acquired values and mask natural tendencies.

"Actions speak louder than words" is your best guidepost. If actions and words don't match, the words are probably not a reliable indicator of thinking style. But, taken in conjunction with other indicators in this chapter and with careful observation of behavior, the following list may be a helpful guide.

Your task: In the following chart, put a check to the left of the *one* expression in each numbered pair that resembles what you hear the other party say most often.

Typical Vertical and Horizontal Communicode Phrases

	Vertical Communicode	*Horizontal Communicode*
1.	____ "Staring us right in the face is the fact . . ."	____ "If we'd only look slightly beneath the surface . . ."
2.	____ "A practical consideration is . . ."	____ "Down the road . . ."
3.	____ "This situation is loaded with minefields."	____ "This situation is filled with opportunities."
4.	____ "Why second-guess the future?"	____ "Why limit our sights?"
5.	____ "Let's get rid of this mess."	____ "Hasn't this happened before?"
6.	____ "If there are any other problems, let's handle them as they occur."	____ "Let's try to figure out what could go wrong."
7.	____ "What can we drop and still achieve our present objective?"	____ "What must we include to meet our foreseeable needs?"
8.	____ "Get started and finish by . . ."	____ "Find a better . . ."
9.	____ "Nothing else matters if we don't fix this today."	____ "If we don't achieve the response we're after, we might as well not do this."
10.	____ "At any rate, to proceed we need to do this . . ."	____ "There are several ways we can go—depends on . . ."
11.	____ "Our immediate need/most pressing concern is . . ."	____ "Let's look at the bigger picture . . ."
12.	____ "There's no time left for changes . . ."	____ "A few minor changes could really improve . . ."
13.	____ "That reminds me of the time Willie Mays . . ."	____ "It's like a no-hitter—well-planned and beautifully executed."
14.	____ "Let's try to fit it to our budget and see where we have to cut . . ."	____ "Let's project what we'll need over time . . ."

Scoring: For each vertical Communicode phrase you checked, score +1; for each horizontal phrase, −1. Total the positive and negative scores and then combine the totals. Possible points: +14 or −14. The greater the positive tally, the greater the indication of vertical thinking; the greater the negative tally, the greater the indication of horizontal thinking.

WINDOW 2 TALLY
\+ total = ______
− total = ______
Tally #2 = ______

Analyzing the score: As we pointed out at the opening of this window, people sometimes say one thing and do another, and what they do is more revealing than what they say. So the indicator for Window 2 must be weighed carefully against the others in this chapter. If, for example, your party uses more vertical than horizontal expressions and the other clues fall in a vertical track, you have a strong indication that this party's natural thinking style is vertical. However, if the majority of the other clues point in a horizontal direction, it's more likely that the natural thinking style is horizontal but the mode of expression is being affected by vertical values.

Your tip for Window 2 gives you one way of gauging words against deeds. When you observe a party doing one thing and saying another, Tip #2 will help you use that observation to identify that party's thinking style.

TIP #2:
LOOK FOR THE DOUBLE STANDARD

We all know people who seem to operate under a double standard: "Do as I say, not as I do." They may say, "I expect you to be at the meeting at 9:00 A.M.—sharp!" and then not show up themselves until 9:15. Watch for these "double standard" behaviors. The actions rather than the words may be clues to the party's natural thinking style.

Look for inconsistency. If the party sometimes performs the "expected" behavior and at other times does not, the reason may not be a double standard at all. It may be that the "expected" behavior is an acquired ability, which is highly valued but which becomes hard to carry out, especially when under stress. If, over a period of time, you observe such inconsistency, you can be fairly sure that what this party is saying reflects values and *what the party is doing* when under stress reflects his or her natural thinking style.

WINDOW 3: TELLING ABOUT A MOVIE OR BOOK

As you saw in Chapter 4, the way someone describes a movie or book can be a clue to thinking style. Engage the other party in a discussion about a film or novel he or she recently enjoyed. It doesn't matter whether you yourself saw the movie or read the book; in fact, it may work better if you didn't.

Be sure that your *first* question is: "What was ________ [the movie or book] about?" Pay very close attention to what your party says first. Does he or she stress the story line, the chronology of events, or character depiction? If so, score +5. Or does the party stress the moral, message, or theme? If so, score −5.

WINDOW 3 TALLY
Tally #3 = ______

As Window 3 shows, when recalling or telling a story, vertical thinkers tend to focus on what happened, in what order, and to whom. They pay close attention to how characters are portrayed. Horizontal thinkers tend to focus on how various elements (action, dialogue, lighting, and so forth) are brought together to highlight the author's or director's point of view.

Vertical thinkers are better able to recall details about plot and character because, as we've discussed, their brains tend to perceive *differences*. They see clear lines of distinction between the various events in a chronology, or between various characters. Horizontal thinkers are better able to recall the underlying message or theme because their brains tend to perceive *commonalities*. They see the constant elements that run through the whole story.

How can you use this knowledge about the differing capabilities of the two kinds of thinkers? Tip #3 will tell you how to identify the party best able to deliver needed information.

Tip #3
Opposite Thinking to Your Rescue

Suppose you're working on a project or report that's due tomorrow, and you're stuck. You've misplaced some of your notes, and you're trying to recall specific, concrete facts, such as when a conference took place, what happened, who attended. Or suppose you need to differentiate between various product lines, recommendations, or investments, and you're having trouble identifying the distinctive attributes of each. A vertical colleague probably will be able to supply the information you need, quickly and easily.

On the other hand, if you're going crazy trying to draw out underlying assumptions or principles from a mountain of data, or if you need an immediate read on what various product lines, recommendations, or investments have in common, a horizontal thinker probably can save the day.

HALFTIME

What's the score so far? Let's add up the indicators. Possible points: +29 or −29.

Window	*Tally*		*Halftime Totals*	
1. Labels	______		+Total =	______
2. Telltale Phrases	______		−Total =	______
3. Movie or Book	______		**Halftime score** =	______
Halftime indication	______ Vertical (if +)	or	______ Horizontal (if −)	

Are you getting a fairly clear picture yet? If not, don't worry; as you continue moving through the "windows," your ability to identify the opposite thinker will undoubtedly improve. Also, using the tips should help clear the view. Look up odd behavior in your "fictionary" . . . watch out for the "double standard" . . . see who's good at doing what on the job. Then take another look through the "windows" and see whether your vision has sharpened.

Don't forget: After you finish getting the picture of your first candidate's thinking style, you should try a second or third candidate to see whether you can discern a pattern of opposite thinking in your communication snafus. The more people you view through the "windows," the better able you'll become to spot clues and identify patterns in foreign thought.

t Thinker

P. to Manager

to arrange a meeting with week. I want no slip-ups. im the prospectus on the deal :e him with the specifics . . ."

V or H

b. "Much of our Midwest business depends on how our meeting with Larson is handled. I'm planning major expansions, and this meeting will pave the way . . ."

V or H

oach to Racquetball Player

ay to improve your game is to d play the corners . . ."

V or H

b. "The key ingredient in racquetball is speed. The faster you are on your feet, the more opportunities you have . . ."

V or H

octor to Patient

ant to take this medicine to inuses . . ."

V or H

b. "You'll breathe better if you take this three times a day for a week . . ."

V or H

hairman of Board to CEO

want to double our asset

V or H

b. "I want to really increase our power base in the industry . . ."

V or H

epartment Manager to Assistant

to help figure out a way to staff to really benefit from this etreat . . ."

V or H

b. "We need to decide on issues to be discussed at the staff retreat, when and where to hold it, and who will be included . . ."

V or H

oss to Secretary

ing to improve our tions to the East coast. There oney to be made if we can e this letter and show it to me et it out right away . . ."

V or H

b. "I want this letter typed and Fed Ex'd to New York before the end of business today. Remember the time difference! . . ."

V or H

EO of Merging Company to Management Team

ensure a smooth and orderly t's important to delineate all e're likely to encounter next three months . . ."

V or H

b. "This merger is about collaboration—combining resources to gain market share. I want to ensure positive receptivity internally and externally . . ."

V or H

arent to Child

come home from school t you to do your homework e your piano immediately. We for dinner at 5:30 . . ."

V or H

b. "I am really looking forward to an enjoyable dinner out tonight. I want us all to have a good time without fights. Be sure to take care of all your business before we leave . . ."

V or H

WINDOW 4: GIVING INSTR

You are frequently in situations in whic receiving instructions. It happens so often th how the instructions are presented. What yo that some people's instructions are easier for The reason: the two kinds of thinkers have d going about the same simple task. Horizon tactics—the WHYS and HOWS of accompli stress execution and logistics—the WHATS a

Study the accompanying chart. Then we'll to recognize vertical and horizontal clues we it in a real-life situation.

Giving Instructions: Vertical and Horiz

What Vertical Thinker Includes	*What Horiz*
THE WHATS:	THE WHY
■ WHAT has to be accomplished . . . *the desired result*	■ WHY de
■ WHAT has to be eliminated . . . *the obstacles*	■ WHY de
■ WHAT has to be done . . .	■ WHY ce
THE WHEN:	THE HOW
■ WHEN desired result must be achieved . . . *the logistics*	■ HOW to

WARMUP TIME

Before taking the chart on the road and u horizontal clues, you may need an oppo warmup exercise will demonstrate how a sin important clue to a party's thinking style.

Each of the following categories represe which people give instructions (vice-presid patient, and so forth). One of the two instru more typically vertical; the other, more typ quickly you can identify which is which. Ci "Giving Instructions: Vertical and Horizontal

EXERCI

Name

Category
a. "I want Larson Overnig to fami

Category
a. "The be hit lowe

Category
a. "It's imp open yo

Category 4
a. "This ye size . . .

Category 5
a. "I want enable c upcomir

Category 6.
a. "We are commun is a lot o deliver. so we ca

Category 7:
a. "We neec transitio the snag during th

Category 8:
a. "When y today, I w and prac are leavi

ANSWER KEY: NAME THAT THINKER

1. a. V	5. a. H
b. H	b. V
2. a. V	6. a. H
b. H	b. V
3. a. H	7. a. V
b. V	b. H
4. a. V	8. a. V
b. H	b. H

How did you do on the warmup? Ready to try a real situation? Use the accompanying worksheet to help you recognize whether the party you're trying to identify gives instructions in a horizontal or vertical manner. Remember, verticals usually begin with the WHATS and WHENS; horizontals usually begin with the WHYS and HOWS.

Follow the Instructions

Instruction-Giver ____ (your candidate's name)

Write down three instructions the above party gave you. Pay close attention to the way the instructions were presented—what was included, what was not included, what was told first, what was told next. For example, if the instructions were about preparation of a report, did your party start by telling you what to include and when the report was due? Or did he or she start by telling you the purpose of the report and how it would be used?

Instruction #1:

Instruction #2:

Instruction #3:

Reread the three instructions you wrote on your worksheet. Give each instruction that stressed the WHATS and WHENS a score of +3. Give each instruction that stressed the WHYS and HOWS a score of −3. (Of course, there will be some overlap. Look for what is being stressed first and most often.) Then combine the three scores for the Window 4 tally. Possible points: +9 or −9.

Instruction #1 ______
Instruction #2 ______
Instruction #3 ______

WINDOW 4 TALLY
Tally #4 = ______

Now that you see how the two kinds of thinkers give instructions, you can use this information as a clue to opposite thinking. In addition, Tip #4 will show you how you can smooth the process of giving instructions to or receiving them from a foreign thinker. The strategy applies to presenting information as well.

TIP #4
AVOIDING SLIP-UPS

In giving instructions or information to an opposite thinker:

Start with what the opposite thinker expects to hear. This helps engage the other party's brain—puts him or her on the right track. If you're a vertical giving instructions to a horizontal, start with the WHYS and HOWS. If you're a horizontal giving instructions or information to a vertical, start with the WHATS and WHENS. After you've supplied what the other party expects, you can add the rest.

In receiving instructions or information from an opposite thinker:

Remember, the other party probably will give you what you're not expecting. For that reason, you may have difficulty remembering what you're told. If possible, write down what the other party is saying so you won't forget or lose sight of the details. If you still need what has been omitted—either the WHATS and WHENS or the WHYS and HOWS—ask for that information. Don't be impatient; verticals can fill in what you need to know about tactics and strategies, and horizontals about execution and logistics, but they may not be able to come up with immediate answers. They may need a few minutes, an hour, or even a day or so to think.

WINDOW 5: QUICK MENTAL CHECKLIST

In trying to detect foreign thinking, the true test is time. Careful observation over a period of days or weeks, using the information given throughout this book and the specific indications given in this chapter, will enable you to make a confident identification of your party's thinking style.

However, there are times when an immediate assessment comes in handy. When you suspect that opposite thinking is at the root of your communication difficulties, the Quick Mental Checklist on the next page gives you a quick way to check whether your suspicions appear to be justified, before going on to a more thorough observation.

Scoring: For each vertical tendency you check, score +1; for each horizontal tendency, −1. Total the positive and negative scores and then combine the totals. Possible points: +10 or −10. The greater the positive tally, the greater the indication of vertical thinking; the greater the negative tally, the greater the indication of horizontal thinking.

WINDOW 5 TALLY
+ total = ______
− total = ______
Tally #5 = ______

TIP #5
USING THE QMC

You may want to keep a copy of the Quick Mental Checklist, or QMC, on a 3×5 card to be used for quick assessment when the need arises. The checklist provides easy-to-remember, readily identifiable behaviors that you can spot during a conversation, at a business meeting, or over lunch. If you use it regularly, you'll soon find that you've committed the list to memory, and you'll be able to run through it in your mind whenever you're talking with someone who shows signs of being a foreign thinker.

Quick Mental Checklist

For each question in the following list, put a check to the left of the tendency that most accurately describes what this party does when communicating with you.

Question	*Vertical Tendency*	*Horizontal Tendency*
1. Does he/she talk about:	_____ Whats and whens?	_____ Whys and what ifs?
2. Does he/she start telling a story, problem, or idea:	_____ With a conclusion?	_____ With some background information?
3. Is he/she more focused on:	_____ What is happening?	_____ What could be happening?
4. When the conversation drags, is he/she:	_____ Getting hung up on specific details?	_____ Going off on tangents?
5. Does he/she seem more concerned about losing:	_____ Time?	_____ Options?
6. When confronted by a specific problem, is he/she more concerned about:	_____ Elimination?	_____ Recurrence?
7. Does he/she more easily forget:	_____ The historical context of an event?	_____ The specific details of an event?
8. In a deal, is he/she more likely to:	_____ Protect the downside?	_____ Maximize potential gain?
9. When working on a project, is he/she more likely to:	_____ Eliminate actions, steps?	_____ Add possibilities, directions?
10. Is the fastest way to get his/her attention:	_____ To state the problem?	_____ To state the benefits?

COUNT THE CLUES

Now it's time for the final count. Tally the indicators from all five windows and see how clear a view they give you of your party's natural thinking style. Record all five tallies below and combine the positive and negative totals to get the final score. Possible points: +48 or −48.

Window	*Tally*	*Final Totals*	
1. Labels	______		
2. Telltale Phrases	______	+ Total =	______
3. Movie or Book	______	− Total =	______
4. Instructions	______	**Final score** =	______
5. Checklist	______		
Final indication	______ Vertical (+)	or	______ Horizontal (−)

ANALYZING THE FINAL SCORE

What does the final score tell you about the cause and cure for the clashes you've found so perplexing? Do you seem to have spotted foreign thinking? Is the mystery clearing up? Does the behavior seem less bizarre? Are you beginning to suspect that opposite thinking may be at the heart of your communication difficulties not only with this party but with others in your life? Try looking through the windows again at other people who have caused you trouble. See if you notice a pattern of clues developing.

If the final score indicates that your "difficult" party is *not* a foreign thinker, you've still gained important information. If the indication is strong enough, you can assume that opposite thinking is *not* the source of the problem and seek some other explanation. (As the New Rule of Communication directs, thinking style differences are the *first* place, not the only place to look.)

But first, how reliable are your deductions? How clear is your view? Let's check it out.

IF the final score you got for the other party is:

± 25 or more **CLEAR VIEW.** The clues have given a strong indication of this party's thinking style.

- *If indication is opposite to your own:* You are definitely reading the right book! Communicoding dilemmas are almost certainly at the root of your discord! To prevent future clashes, go to the Thinking Style Scanner on page 121, a thumbnail guide exposing the "customs" of the foreign thinker. You may want to speed ahead to Chapters 8–10. These chapters will help you resolve conflict with foreign thinkers, especially those with whom you've been engaged in long-running battles.

- *If indication is same as your own:* You have almost certainly ruled out opposite thinking. Time to look for other possible explanations. Unless your view of yourself in the Chapter 4 windows was unclear, factors other than thinking style are most likely at play in your miscommunication with this party. It may be wise to brush up on your listening, clarifying, and restating skills. If these don't eliminate the clashes, your subjective explanations may be correct!

± 15–24 **CLOUDED VIEW.** Although the view is somewhat hazy, what can you deduce from the clues?

- *If indication is opposite to your own:* There is a strong possibility that you are dealing with a foreign thinker, but the other party may be giving mixed signals that are hard to decipher. You need a litmus test—a way to gather more evidence to confirm the indication. Immediately apply the Thinking Style Scanner. Start following the guidelines for the indicated thinking style. If tension between you and the other party is eased, you have your answer: opposite thinking is confirmed.
- *If indication is same as your own:* Did you have a clear view of yourself in the Chapter 4 windows? If not, your communication difficulties may be the price you're paying. The more clouded your view of yourself, the more likely that you're miscommunicating with a same-style thinker. The Thinking Style Scanner should help clear the view. Use the guidelines for *your own* thinking style. If tension is eased and your assessment is confirmed, you need a better picture of yourself so you can lead with your natural abilities. Review Chapters 2–4. Be sure to retake the Self-Observation Inventory.

± 14 or less **OBSTRUCTED VIEW.** Are your party's signals hard to read? Or could you be having trouble reading the clues accurately? To check your ability to read the clues, go to the Code Detection Quotient (CDQ) on page 123. If your CDQ is low, review the material in Chapters 1 and 2. If you're having trouble observing what your party is actually doing, you need an observation aid. Try carrying a small pocket notebook to record interactions with suspected foreign thinkers. Write down, as accurately as you can, what occurred. Be sure to record what happened, not your reactions to what happened.

When you've completed your assessment of the chosen party, be sure to try it again with someone else. The more you use the "windows," the clearer view you're likely to get. The purpose of Communicoding is not merely to relieve the strains with one party but to identify opposite thinking as a possible, unsuspected cause of many of your communication difficulties.

THINKING STYLE SCANNER

When in Rome, do as the Romans do. In order to get through to foreign thinkers, you need to learn something about their culture and customs. You need to adopt those customs if you want to survive in their land without constant, time- and energy-consuming hassles.

The Thinking Style Scanner will:

- Confirm the presence of opposite thinking.
- Give you practice talking the way the other half thinks.
- Teach you how to avoid Communicoding dilemmas.
- Ease tension quickly.

The Scanner works because it follows the foreign thinker's code. It tells you how to say what the opposite thinker expects to hear, what's customary in the foreign land. When you follow the foreign code, the foreign brain is able to immediately process the information and stay on the objective path. For example, it's amazing how the order in which you present information can affect the outcome!

HOW TO USE THE THINKING STYLE SCANNER:

1. Look first at the middle column of the chart. Find the situation you're facing.

2. If you're a vertical thinker dealing with someone you believe to be horizontal, do what the right-hand column tells you. If you're a horizontal thinker dealing with someone you believe to be vertical, do what the left-hand column tells you.

3. If you've tried the prescribed tips three to five times and they are not helping, it's time to scan the other side of the chart. You probably are dealing with someone of your own thinking style.

THINKING STYLE SCANNER

Vertical Custom	*Situation*	*Horizontal Custom*
Give conclusion first. Provide background information only if asked.	WHEN MAKING A POINT	Bring other party up to speed—go over past and present events before giving conclusion.
State difficulties blocking execution.	WHEN ANALYZING AN IDEA OR SOLUTION	Present attributes of idea or solution before stating difficulties with it.
Delineate specific actions to be taken—what comes first, second, third.	WHEN PROCEEDING WITH A PROJECT, IDEA, OR SOLUTION	Delineate areas that will be impacted in chronological order—first, second, third.
Do only what you are literally asked for.	WHEN ASKED TO DO SOMETHING	Find out desired effect that is anticipated.
Ask for what you literally want.	WHEN YOU WANT SOMETHING DONE	Make sure your desired impact is known.
Pinpoint best route before giving alternatives.	WHEN ASKED FOR A SOLUTION	Provide various options or alternatives before pinpointing best route.
Ask questions about deadlines and quantities.	WHEN REQUESTED TO DELIVER SOMETHING (RESULT, ASSIGNMENT, PROJECT, ETC.)	Ask questions about purpose and use.
Treat deadline as sacred—"around" the same time is not the same time.	WHEN GIVEN A DEADLINE	"Around" the same time is acceptable. If delayed, supply a reason benefiting project.
Limit your answer to question asked.	WHEN BEING QUESTIONED	Treat questions as sacred—a question half-answered is still not answered.

TEST YOUR CDQ

The Code Detection Quotient, or CDQ, is designed to help you quickly size up how adept you are at recognizing vertical and horizontal thinking. If the windows earlier in this chapter showed an obstructed view, your CDQ may indicate whether you're having difficulty picking up thinking style clues. But even if you're becoming quite proficient at recognizing the vertical and horizontal thinkers in your life, you may have fun determining your CDQ.

Your task: Suppose you're involved in each of the situations below. Decide, based on the knowledge you've gained thus far of vertical and horizontal thinking, in which direction the other party's behavior appears to be leaning. Circle V or H.

Situation	*Leaning*
1. You have just asked a subordinate a question. He/she responds with three more questions.	V or H
2. A higher-up in your company doesn't seem to recall a situation you salvaged or what you did to turn it around.	V or H
3. A lecturer is describing the early years of a famous historian's life in intricate, specific detail.	V or H
4. Your spouse proudly shows you a pile of "junk" extracted from the front hall closet.	V or H
5. Your hockey coach has just taught the team a new play by describing what to do and when.	V or H
6. Your department manager has revamped the overloaded work schedule by taking away aspects of previously assigned projects and revising the due dates.	V or H
7. The manager of one of your departments wants to discuss the source of a brewing crisis.	V or H
8. You and a friend are having a quarrel, and the friend is connecting this incident to a similar one that happened before.	V or H
9. An associate is trying to convince you to read a novel by describing the action and characters.	V or H
10. A marketing manager investigating new product lines starts by doing a comparative analysis of four possibilities.	V or H

ANSWER KEY: TEST YOUR CDQ

1. H	6. V
2. H	7. H
3. V	8. H
4. V	9. V
5. V	10. H

Scoring: Give yourself 10 points for each correct answer. Your total score is your CDQ. The more clues you correctly identified, the better able you are to detect vertical and horizontal codes in operation.

TO SUM UP

You've pulled aside the curtains and peered through the windows. You've focused on the difficult people in your life and looked them up and down and side to side. By keeping your emotions out of your sightlines and letting unbiased observations shine through, you've deduced whether opposite thinking is behind your communication dilemmas. You've demystified the bizarre, scanned for foreign customs, and begun to crack the foreign code.

Nevertheless, your Communicoding dilemmas will continue. No matter how high your CDQ, how diligently you practice your scanning tips, you will be hit with unexpected behavior or reactions. After all, you're trying to think in a foreign "language"—one you're just learning. Whether you're first dealing with a foreign thinker or whether the party is someone with whom you've had a long history of misunderstandings, it's not going to be easy. The information coming up in Chapters 8–12 will show you how to resolve the inevitable conflicts that still will arise.

Then, too, not all Communicoding clashes are one-to-one. Sometimes a whole department—even a whole organization—favors one thinking style over the other. What happens if you're in such a department or organization and you happen to be of the *un*favored thinking style? What happens when opposite thinkers compete within an organization or department to show how smart or wise they can be? What happens if the department or organization has a problem that the dominant thinking style is ill-equipped to solve? What happens if someone of the other thinking style is brought in to solve the problems that then result? The next chapter will reveal how organizations "think."

7 MINDING THE ORGANIZATION

The trouble with being a leader today is you can't be sure whether people are following you or chasing you.

—ANONYMOUS CEO

There's a war going on in American business. A war so subtle, so disguised that hardly anyone realizes it's under way. Its fallout has been mistakenly attributed to personality clashes, communication difficulties, sabotage, and incompetency. Its victims are found in failing deals, partnerships, and businesses. What's not seen, what's not known, is that these are signs of a war between foreign thinking styles.

In this insidious and costly war, the battles are fought not only *between* companies but *within* companies. The issue is which thinking code will dominate: which will govern the company, select the management team, make the critical decisions, and, yes, make the mistakes.

In a thinking style war—whether the adversaries are individuals, companies, or departments—nobody wins. Because each thinking style has its own brand of creativity and logic, each inevitably raises different questions, anticipates different dangers, solves different problems, attends to certain details and neglects others. Thus each is capable of contributing something distinctively valuable, distinctively different, and equally necessary to a company's survival, health, and growth.

Can business afford to continue operating with battle lines drawn between opposite thinkers?

THE WAR NOBODY WINS

A classic cautionary tale of corporate downfall due to a "personality clash" is told in Ken Auletta's best-seller, *Greed and Glory on Wall*

Street. But might the fatal clash between Peter ("Pete") Peterson and Lewis Glucksman, co-captains of "the street's" oldest investment banking firm, have had more to do with a mismatch of thinking styles than of personalities?

The promotion of Glucksman from chief operating officer to co-chief executive officer of Lehman Brothers in May 1983 seemed auspicious for the company's future. Glucksman, who had labored in the trenches and knew the company inside out, would share power with Peterson, who had led the investment house from imminent collapse to five consecutive profit-breaking years. Yet, within three months, Glucksman got Peterson ousted. Nine months later the company, now losing money, was sold.

Auletta's book attributes the disastrous effects of "irreconcilable conflict" in the boardroom to "human folly and foibles." We read of Peterson, former Secretary of Commerce in the Nixon administration, too engrossed with such great issues as foreign debt to keep tabs on his power base or to see Glucksman's rising hostility; and of Glucksman, the ambitious "operator," who resented Peterson's place at the head tables of finance and statecraft.

Certainly there can be no two more opposite personalities than Peterson (cool, cerebral, and imperious) and Glucksman (passionate, prickly, and unpolished). But could there be another way to analyze what happened? What if there was another factor, an unseen difference between the two men that caused much of the misunderstanding and misinterpretation of each other's motives and character? What if Pete Peterson was a horizontal thinker, whose primary focus was to broaden the business base and increase the demand for the company's services? What if Lew Glucksman was a vertical thinker whose primary focus was on a smooth, orderly operation that produced a consistent standard of service to the customer? Isn't it possible that each might have felt that the other was deliberately following a private agenda and trying to usurp power? That each failed to recognize the complementary skills the other provided?

Further, what if it was the complementary nature of these two distinct thinking styles that was responsible for the record-breaking five-year profit the firm experienced while both men held key positions? What if, ironically, it was the lack of understanding of these two equally valuable but opposite ways of thinking that led to antagonism between the two men and ultimately to Glucksman's takeover? Most importantly, what if the "fall of the house of Lehman" can be directly linked to the withdrawal of the horizontal component of this successful team?

Although this interpretation of the Lehman saga may seem simplistic, it has been our observation that the most complex issues frequently have simple origins. Of course, personality issues may well have come into play. As we showed in Chapter 1, clashes touched off by thinking style differences frequently escalate into personality conflicts.

If unrecognized thinking style differences were indeed at the root of Lehman's collapse, what lessons can American business learn from it? If issues like those between Glucksman and Peterson can be reduced, early on, to thinking style differences, it may become easier to resolve them, and even, possibly, to profit from them.

We contend that internal strife like that at Lehman Brothers often represents a struggle of opposite thinking styles for control of the organization. Failure to capitalize on the merits of *both* styles is seriously weakening American business as it girds for the crucial battles of the 1990s. The real winners in these broader struggles are most likely to be the companies that stop the thinking style war and learn to successfully mesh the strengths offered by the Petersons and Glucksmans.

THE CHANGING WINDS OF WAR

This chapter is based on a simple premise: Organizations, like people, have thinking styles. Most companies, at any given time, are dominated by either vertical or horizontal decision-making. Of course, companies are composed of both vertical and horizontal thinkers. However, one type of thinking usually prevails, strongly influencing membership in the inner circle.

When an organization has a thinking style bias, the costs become most evident in a period of rapid change. A company may achieve significant success by following the strategies and tactics of either code, vertical or horizontal. But to *remain* profitable, companies must be able to anticipate and respond to changing demands: market demands, customer demands, operational demands, or regulatory demands. Companies driven by one kind of thinking, whether vertical or horizontal, have trouble shifting course; and when they do, they generally make the mistake of rotating a full 180 degrees. Instead of finding ways to utilize the strengths of both thinking styles simultaneously, they continue to use only one or the other at a time.

Following the steer of either thinking style worked stunningly during the post–World War II decades, when corporate America sailed ahead of the competition. There was no realistic need to challenge American business strategies, to ask what weaknesses might flow from their obvious strengths.

However, strategies appropriate to a clear front-runner are no longer apt. American business confidence is becoming wobbly, not so much because corporate America is falling behind but because its strategies for getting ahead aren't working. In order to stay ahead, business leaders must be prepared to tackle the complexities of balancing long- and short-term concerns, maintaining a knowledgeable and stable work force, and struggling to compete in an international marketplace.

Is the predominance of one thinking style alone enough?

FRONT SEAT FOCUS

The driving force behind the company's success is its Front Seat Focus: the pervasive philosophy that influences the shaping of goals and decisions. Each thinking style has its own focus: its own strategy for winning, its own tactics for each round, and its own structure for organizing the troops (which we'll describe later in the chapter).

When one thinking style predominates, management attends to certain kinds of details and neglects others. The Front Seat Focus determines which matters will get attention first and foremost. When problems arise, solutions that fit the focus are seen as paramount; others are shunted aside, relegated to the Back Seat. (See accompanying chart.)

Front Seat Focus and Back Seat Shunt

- To find Front Seat Focus for each thinking style, read down.
- To find Back Seat Shunt for each thinking style, read up.

Vertical Front Seat Focus Details attended to *(Read Down)* ↓	*Horizontal Front Seat Focus* Details attended to *(Read Down)* ↓
• Maintain lean machine • Develop mission statement—standards and procedures • Separate different departments, markets, products • Increase consistency • Reduce operating costs • Eliminate waste • Protect downside (what's up must come down) • Secure investment	• Maintain well-oiled machine • Develop mission statement—goals and guidelines • Integrate different departments, markets, products • Decrease duplication • Increase demand • Eliminate redos • Protect upside (keep motion upwards) • Maximize return
(Read Up) Details not attended to *Horizontal Back Seat Shunt* ↑	*(Read Up)* Details not attended to *Vertical Back Seat Shunt* ↑

The Front Seat Focus can make or break a company. When the details attended to are necessary for growth, the company soars. But when the conditions for growth require attention to the details that have been neglected, the company is likely to get stuck. The company may try rescue strategies that fit its focus (we'll describe typical vertical and horizontal rescue strategies later in this chapter). But if those strategies fail, what then?

In walks THE SAVIOR, someone of the opposite thinking style, someone with the Midas touch. An "alien" thinker, either from within or outside the company, moves in and changes the focus. The change works. Renewed life is breathed into the company. Of course, the savior is seen as brilliant. From that point on, anything the savior says goes. Eventually the foreign ways take over. The Front Seat Focus shifts. Now the formerly neglected details get high priority. And, over a period of time, the formerly attended-to details begin to be neglected. Of course, these neglected details can ultimately become the seeds of a different set of problems. A new savior may then appear, someone of the formerly dominant thinking style.

We call this phenomenon the Organizational Shuffle.

THE ORGANIZATIONAL SHUFFLE

The following brief vignettes, selected from recent newspaper accounts, strongly suggest shifts in the making:

- For a quarter of a century, Polaroid Corporation's horizontal focus, based on the vision of its founder, Edwin Land, made the company a raging success. It had "the right product at the right time"—instant pictures in a booming postwar era of instant gratification. But market conditions changed. When consumers could get high quality 35mm. photos professionally developed in an hour, expensive instant snapshots lost their luster, and Land's mission lost its focus. Frozen in its perspective, Polaroid failed to develop new products or marketing approaches. Following Land's 1982 resignation, the focus shifted. Now vertically driven, the company is expanding into diverse markets, cutting costs, and targeting untapped, specialized market applications of its technology. Progress has been made, but Shamrock Holdings, Inc., which has mounted a takeover bid, scoffs at the improvements as "short-term fixes." Could a horizontal reshuffle be ahead?
- When Steven G. Rothmeier became chairman of Northwest Airlines in 1986, his focus was highly vertical. He promulgated strict standards and procedures. (Memo One: Executives' workdays to begin at 8:00 A.M.; officers to be in the office at least two Saturdays a month.) Was the new boss stifling creativity (as some employees griped) or merely

playing it straight, putting expectations on the line? Rothmeier's biggest challenge arose from what was initially seen as his masterstroke. Faced with stiff competition from United Airlines, which was feeding passengers into competing Pacific routes, he solved the problem by acquiring Republic Airlines routes that fed into Northwest's Pacific system. But morale suffered when Rothmeier tried to blend the two operations too quickly. Might horizontal integration skills have been in order? Recently takeover talk has surfaced. A shift to horizontal thinking may be coming.

- After fifty-nine years of promoting from within, Gerber Products—following two years of hemorrhaging losses—brought in its first chief executive from outside the ranks. When David Johnson took over in October 1987, he quickly moved to maintain a well-oiled machine by increasing demand and decreasing duplication. Johnson sold off or consolidated limping subsidiaries that had been draining the company's traditional strength—baby food. He nearly doubled the earnings of that division through an increased commitment to research, advertising, and marketing of new products, such as a new line of extra-finely strained foods for the under-six-months crowd and, at the other end of the age spectrum, flavored applesauce for the senior market. The company also is developing transitional foods for toddlers, looking into markets for packaged milk and bottled water, and moving into foreign baby food markets. All this adds up to what has been hailed as a "remarkable surge," thanks to a horizontal shuffle. But might the winds shift again—and when?
- Might this same phenomenon be occurring at Disney studios? Could its vertical creativity, which revolutionized the film industry, be giving way to a horizontal focus, an emphasis on increasing demand? When its new animated features failed to match the success of its early classics, the company's endeavors shifted into family-oriented, PG-rated films under the Touchstone label. Expanded lines of Disney clothes and toys and the opening of new markets in Japan and France may be further signs of a horizontal focus at work.
- Could Sears Roebuck and Company's horizontal focus have been responsible for its difficulty in competing with the Wal-Marts and K-Marts? Would a more vertical focus have enabled Sears to more easily pull off plans for segmenting its stores into a boutique format? Perhaps a vertical focus is now coming into view, with price cuts and the addition of more brands and products.

The organizational shuffle normally works. When a new thinking style takes over, it generally does save the day. But for how long and at what cost?

CASUALTIES OF THINKING STYLE WARFARE

Although our descriptions of thinking style warfare are necessarily simplified, they show how the Front Seat Focus can lead a company alternately to victory and defeat. No matter what the shuffle accomplishes for the organization, the gains cannot be sustained. Sweeping away one thinking style (rather than integrating both) is bound to intensify the war.

The "alien" thinker who bails out the company and cleans up after the old regime does strengthen the organization. But, in the process, precious contributions are lost—contributions made by followers of the other thinking code, often those who built the company. These once-successful methods are summarily replaced. The result is a periodic redistribution of the spoils: vertical in, horizontal out; horizontal in, vertical out.

Wouldn't it be simpler and better to join forces?

Instead, the buzz word is "leadership."

IS "LEADERSHIP" THE ANSWER?

Experts suggest that 90 percent of business failures are due to managerial incompetence. The conventional answer to internal strife, external conflict, and rising competition is to find effective leaders who possess the qualities that ensure success. What's not realized is that those very qualities are intimately related to thinking style.

According to Kenneth Labich, writing in the October 24, 1988, issue of Fortune, there's general agreement among CEOs, management consultants, and business school professors as to "The Seven Keys to Business Leadership." The seven principles he listed were:

- Trust your subordinates
- Develop a vision
- Keep your cool
- Encourage risk-taking
- Be an expert; become more knowledgeable
- Invite dissent
- Simplify, so as to keep the big picture in view

We believe that most leaders are more than competent and earnestly attempt to follow these guidelines. The catch is that the interpretation and implementation of these key principles varies widely—and not merely because of disparate personalities or "leadership styles" but because of thinking styles. (See accompanying chart, "Seven Keys: Vertical and Horizontal Codes.") A horizontal executive's vision will be markedly different from that of a vertical executive, and the way those

SEVEN KEYS:

Vertical and Horizontal Codes

Although most business leaders would agree on the seven keys to successful management outlined in Fortune magazine, they follow different codes in applying those principles.

Key	*Vertical Code*	*Horizontal Code*
TRUST YOUR SUBORDINATES	• Develop army of separate departments • Expect them to do their jobs independently	• Develop squads of integrated functions • Expect them to work together cooperatively
DEVELOP A VISION	• Look at what you want company to be doing in next three to five years • Identify differing tactics—actions that can be taken • Specify future actions on structured, step-by-step timetable	• Look at where you think industry is heading in next three to five years • Develop common goals your company can strive toward • Specify future options to see which ones capitalize on direction of industry
KEEP YOUR COOL	Remove obstacles: • Isolate and contain problem • Anticipate obstacles that block elimination of problem	Prevent obstacles: • Convert problems to opportunities • Anticipate any obstacles that may lessen opportunities
ENCOURAGE RISK-TAKING	• Find best time to buy into an opportunity or bail out of a disaster • Watch for starts and stops	• Find the direction in which the current wave is flowing and ride it • Watch for ebbs and flows
BE AN EXPERT	Be a specialist: • Know your field • Have extensive, specific, field-related experience	Be a generalist: • Have a broad base of interrelated skills • Be able to apply a variety of skills in a given situation
INVITE DISSENT	• Encourage differing answers regarding: What should we do more of? What can we do faster? How can we trim?	• Encourage differing answers regarding: What should be integrated, coordinated? What's the competition doing? What should we add?
SIMPLIFY	Reduce specific steps to destination: • Ask: What steps have to be taken? How can they be rearranged or eliminated?	Increase speed to destination: • Ask: What direction is the current flowing? What can break the flow? How can it be prevented?

divergent visions play out will have a profound effect on the entire company's operations. Each of these executives will consider different kinds of knowledge important and will encourage the taking of different kinds of risks. And what each encourages or considers important may or may not be what's needed at a critical juncture. Pete Petersen and Lew Glucksman, for example, saw their roles as CEOs quite differently, though both probably would agree with Fortune's seven keys.

Can you now see how the cry for "fresh leadership" may in fact exacerbate a company's difficulties?

Is thinking style warfare beginning to sound like something you've experienced on the office front? Are you starting to recognize the signs? Let's see whether our descriptions of how vertical and horizontal companies operate look familiar.

ORGANIZING THE TROOPS

Quick review: As we explained in Chapter 2, vertical thinkers find distinctions; horizontal thinkers find commonalities. Vertical thinkers draw lines; horizontal thinkers draw circles. Vertical logic identifies fast paths by climbing ladders; horizontal logic identifies fast paths by spreading and then tightening nets. Vertical creativity sets new directions by rearranging the old; horizontal creativity sets new directions by making novel associations.

When the two kinds of thinking styles use these tools to establish company organizational structures and policies, the results, as you might imagine, look quite dissimilar.

THE VERTICAL COMPANY

Because vertical thinkers manipulate differences, a predominantly vertical company divides functions into separate and distinct areas of specialization. It's usually quite clear where the responsibility of one department ends and that of another begins. Vertical management has definite lines of authority. Turf battles are generally resolved by further delimiting authority and subdividing responsibility.

Early in 1989, an internal rift surfaced between audit partners and consulting partners of Arthur Andersen, the second largest of the Big Eight accounting firms. The traveling consultants, who service farflung clients and account for a rapidly growing share of the firm's total business, felt they were getting too little pay and had too little power in comparison with the auditors, who handle work that comes into a particular office. So, the board ordered a restructuring of the company.

The solution was a highly vertical one. The auditing and consulting operations were separated so as to give the consultants more self-determination. Consultants would no longer report to the same regional managers as auditors. In addition, they would draw compensation from a separate income pool. As the firm's revenues from consulting increased, the consultants would receive a bigger piece of the pie.

While decision-making in a vertical firm often goes from the top down, it also can move in the other direction. A middle manager may have an idea about how to streamline a procedure and may discuss it with the vice-president in charge of the department. If the idea affects the organization as a whole, the vice-president may discuss it with the CEO. Thus the decision-making path goes up as well as down the rungs of the organizational ladder.

THE HORIZONTAL COMPANY

As you might expect, a predominantly horizontal company has a circular rather than linear structure. Authority is generally more diffused than in a vertical company. Functions tend to be shared or integrated, creating overlapping areas of responsibility. Activity flows as on a conveyor belt. Departments maintain constant communication and form networks united around common goals.

A horizontal company generates ideas through interaction of people from diverse backgrounds. S.C. Johnson & Sons, Inc., makers of Johnson's Wax (one of the largest family-owned companies in the United States), utilizes "sponsor groups," which combine the expertise and ideas of people from a variety of disciplines, like technology, marketing, manufacturing, and sales. These groups meet regularly and sponsor ideas, which they carry through to implementation. The company consciously seeks to avoid what Chairman Samuel C. Johnson calls "bureaucratization of research" by spreading its research divisions around the world. If a European chemical company comes up with a new material, Johnson's people are on the spot and can find out about it early.

Of course, there are advantages and disadvantages to both linear and circular organizational structures. The cleaner the lines, the clearer the parameters of responsibility or authority. On the downside, these clean, clear lines often provoke territorial battles, discourage cooperation and sharing of resources, and create duplication of effort. Circles, on the other hand, encourage shared responsibility but also make it difficult to hold individual people or departments accountable for certain functions.

What Kind of Company Do You Work For?

Look at these two organizational charts. One is strictly linear; the other is circular. Which one more closely resembles the structure and functioning of your company?

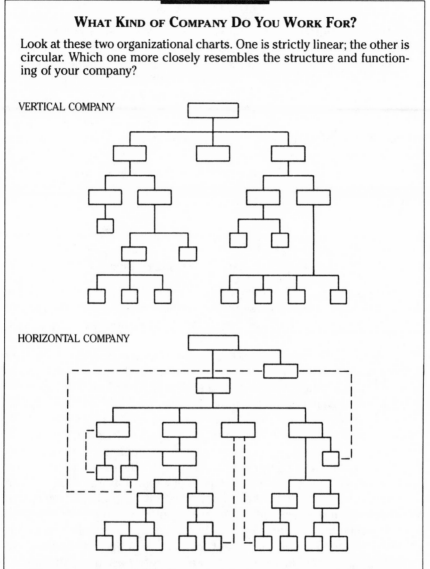

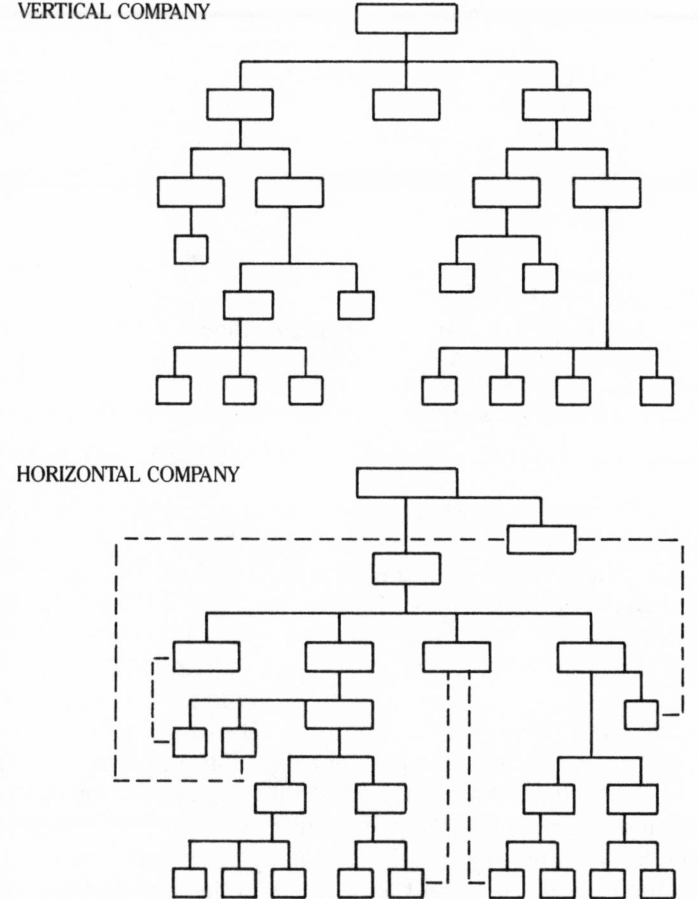

The more clear, straight lines of authority and responsibility in your company's organizational structure, the more likely it is to be vertical. The more continuous or overlapping areas of authority and responsibility (the dotted lines), the more likely the company is to be horizontal. A word of caution: If your company has undergone frequent restructuring, you may see remnants of past structures alongside the current setup. Look for what predominates, or where the current restructuring is heading.

FIELD MANEUVERS

Vertical and horizontal companies engage in different maneuvers to improve their positions in the field. They start by asking different kinds of questions, hoping the answers will advance them to their target.

THE VERTICAL COMPANY

When a vertical company seeks to boost sales, expand markets, or increase profitability, its management most often looks at questions like the following:

- Which products or services are most profitable or unique to this company?
- Which new products or services could be launched with the greatest speed and efficiency?
- Which products or services could be eliminated with minimal impact on bottom-line profitability?
- Which expenses are incidental to the primary focus of the business?

A few years ago, a large Midwestern metropolitan newspaper publisher decided to expand in hopes of further consolidating its already strong profit picture. The issue was: What form should the expansion take?

The conclusion reached was that all profits emanated from the success of the basic daily newspaper. Therefore, the consensus was to expand into an area that would help ensure the continued profitability of the basic newspaper, rather than (for example) add another special section or expand into an unrelated field. How to do it?

The answer, from a vertical point of view, was obvious. The way to expand was upward and downward in the production channel, to gain more control over both supply and distribution. By acquiring the paper mills, newsprint supplier, and independent distributors on which the publisher was dependent, the company could both ensure access to raw materials and guarantee stable pricing of its product.

This solution not only enabled the company to ensure the newspaper's continued profitability but strengthened its position in the publishing field and allowed it to realize revenues from the added supply and distribution operations. At the same time, the newly acquired suppliers and distributors were guaranteed stable businesses and continued profitability.

This solution also serves as an example of vertical creativity. The publishing company was seeking a new direction in which to expand. The vertical solution was to take apart what was already being done and rearrange the pieces in a different way, by bringing both ends of the production channel under ownership and control of the publisher.

THE HORIZONTAL COMPANY

What if the publishing company's dominant thinking style had been horizontal? In that case, management undoubtedly would have approached the expansion issue quite differently.

The questions horizontal companies are most likely to ask themselves when trying to boost sales, expand markets, and increase profitability are:

- In what direction is the industry headed?
- Into what areas or markets are our competitors moving?
- How can we better satisfy consumer needs through new products or services?
- How can internal production functions be integrated or coordinated more smoothly or more efficiently?

In our newspaper example, management would have seen that newspaper circulation nationwide was dropping, that in-home entertainment was eating into readership, that many urban newspapers were going under but rural newspapers continued to show strength. The managers would have identified the common thread: "People are reading less and will continue to do so."

To ensure against a decline in profitability, management then might have outlined three options: 1) adopt the *USA Today* strategy: play to the changing marketplace with shorter, snappier stories and stronger graphics; 2) buy rural newspapers whose sales and profitability are growing; 3) buy out competitors, gain monopoly control over the metropolitan marketplace, and then raise the price of the newspaper and its advertising rates. Any of these solutions would have been a good example of horizontal logic. Identification of a constant (the trend away from reading) would have assisted in finding a fast path to continued profitability.

Thus, by asking different questions, a horizontal company most likely would have come up with a different answer than the vertical management did. Which maneuver would probably be more successful? Each would have certain pluses and certain minuses. The two solutions would provide different advantages and create different problems.

About now, you may be getting the feeling that you're back in business school. You may be thinking, "These stories aren't about thinking style, they're about vertical and horizontal integration." Our observation is that companies with a vertical focus are more likely to expand their marketplace through a vertically integrated approach, while horizontal companies are more inclined to try horizontal integration.

In fact, we would suggest that many of the tenets learned in business school are selectively followed, depending on a company's dominant thinking style. The obvious drawback is that companies tend to reject useful tenets because they are foreign to the prevailing code, rather than objectively choosing the most effective approach to the situation at hand.

How Does the Company Think?

Closing a sale? Negotiating a deal? Angling for a management spot? Use this checklist to assess thinking style so you can talk the way the company thinks. (Remember, the tips in Chapter 6 can apply to organizations as well as to individuals.)

	Vertical View	*Horizontal View*
Ideas that are praised generally reflect ways to:	__ Decrease waste, increase consistency	__ Decrease duplication, increase demand
If profits are dropping, the company is more likely to:	__ Manage waste better	__ Manage the work flow better
When negotiating a deal, the company is more focused on:	__ Protecting downside	__ Protecting upside
Lines of authority are more likely to be:	__ Clear	__ Overlapping
The way to go in this company is to:	__ Specialize	__ Integrate
A smart politician is someone who tries to:	__ Stay within the lines	__ Stay well connected
A well-run department has:	__ Smooth operations	__ Few redos
The company motto is:	__ "Make each and every dollar count"	__ "Get the biggest bang for the buck"

RESCUE MISSIONS

Just as vertical and horizontal companies engage in different maneuvers to get ahead, they apply different strategies when things go wrong. Often a setback will occur after a period of rapid growth. Management's initial self-help reaction may be to intensify the Front Seat Focus that originally brought success.

THE VERTICAL COMPANY

When vertical companies run into difficulty, they usually respond by drawing tighter organizational lines, shortening the ladder. A department or division may be broken into two or more smaller ones to increase personalized service and responsiveness. Management will probably work hard to cut out inefficiencies that may have cropped up during the growth phase. It may sell off a division that shows weak promise or performance, or it may reduce staff overall.

Millipore, a materials separation company, was one of the high tech superstars of the 1960s and 1970s. By 1979, the company achieved profits just short of $20 million. Two years later, in 1981, profits dropped a precipitous 43 percent. By 1984, profits had snapped back, up 48 percent.

How did management achieve such a dramatic upturn in just three years? By using vertical rescue strategies. The top brass cut back staffing, reduced expenses, and sold off a subsidiary, using the proceeds of the sale to retire long-term obligations. They set goals for profitability of each product and each segment of the market and then watched to make sure those performance goals were met.

THE HORIZONTAL COMPANY

A horizontal company's rescue strategies are quite different. They usually are strategies of inclusion rather than exclusion, addition rather than subtraction or elimination.

When a growth spurt is followed by a sag, a horizontal company—instead of breaking up a division—may reorganize by combining departments that produce similar products or aim at similar markets. Whereas a vertical company will concentrate on cutting costs, a horizontal company may *increase* expenditures for research and development in hopes of recapturing momentum. It may add new product lines or create new divisions.

Thermo Electron's earnings were evaporating. Revenues dropped from $231 million in 1982 to $182 million in 1983. So this Boston area thermodynamics conglomerate used horizontal rescue tactics to cool off its overambitious operations. The senior management team halved the number of business units by sizing up each one and evaluating whether it should be sold, closed, consolidated, or left intact. They cut staff by eliminating duplication, and they boosted research and development funding, drawing on technical and marketing staff to pinpoint priorities. By 1984, sales were up 29 percent, and revenues had climbed to $235 million.

■

We've described vertical and horizontal success stories. Obviously, both kinds of rescue strategies can work, sometimes brilliantly, if conditions are right and a company is unified behind one or the other style of command. But the strategies are not always so successful. What happens when rescue missions fail or fall short? Eventually, as we've shown, "new blood" of the opposite thinking style may be brought in to attempt to reverse the fortunes of war. What happens when this organizational shuffle has been played out too late and possibly too many times? What next?

THE MERGER: THE ULTIMATE RESCUE

Most mergers happen simply because both sides need each other. Merging companies usually talk about complementary strengths, rescues, or expanded growth potential. They rarely talk about the real issue, the real need: survival.

In our experience, mergers—especially those involving "complementary strengths"—often inadvertently unite companies with opposite thinking styles. Vertical companies looking for missing lines, horizontal companies looking to better integrate networks. For example, a vertical company that sells to five industries acquires another firm that sells to three other industries. The missing piece the vertical management is looking for is more lines. What the vertical management doesn't realize is that the partner may be horizontal and, instead of extending lines, may form circles.

In order for this type of merger to be successful, live up to promises made and goals set in pre-merger talks, the parties would need to acknowledge their weaknesses: "How are neglected details stunting us?" This is one of the most difficult questions for a company—especially the stronger (more financially sound) of the parties—to address. Failure to answer this question accounts for much long-term loss.

If the question is addressed and weaknesses exposed, the parties can then join forces to overcome the weaknesses and realize their goals.

Instead, what often occurs is a war for thinking style dominance in the merged organization. Both parties chant, "I'm OK, you're OK, but we're going to do it MY way." The stronger of the two usually wins and tries to remake the other party in its own image. The result: both ultimately lose. The reason: The strengths of the acquired company get lost or downplayed, and the weaknesses of the stronger party never get exposed. Could this be why so many mergers fail—why 50 to 80 percent of mergers, according to studies, are financial disappointments?

Favorite Game: Change the Structure

When Eugene Allen took over AT&T after James Olson's premature death, one of his first vertical moves was to reorganize Olson's consolidated structure into nineteen autonomous business units.

Are you part of a merged company, or one that has just hired a new CEO? Or is your company about to be taken over? Want to figure out whether the new management is going to take the company in a horizontal or vertical direction?

Look for early clues in the ways the new management changes the organizational structure. Check it out:

	Vertical View	*Horizontal View*
Is management trying to integrate or separate functions?	__ Separate	__ Integrate
Is management making the lines of responsibility and authority clearer or is it consolidating them?	__ Clearer	__ Consolidated

A CASE IN POINT

A vertical computer sales company, in hopes of improving its credibility in the industry, took over a horizontal computer consulting firm. Nine months after the papers were signed, 65 percent of the acquired company's consultants left the firm, taking their clients, professionalism, and good reputation with them.

The trouble began when the vertical company, desiring consistency, quickly standardized procedures used with clients of both companies. Seeing no need to examine the procedures the consulting company already had in place, the vertical company instituted procedures utilized by its own sales force, procedures the consultants regarded as time-consuming and pointless.

Unfortunately, no discussions of the consulting company's procedures or needs ever were held. Possibly, if they had been, the vertical company's management would have learned something about the techniques used to attain the professional image they sought. As it was, a merger that had been intended to enhance the acquiring company's growth and reputation ended up a drain on its time, assets, and energy. In a little less than two years, the consulting company was resold for a fraction of the original purchase price.

This theme, with variations, is repeated endlessly on the financial pages of newspapers and in business periodicals. Yet hardly anybody seems to learn. Valuable opportunities to adopt the "smart ways" of both sides are lost. Instead, these "smart ways" become hidden land mines that can blow up into costly litigation.

THE BITTER AFTERMATH

Take Ross Perot's sale of his Electronic Data Systems to General Motors in 1984. Could the debacle created by that merger be traced to vertical and horizontal styles of doing business?

Perot, described as "the hottest entrepreneur in America," reportedly was enticed by the challenge of combining GM's immense resources with his own dynamic style of leadership. He hoped to create an unbeatable colossus to lick the Japanese. Instead, no sooner had the ink dried on the contract than the two companies began squabbling. GM viewed EDS as a subsidiary; Perot did not. He insisted, for example, on a separate compensation plan for EDS people and fought to prevent a GM audit of his company's books. GM and EDS staffers were constantly sniping at and ridiculing each other's way of running a business.

After two years of constant public dissension, both sides recognized their mistake. In 1986, GM bought out Perot, then the corporation's largest stockholder.

Of course, there's nothing unusual about a clash of corporate cultures. But what if the source of this clash was, at least in part, a difference in corporate thinking styles? The Front Seat Focus at EDS bore strong horizontal earmarks. As the editors of Inc. observed in January 1989, the power of Perot's organization was based on its flexible structure: "The company had been built as a shifting collection of loose teams, assembled and dismantled as challenges were overcome. Their strength came from their ability to focus, and their loyalty to a shared cause." After Perot's departure, according to staffers who later left EDS to join his newly formed Perot Systems, "the old EDS brotherhood had dissolved . . . drowned in a sea of memos, sign-off sheets, and procedures. . . . Gone, too, was the loose organization that could reorganize in a weekend—replaced by committees and consultants."

scene dominated by the other thinking style. Due to their particular Front Seat Focus, both vertical and horizontal companies attend assiduously to certain aspects of operations and neglect other aspects. Workers who attend to the aspects at which the company does well are seen as having the right stuff.

Foreign thinkers entering a company normally excel at what the company is currently neglecting. They are drawn to those areas where they see problems not being attended to. They see lights flashing, "DANGER! DANGER!" They quickly attend to these unattended details, expecting praise for their efforts. However, more often than not, their actions are misunderstood. Instead of being applauded, these efforts are seen as unnecessary and time-wasting.

So, on minor as well as major fronts, the battle between the thinking styles goes on. Foreign thinkers are seen as having the wrong stuff—not having what the company needs in order to get where it wants to go. People whose individual thinking styles fit the dominant one tend to rise; those whose thinking styles don't fit soon reach dead ends or are forced out.

Might companies react differently to foreign thinkers if their thinking methods were better understood? If managers paid as much attention to methods as they do to results, might they get better work products? If—instead of automatically rejecting thought that doesn't follow the prevailing mode—they examined how the foreign methods might work in a particular situation, might they learn something valuable?

Warning Signs of Thinking Style Warfare

When is your company caught in a thinking style war? When everyone knows:

- What questions can't be raised
- What criticisms, excuses, complaints can't be uttered
- What kinds of solutions get no recognition
- What talents aren't appreciated

BOGGED DOWN IN BUREAUCRACY

What happens when the "wrong stuff" is excluded from the inner circle, discouraged from initiating suggestions, viewed as incompetent and uncreative—and there is no external pressure to change? Bureaucracy sets in.

Bureaucracy is nothing more than rigid adherence to established ways of doing business. Either a vertical or a horizontal culture can become stale, set in its routines, when one style of thinking has been dominant too long and its natural talents are overused.

A vertical company with too many rigid lines can't break through and get a broader perspective on the industry, see in what direction the current is flowing. A horizontal company with too many circles can't see when something has ended—when the trend is over. Managers delude themselves into believing the mythology: that the company way works, and works *best,* if they just hang in there long enough. What happens, however, is that while they conform to their established procedures for attending to the details of the Front Seat Focus, the neglected details pile up. Too busy watching the front seat to pay attention to the rear, they get blind-sighted and stuck.

Typically, horizontal bureaucracies become mired in inflexible missions, sloppy operations (such as late billing, inaccurate inventory information, and out-of-control expenditures), and poor performance tracking. Vertical bureaucracies, on the other hand, may lose clear direction, develop sloppy work habits (such as excessive duplication of effort, too many redos of assignments and projects, and too many forms to fill out), and fail to properly coordinate services or products. Of course, management doesn't recognize that it's trapped in its own procedures.

THE HIDDEN COSTS OF THINKING STYLE WARFARE

The costs of getting bogged down in bureaucracy and rejecting the "wrong stuff"? See the accompanying chart.

Millions of dollars a year in turnover, lost sales and contracts, and dissolved partnerships may be attributable to lost or misunderstood information. Consider:

- Americans attend at least 12 million business-related meetings per

The Hidden Costs of Thinking Style Warfare

Problems	*What Happens*	*Company Cost*	*Personal Cost*
Same words have different meanings	Assignments are done incorrectly due to misinterpretation	Assignments are redone and redone, resulting in WASTED TIME	Person feels ineffectual
Ideas get discounted	Value of ideas depends on who is listening	Creative ideas are lost, resulting in WASTED MONEY	Person feels discouraged
"My way's better than yours"	Thinking styles struggle for territorial control	Focus is on differences rather than capitalizing on strengths, resulting in WASTED ENERGY	Person feels exhausted

day. The average manager devotes up to half of his or her working life to meetings, conferences, and consultations, which may consume more than 35 percent of an organization's personnel budget.

- The average corporate worker spends 61 percent of an eight-hour day initiating or receiving communications in one form or another. Some managers spend up to *100 percent* of their time sending or receiving memos and reports.
- Some 70 percent of internal and external communications—within and between companies—are oral.

If only *half* of these communications involve embattled foreign thinkers—if even *one-third* of the time spent in meetings or on memos and reports is wasted on thinking style battles—how much critical information is lost!

TO SUM UP

We're not saying that thinking style wars are the sole cause and Communicoding the sole cure for organizational ills. Hardly. Communicoding is not a goal, it is not an end in itself, it is not a panacea. Communicoding is a technique that accelerates the journey and enhances the vision of where individuals and companies want to go.

As we all know, companies are seeking to increase:

- Quality of products
- Customer satisfaction
- Worker participation and performance
- Opening of new markets

Thinking style wars are interfering with the ability to reach these goals. Thinking style wars are sidetracking and distracting companies from keeping their eye on the ball.

Could Communicoding be the fastest path to a new direction?

A LOOK AHEAD

In the chapters that remain, we'll show you how to wind down the war with foreign thinking, both on the personal and organizational levels. How to decipher the logic of the foreign mind . . . see the value and creativity in the foreign solution . . . gain influence with the foreign thinker when your own thoughts fall on deaf ears. Lastly, we'll show you how to marshal the forces by blending thinking styles for optimal results.

American business needs new answers, and these answers require asking different questions. How to work with rather than against foreign thinkers may be the key question that provides the answer corporate America is searching for.

8 DECODE

Half the controversies in the world are verbal ones; and could they be brought to a plain issue, they would be brought to a prompt termination.

—JOHN HENRY CARDINAL NEWMAN,
Oxford University Sermons

How many meetings have you attended in which the same arguments and epithets were bandied back and forth until the side with more power or more endurance won the hollow victory of having the other side reluctantly agree? Decisions may be reached in this way, and disputes may appear to be resolved. But, as with the endlessly self-propagating broomstick in *The Sorcerer's Apprentice,* no sooner does the dissension seem to be cut off than it pops up again in a dozen different places. Why? Because the core conflict remains untouched. A resolution that works must be based on mutual respect; it must take account of the *legitimate* difference in thinking that's the source of the friction.

This chapter and the next two will show you how you can use Communicoding to transform a clash into a click. Our proven Communicoding formula has three parts:

COMMUNICODING: THE FORMULA

1. *Decode:* Decipher the foreign logic
2. *Encode:* Reveal the creativity of the foreign solution
3. *Recode:* Show your value to the foreign thinker

Have you made a request and received a response that seemed off base? That's your signal to *decode*: to decipher the logic behind the incongruous response. This chapter tells you how.

Have you asked someone to solve a problem and gotten back an absurd solution? That's your signal to *encode*: to look for the potential value, or benefit of the solution. (See Chapter 9.)

Has someone trashed *your* ideas? That's your signal to *recode:* to state your view in a way the other kind of thinker can gain from. (See Chapter 10.)

More often than you'd imagine, these three techniques, used singly or in combination, will amicably resolve the issue.

THE NEED TO DECODE: ENTERING THE FOREIGN LAND

The need to decode begins with an unwelcome surprise. Someone has responded to your request in a way you didn't anticipate. The unexpected response is odd, unsettling—an intrusion on your vision of what was to happen or what was to be done. This unsettling experience is a very important clue that you may have entered the land of the foreign thinker.

We human beings are ethnocentric: we tend to regard foreign cultures and customs as inferior to our own. Similarly, whether we're vertical or horizontal, the logic of a foreign thinker is likely to look faulty. We can't see any good reason for anybody's responding to our request in that way! This is especially true because we don't *realize* we've stumbled onto foreign soil. The other party *seems* to be speaking our language, so why does the response come out like gibberish?

Surprise entrances into foreign territory occur quite frequently both in business and in our personal lives. We ask for one thing and receive another. At best, we assume that our request was not understood; at worst, that it was deliberately ignored. Either way, the response seems unresponsive. Hostility rises, mislabeling begins, and the opportunity for resolution is lost.

Is it possible that the other party not only understood the request but actually *fulfilled* it—in a different way then we expected? That the exasperating response was, in reality, a perfectly logical, predictable one—in fact, was the *expected* response to such a request in the land of the foreign thinker?

What a surprise *that* would be!

DECODING: DEFYING CONVENTIONAL WISDOM

Foreign responses are surprising because they challenge our conventional wisdom. We believe, when we make a request, that it's obvious what we're looking for. But that's not what we get back.

Jan was Mike's supervisor at a small insurance company. Sales had been faltering, and Mike, an experienced insurance salesman, had been hired to develop new business opportunities. When Mike first came on board, Jan sat down and spent time with him, giving him an overview of the various products in the line and outlining the goals of the development plan. She suggested several sources for lists of prospects he could begin to contact. They also agreed that much of the sales literature needed updating and repackaging. Jan told Mike to start implementing the plan immediately and report back to her in two weeks.

Two weeks later, Jan called Mike into her office to check on his progress and was stunned to hear that he hadn't made a single contact. "I can't believe it!" she exploded. "You were hired to develop new business. I told you to get on the stick and start implementing the plan. You haven't even picked up the phone!"

Mike was defensive. "I didn't see any point in going out to see customers until I was ready to sell them."

"Ready to sell!" Jan fumed. "We have more than fifteen products, and you're not ready? We have to get out there and get our name before the customer! It's obvious what needs to be done. Why are you dilly-dallying?"

Was Mike really dilly-dallying? Or was the rationale behind his response to Jan's request simply foreign to her? Was his thinking inferior—or was his view of the "obvious" just different?

If Jan had known how to decode, she might have discovered that Mike *was* satisfying her request to implement the plan and, in fact, was working quite hard. To Jan (horizontal), the obvious first step was to get name recognition. She would get on the phone, make contacts, spread good will, and identify possible prospects. To Mike (vertical), the obvious first step was to review the literature, update and repackage the materials before making calls.

Of course, both steps were necessary to develop new business opportunities. If Jan could have decoded, she would have seen that they were arguing not over *what* should be done—they agreed on that—but over the *order* in which it should be done. Mike's vertical brain automatically went first to fixing what was "broken" (the brochures), while her horizontal brain automatically went first to the root of the problem (lack of exposure).

To decode is to reveal the logic behind a foreign response that at first blush appears odd, inferior, or faulty. Decoding teaches you to stop believing that any smart brain automatically goes to the response you expect. It teaches you that what's expected depends on the customs of the particular land.

Decoding allows you to defy the conventional wisdom: to recognize that there may be another way to satisfy a request besides the one that's "obvious" to you. Decoding requires you to acknowledge that there are really *two* different "conventional wisdoms"—that what's obvious to a vertical brain isn't the same as what's obvious to a horizontal, and that both kinds of responses may be equally sound and sensible within the framework of different thinking styles.

Without decoding, you have no basis, other than your own view of the world, for evaluating foreign ideas, suggestions, information, or behavior. Although, over time, your thinking may change or broaden through experience, it's still your own thinking that you use as a yardstick to measure the logic of others. And foreign thinking—when measured against this unfair yardstick—will almost always fall short.

If you attempt to translate a foreign response into your own Communicode without decoding it first, the foreign response will appear inferior. Jan might have thought, for example, that Mike was unimaginative and needed to rely too heavily on the printed word. In order to accurately translate the logic of foreign thought, you must *put your own thinking aside* and attempt to look through the eyes of the foreign thinker. Only then can the smartness of that person's thinking penetrate your brain.

Since decoding requires a mental leap into the other person's head, how can you break through the boundaries of your own thinking style and enter the logical system of the foreign thinker?

DECODING: THE WORK AT HAND

- Find what's odd
- Verify the anticipated result

You suspect, from that uncomfortable knot in your chest or in the pit of your stomach, that you may be dealing with a foreign thinker. You've closed your eyes, counted to ten, and tried to turn off the negative labels that keep blinking in your brain. But you still can't fathom that weird response to your request!

Your task in decoding is to do just that, and no more. Restrain your impulse to jump to conclusions about the value of the other party's response, or to focus on what the response leaves out. How can you determine the value of something, or identify what it lacks, until you're sure what it is you're evaluating? Decoding a foreign response isn't the same as accepting that response. Right now your job is simply to decipher the logic of the unexpected response.

To complete the Work at Hand, you'll need answers to the following questions:

1. *What was unexpected about the response to your request?* First you need to examine your own reaction: diagnose your general feeling of queasiness and pinpoint the specific source of your distress. Zero in on what seems odd, appears faulty, or makes little or no sense to you—what alerts you to the probability that you're dealing with foreign thought.

2. *How does the other party believe the response satisfies your request?* What result is he or she anticipating that's different from what you foresee? You're not a mind reader; you could make an educated guess, but you'd most likely be wrong. Foreign logic is difficult for you to readily comprehend. So, go to the source. Ask (politely, of course) what the other party had in mind. Then verify your understanding: restate it and check to see whether you've got it right. It doesn't matter at this point whether you agree or disagree; you're simply trying to find out whether the other party was attempting to meet your request in a different way than your conventional wisdom dictates.

3. *Does the answer to Question 2 fall into a vertical or horizontal track?* Now that you know how the other party sought to meet your request, ask yourself: Does that response fit into the mental set of a foreign thinker? In what way? What's the logic behind it? (You have several tips to assist you in Chapter 6, if you need them.) Remember: Vertical thinkers are concerned about the here and now. They talk in terms of what's practical, functional, and needs to be fixed. Horizontal thinkers are concerned about the overall impact. They talk in terms of benefits and possibilities, problems down the road.

More than likely, the answers to the three questions will confirm that the source of the misunderstanding was indeed a difference in thinking styles and that the response that upset you was a perfectly appropriate and expected one in the foreign context—a legitimate, smart response rather than the silly, dumb response you originally saw it as.

Note that successful decoding requires verbal interaction. You can do the first part of the Work at Hand—*find what's odd*—by yourself, because it deals with your reaction to the foreign behavior. You can try to deduce what result the other party may have been anticipating, especially if you know his or her thinking style. However, if the process has taken place in your head, your translation will frequently fall short. After all, it's the other party's language, not yours! That's why the second part of the Work at Hand—*verify the anticipated result*—is essential. Only through direct verification can you be sure that you are dealing with a foreigner and that you really understand the foreign thinking.

SUCCESSFUL DECODING: AN EXAMPLE

Let's walk through an example of successful decoding. Later in this chapter, you'll have a chance to practice it yourself.

We'll take a small, everyday occurrence—the sort that bothers many of us more than we like to admit. Martha was an audit partner at a Big Eight accounting firm. Neil, also a partner, was based in another city. Martha (vertical) was disturbed by Neil's apparent reluctance to get back to her with information she needed when she asked for it. One day she left an urgent message: "Call me with pension plan info as soon as possible." The message referred to information Neil had been gathering for her, which she wanted to present to a client who happened to be coming in the next day. She didn't hear from Neil for three days, even after she left a second message. "What a slacker!" Martha said to herself. "This isn't the first time he's pulled something like this!"

Martha phoned Neil, intending to give him a piece of her mind. But first, to be fair, she clarified to make sure he had actually received and understood her request. She asked in a neutral tone of voice, "I'm wondering whether you received my message about the pension plan information. I asked you to call me with it as soon as possible."

"Yes," Neil replied. "I was going to call you tomorrow."

This simple kind of clarification is a tried-and-true technique that often clears up misunderstandings when thinking style differences aren't involved. But with opposite thinkers, it can serve to inflame the situation. If the other party understood our request and still responded in this incomprehensible way, there must be something wrong with him! Thus, ironically, the "clarification" leaves us free to criticize and mislabel the opposite thinker to our heart's content.

Martha was about to reply, in her iciest tone, "And just what was so earth-shakingly important that it kept you from responding to my message for three days?" But instead, having just taken one of our Communicoding courses, she caught herself, took a deep breath, told herself to slow down, and decided to try to decode.

Having already identified what was unexpected in Neil's behavior—his failure to call her promptly with information she had requested—she went right into the second question: "I was surprised that I didn't hear from you sooner. I'm sure you had something in mind in waiting to call me back. Can you tell me what it was?"

"I knew what information you were looking for," Neil explained. "I figured it would be a waste of your time and mine to call you unless I had the whole picture for you, and it just wasn't possible to get together all the data any sooner."

Martha now saw that the result Neil was anticipating by delaying his return call was a thorough report and more productive use of time for both of them. Rather than slacking off, she concluded, Neil was actually acting conscientiously. To verify her understanding, Martha restated it in her own words, as accurately as she could: "So you're saying you anticipated that it would be more efficient to wait to call me back until you had all the facts you believed I needed?"

"That's right," said Neil.

Martha now reflected on the third question: how Neil's response might fit into a vertical or horizontal thinking style. "As soon as possible," to a vertical thinker like herself, meant "as soon as you can get to a phone." To Neil, it meant, "As soon as you have the whole picture"—a typically horizontal translation. Although Martha knew that even a limited amount of information might have been enough to allow her to move ahead with this particular client, it had never dawned on Neil that a less-than-complete picture might suffice. Furthermore, it had never dawned on Martha that the value of giving partial information, rather than none, might not be obvious.

Decoding accomplished, Martha found it quite easy to resolve the problem. In the future, she would word her requests more explicitly, giving an exact time when she needed the information. She asked Neil, when he got such a message, to check back with her and let her know how soon he expected to have the material. "If I can wait, fine," she said, "If not, I'll let you know that I prefer a partial report."

Without decoding, it's easy to imagine how this simple difference could have blown into a major clash. Imagine the fight that might have ensued—Martha accusing Neil of shirking responsibility, Neil defending himself, Martha insisting on punctuality, Neil calling her a nag! Fortunately, Martha recognized the unexpectedness of Neil's response and her negative labeling of him as signals to decode.

REQUESTS CAN HAVE DOUBLE MEANINGS

Often, when you're greeted by an unexpected response, it's at least in part because the words used in your request have different meanings in the two Communicodes—meanings that seem equally clear and equally obvious to the respective thinkers. *As soon as possible* is one example. Here's another:

Bill, the president of a small corporation, came to us with a problem. He had asked his board of directors for help in dealing with an important customer on a sensitive issue involving company policy. Louise, a board member who wanted to be helpful, had offered to call the customer herself. Bill, offended, interpreted Louise's offer as a vote of no-confidence. Louise, in turn, was miffed at Bill's reluctance to accept the help he had asked for. "Do you want help or don't you?" she demanded.

The truth was, Bill *did* want help, but not in the way Louise took him to mean. *Help,* to her, meant relieving someone of part of a function or task. To a vertical thinker like Louise, the word *help,* translated, was tantamount to doing it herself. To Bill (horizontal), *help* had a different connotation. When he asked for help, what he wanted was advice and

VERTICAL AND HORIZONTAL PROGRAMS FOR TYPICAL REQUESTS

Typical Request	*Vertical Program*	*Horizontal Program*
Give me your reading on this	Tell me what we should do	Draw a picture of what we know
Cover all the bases	Pinpoint the essentials to begin	Pinpoint essentials for completion
What's the problem?	Find what's stressful	Find what's causing the stress
What's the bottom line?	Where do we stand?	What do we have to do?
Follow my lead	Do exactly what's told	Ensure the impact agreed upon
Get me the facts	Give me information surrounding the start and finish	Give me information surrounding the past and future
What's the downside?	What factors hinder start?	What factors hinder finish?
Get to the point	Tell what you want done	Tell the reason you're here
Make it short and sweet	Minimize the effort	Maximize the aim
Do it right away	Do it the instant we finish talking	Give it high priority among other tasks
Tell me your strategy	Delineate actions to be taken	Delineate how to maximize gain
Where's the payoff?	What will be eliminated or saved?	What will be gained or enhanced?

counsel—not for someone to take over what he saw as *his* job. Thus *help* functioned as a code word with two disparate meanings.

Once we helped Bill decode, he was able to handle Louise, as well as other vertical board members, more smoothly. He understood that they were, in fact, giving him help—but in a different manner than he expected. He even realized that sometimes this type of help might be worth considering. He also learned how to get the type of help (advice) he sought from vertical thinkers. We suggested that he make his requests *more specific:* "Can you tell me what you would say to the person in that situation?" After trying that technique, Bill reported with delight that he had received excellent suggestions. Armed with two types of help to draw upon, Bill realized that, in the future, it would be useful to make clear which type he wanted.

As soon as possible and *help* are only two of many typical requests that, for vertical and horizontal thinkers, have different intended responses. Vertical and horizontal brains automatically go to what's most essential according to their own thinking styles—much like computers that have been programmed to give different responses to a particular command. The chart on the preceding page shows common phrases often used in requests—phrases that, based on our research and observation, call for different responses in the two Communicodes.

MORAL OF THE STORY

Were you surprised that each of these requests could call for two such different responses? Did you see how each response could be a legitimate way of responding to the request?

This chart may be a useful reminder next time you're hit by an unexpected response. You may want to refer back to it to assist you in seeing where the responding party's brain is heading.

The point to remember is that just because a word or phrase has a certain meaning to you, it doesn't necessarily mean the same to a foreign thinker. Vertical and horizontal brains go in different directions when they hear a request. So, if you're making a request and you have a particular response in mind, make sure you clearly state what it is—or go back and make sure the other party understands what you're looking for. Don't assume that what's obvious to you is obvious to a foreign thinker.

WHEN TO DECODE

Now that you see how helpful decoding can be, and you know how to go about it, how do you know when it's time to decode?

Ideally, *before* a disagreement becomes disagreeable. You should start decoding when the first pangs of oddness strike you: the first subjective reaction on your part, which you now can correctly interpret as an indication that you may be on foreign ground.

Many times, though, people don't become aware of the need to decode until they're already embroiled in a seemingly intractable clash. It's in such situations that thinking style differences most clearly show up. Of course, not all conflicts are due to thinking styles. Decoding will tell you whether or not thinking styles are the source of the problem.

Watch for the following signals that decoding is called for:

- *You are criticizing or negatively labeling the other party.* Remember, foreign thinking, when compared to your own, will most likely appear inferior or faulty. Be highly suspicious of your quickness to explain an odd response by reaching negative conclusions about the other party's thinking or personality. Decode instead.
- *This isn't the first time you've had an upsetting response from this party.* Constant irritation and disappointment are likely indications of a thinking style clash, which can be resolved by decoding.
- *You are repeating the same arguments or criticisms over and over.* If you can't make the other party see what's wrong with the response, and the other party can't make you see what's right about it, it's likely that a thinking style difference is keeping you from considering each other's view. You can find out by decoding.

Criticism, frustration, and repetition all signal the need to decode. What starts as a request may turn into a tirade. The same is true on the other side; the other party can't understand why the virtue in the response isn't clear. A battle often breaks out, with each side endlessly upholding a fixed point of view. Decoding requires you to STOP the battle and separate the request and its anticipated result from the criticism. The following exercise will give you practice in doing that.

EXERCISE: CUT THROUGH THE CRITICISM, REVEAL THE ANTICIPATED RESULT

The purpose of this exercise is to give you practice in recognizing your arrival in the foreign land.

When you criticize an opposite thinker's response, it's usually because it's not clear to you what result that party is anticipating. (By the same token, when an opposite thinker criticizes *you,* it probably reflects lack of recognition of what result *you're* anticipating.) When emotions run high, discerning the logic behind the foreign response isn't easy—you're blinded by your own criticism and by the battles that unfold. However, if you stop and recognize that you are anticipating different results, decoding can be simple.

We'll describe three scenarios based on typical vertical-horizontal battles our clients have told us about. We've scripted the scene, the surprise, and how the battle unfolded after the surprise. As you'll observe, requests have turned into criticisms. What has gotten lost is the fact that the parties are anticipating different results.

Your task is to identify the request being made and its anticipated result.

1. Carefully read each scenario.
2. Underline the criticism. Notice how easy it would be to get sidetracked by the words and the tone.
3. In the blanks provided, fill in the request and the result the requesting party anticipated.
4. Turn to the answer sheet and compare the result the requesting party anticipated with the result the responding party anticipated. Because you don't have the other party to decode with, we've identified the latter for you.

Scenario 1

THE SCENE: Vertical partner (V) asks horizontal partner (H) to do him a favor.

THE SURPRISE: H partner asks V partner several questions about the favor he wants done.

THE BATTLE:

V partner: Why is it that every time I ask you to do a simple favor, I have to play Twenty Questions? If you don't want to do it, just tell me.

H partner: You have the attention span of a five-year-old. If you have to stay focused for more than a minute, you freak out. What's so wrong with wanting more information?

V partner: Just forget it. It's easier to do it myself. It takes less time than discussing it with you.

NOW, FILL IN THE BLANKS:

What was the request?

What result was the requesting party anticipating?

Now look at the answer sheet. Compare your answers with ours. Then notice the difference between the results anticipated by the request and the results anticipated by the response (which, as promised, we've provided for you).

ANSWER SHEET:

Scenario 1

What was the request?

That the horizontal partner do a favor.

What result was the requesting party anticipating?

That the favor be executed with no questions asked. The vertical partner had already identified what he wanted. Therefore, asking questions wasted time, undermining the purpose of asking the favor.

What result was the responding party anticipating?

That by understanding the whole story, he could do the best job—maybe even more than was asked.

Now, do the second and third scenarios, following the same procedure as in the first.

Scenario 2

THE SCENE: Horizontal wife asks vertical husband to find a babysitter who can work Saturday nights.

THE SURPRISE: Husband makes one phone call to the teenager on the corner, who has mowed their lawn, and finds out that he babysits and is available on Saturday nights.

THE BATTLE:

H wife: Well, you really put yourself out on this one. What kind of babysitting experience does he have? Is he our only choice? If I put as little effort into raising our child as you put into finding a babysitter, we'd really be in trouble.

V husband: There you go again, making mountains out of molehills. You wanted a babysitter for Saturday nights and we have one. He even lives close by.

H wife: Well, if that doesn't say it all! "He lives close by." So you won't have to be inconvenienced by taking him home!

NOW, FILL IN THE BLANKS:

What was the request?

What result was the requesting party anticipating?

Now compare your answers with ours:

ANSWER SHEET:

Scenario 2

What was the request?

That the husband find a babysitter who was available Saturday nights.

What result was the requesting party anticipating?

That the husband have specific criteria for selecting a competent sitter (including experience and background) and that he locate a few prospects to compare with each other.

What result was the responding party anticipating?

That he find someone in the neighborhood with whom they'd had personal experience and who was available Saturday nights.

Scenario 3

THE SCENE: Vertical boss asks horizontal manager to report the highlights of a conference the manager attended.

THE SURPRISE: H manager gives V boss a ten-page report with a ten-page appendix of supplementary material.

THE BATTLE:

V boss: Don't you know what *highlights* means?—Summarize the key points, the main ideas. Can't you see how much of my time and money you're wasting? If you're trying to impress me this way, it's not working.

H manager: I only gave you what I thought you wanted. Any less would have given you an inaccurate picture of what took place.

V boss: If I wanted such an accurate picture, I would have gone to the conference myself. Your job is to make my life simple, not to complicate it!

NOW, FILL IN THE BLANKS:

What was the request?

What result was the requesting party anticipating?

Now compare your answers with ours:

ANSWER SHEET:

Scenario 3

What was the request?

That the manager report on the conference.

What result was the requesting party anticipating?

That a brief, one-page or two-page synopsis—possibly bulleted—would provide all the salient information.

What result was the responding party anticipating?

That a comprehensive summary, highlighting essential conclusions and including support material to aid understanding, would be most useful to the boss.

You've seen, though various examples in this chapter, as well as in this exercise, that a request can produce distinctly different responses. Yet, no matter how much we explain and demonstrate this phenomenon, we cannot overstate the amount of damage that can be caused by failure to realize when you've entered the foreign land. Isn't it too bad that so much misunderstanding and mistrust can grow out of unawareness of thinking styles?

Aren't you also beginning to see that each of these responses had legitimacy within the context of a particular thinking style—that there was a logic on both sides? Go back to the scenarios. Try to decipher the vertical and horizontal logic behind the anticipated results. Doesn't each make sense in its own way?

Next time you're struck by an odd or disappointing response—especially if you start being critical of that response—we hope you'll stop, think back to this exercise, slow down, and decode.

DO YOU NEED TO READ FURTHER?

Decoding is simple *if* you can put aside your natural inclination to judge the other party's response by your own standards. If so, you don't need to read the rest of this chapter. Decoding becomes difficult when you encounter interferences that encourage you to continue viewing the other party's thinking as inferior.

So, don't be surprised if you have trouble decoding. In a moment, we'll tell you how to get back on track. But first, a look at some of these interferences that can divert you from doing the Work at Hand.

INTERFERENCES WITH DECODING

Now that you realize foreign thinking exists and that it can appear at the most unexpected times and places, you're on the alert to identify odd behavior wherever it shows up and to decipher the thinking behind it. So what could possibly deter you from your mission? The answer: Entertainment.

The velocity at which odd behavior whizzes past—combined with human beings' computerlike need to make sense of the unusual—contributes to the popularity of the sport of character depiction. This entertaining game is such second nature to most people that often they aren't even aware they're playing it.

Recently we at Marsten were engaged in conversation with a high-powered executive. We were explaining vertical and horizontal thinking and the power of decoding. The executive was totally engrossed in the conversation. He appeared to easily and fully follow the concept and was animated in his agreement. However, as soon as the topic of conversation moved to a marketing strategy session he had been involved in, Communicoding appeared to go out the window. Mr. Executive began to depict one of his subordinates as an overemotional, "me-first" type. There was no identification of odd behavior, no attempt to imagine what result might have been anticipated by an unconventional response. Instead, this bright, talented, well-intentioned executive quickly turned the discussion into a negative characterization of his subordinate's motivations and background.

Without a conscious and deliberate effort to discern the logic of the foreign thinker, many people like this executive move comfortably and automatically into personality analysis and character depiction. If you have any doubts on this point, stop in at any busy lunch spot catering to executives on the go. Eavesdrop. Notice how often you hear criticism of somebody's colleague, boss, or employee, and how easily people relate this criticism to some personality flaw. This is not malicious, it's customary!

Character depiction has three popular variations: the Rush to Judgment, Thinking Style Snobbery, and the Negative Write-Off.

RUSH TO JUDGMENT

"How was the movie?"

"Great!"

"What was the main character like?"

"Conceited!"

How often do you hear people "describe" other people or situations with interpretations? This happens so often that most of us hardly seem to notice that our recitals are filled with conclusions but devoid of facts and descriptions. What's more, our listeners don't seem to be bothered at all; rarely, if ever, do they ask us to fill in the details necessary to bring them along with our thinking. Instead, what generally happens is that someone else in the crowd comes up with another entertaining tale . . . and so on . . . and so on. ("That Johnny's a real . . ." "But I heard . . ." "Yeah, he's sneaky . . .") The frightening effect is that information is seldom expected or well-received. In fact, information—when offered—is taken as an interference. ("Don't confuse me with the facts!")

In this Rush to Judgment, the opportunity to identify odd behavior and to decipher the thinking behind it gets swept away. Decoding isn't even attempted. The foreign view is forgotten; the negative judgment of the person is remembered.

THINKING STYLE SNOBBERY

If you've tried to decode, if you've asked the three questions and you're still coming up with negative explanations, you may be encountering Thinking Style Snobbery.

Thinking Style Snobbery is the tendency to keep supporting, explaining, and verifying your own logic to yourself, to others, and to the foreign party. The rightness of your own logic gets more and more deeply ingrained in your mind, leaving less and less room to let in new and different information.

Many Americans visiting Europe are appalled when they discover that shops and museums close for a couple of hours at midday. This system appears senseless to tourists who must hurry through or even miss out on a landmark attraction because they haven't timed their arrival far enough before the noon closing. Many times, these tourists argue with museum guards or store managers—to no avail, of course—trying to "educate" these obviously irritated personnel to the more convenient hours of operation back home. Rarely do Americans try to understand the logic behind the European system and the results it achieves: long, leisurely lunches followed by midday strolls; a welcome break in the work routine; time to socialize when everyone is fresh enough to enjoy it.

It's the same with thinking styles. If you continue assuming that your way of thinking is right, best, and most logical, you'll slow down or block the flow of information, increase antagonism, and interfere with decoding.

THE NEGATIVE WRITE-OFF

Cutting your losses is an accepted business strategy. Almost everyone has at one time or another reached a decision that rather than try to salvage a losing situation, it was cheaper, easier, and less time-consuming to write it off, get out, and move on. With people who give you continual headaches, it's tempting to do the same thing—to simply write off the foreign thinker. How many times have you said, "Well, you know So-and-So—she did her usual number"?

The Negative Write-off is the antithesis of decoding. How can you understand a foreign point of view if you've already written it off?

Gary is vice-president of Meredith's division. His favorite expression is "Time's at a premium!" Yet, when she asks him for information or advice, he continually wastes time (in her eyes) by going off on tangents. To a knowledgeable Communicoder, Gary's behavior would be a tipoff that he might be horizontal. To Meredith (vertical), Gary's behavior would be a tipoff to write him off—if he weren't her superior.

When Gary telephones Meredith with an answer to one of her questions, the conversation goes on for hours. The last time, she put him on the speakerphone and proceeded to dust her office while Gary droned on.

So Meredith has kept her wits, adapted, and gotten a clean office to boot! And she's learned to go around Gary whenever possible. But the thinking behind Gary's "digressions" has been lost.

ELIMINATING INTERFERENCES

The cost of the Rush to Judgment, Thinking Style Snobbery, and the Negative Write-Off goes beyond the loss of an individual's particular contribution, no matter how valuable that contribution might have turned out to be. The true cost is the loss of a whole different way of thinking—a loss none of us can afford.

To repeat: All of these interferences, which you may very well confront when attempting to decode, spring from a single source: *you have entered the foreign land and are unaware of it.* Most people, when they go abroad, realize that some things will look strange that make sense to the local populace. Even so, many travelers have trouble putting aside their own ways and squelching their ethnocentric reactions. Recently we saw an American businessman stop someone on the street in Paris and ask for directions to the Eiffel Tower. When the Frenchman didn't seem to grasp what was wanted, the American spoke louder and louder, as if the inability to communicate was the Frenchman's failure, not his own. How much more intolerant that tourist would undoubtedly be of foreign thinking spoken in his native tongue!

Your ability to accomplish the Work at Hand is crucially dependent on separating your reactions from the information you're trying to obtain. Difficulty in side-stepping your reactions is a clear indication of the need to slow down your brain, defuse your feelings, and reverse your assumptions.

To neutralize your reactions, defuse feelings:

To get yourself unstuck, you may first need to ventilate your present thoughts. When you've gotten them out of your system, you'll find it easier to begin decoding.

Start where you're at. Identify all the good points about your own view and the bad points of the other.

1. Write down all the benefits you can see in meeting your request as you intended.

2. Write down all the drawbacks in the unexpected response—all the ways in which it's really stupid.

3. Go ahead—have fun and write down all the perverse benefits you can think of that the other party seems to derive from driving you crazy.

Are you calmer now? Good. Because now you're ready to reverse your enthocentric assumptions.

Reverse assumptions:
Right now you believe the other party is illogical, stupid, and/or out to get you. Start over. Forget your list of reasons why the response isn't worth considering. Assume that there's a thinking style difference and that the other party is bright, rational, and well-meaning. Go further: Assume not only that the foreign thinking has legitimacy but that the other party is brighter, more rational, and/or better intentioned than you are.

If, in fact, you perceive the other party to be smarter, you'll want to know what makes this superior mind tick. Suppose, for a moment, that you had the opportunity to sit down with Charles Darwin, Henry Ford, or Marie Curie. Each of these brilliant thinkers undoubtedly possessed certain eccentric qualities that could easily be ridiculed. But you surely wouldn't waste time making judgments about them. Instead, you'd try to absorb as much information from them as you possibly could. That's exactly your job with the foreign thinker.

The Work at Hand now becomes a stimulating exercise to satisfy your intellectual curiosity. Once you've reversed assumptions, you'll no longer see the foreign response as an obstacle. You'll want to know the thinking behind it. You'll want to find the hidden result that the foreign thinker is anticipating. You'll ask clarifying questions to help you grasp this smart thinking.

AND NOW TO DECODE . . .

So now you've come full circle. You're ready to decode. Go back and ask the three questions:

1. What was unexpected about the response to your request?

2. How does the other party believe the response satisfies your request?

3. Does the answer to Question 2 fall into a vertical or horizontal track?

Don't forget to verify the result the other party anticipates. Since you're talking to someone whom you now assume to be smarter than you are, you'll want to be especially careful. Make sure to accurately restate your understanding of the other party's view and to avoid any phraseology that inadvertently incorporates the biases of your own thinking style. Remember, you don't want to show your ignorance to a superior thinker! Watch out for:

- Information you may delete
- Information you may distort
- Judgmental tone of voice

Here are some useful phrases when verifying: "Are you making the point that . . .?" Or, "It sounds to me as if what you're saying is. . . . Is that right?"

A SUMMARY EXERCISE IN DECODING

Are you ready to try decoding? Here's a case study about a disagreement between two men named Walt and Harold. Read the story carefully, putting yourself in Harold's place. Then we'll ask you to decode Walt's behavior.

■

Harold, a name partner in a major Chicago corporate law firm, was having lunch with Walt, the managing partner. Walt mentioned that he'd had a call from the daughter of Charles Dawson, chief executive officer of one of the firm's biggest clients. The young woman wanted an interview for an associate's position with the firm. "She's a recent *summa cum laude* graduate of Yale Law School—" Walt began.

Harold didn't need to hear any more. "This could be very touchy," he cautioned. "Better handle it with kid gloves."

"Don't I know it!" Walt replied.

A week later, Harold was again having lunch with Walt. "How did you get out of that interview with Dawson's daughter?" he asked.

"Get out of it?" Walt replied. "I interviewed her yesterday and was quite impressed. I set up a second-round interview for next week. I hope you can make it."

Harold nearly choked on his coffee. "You actually interviewed Charles Dawson's daughter? Didn't I tell you to handle this situation with kid gloves?"

"You certainly did—and I did. I called Chuck. He wanted no special favors. What did you want me to do—slam the door in his daughter's face?"

"Obviously, I wanted you to find a graceful way out," Harold replied. "It's the only thing that makes sense. Now we're really in a bind! What if we don't want to hire her? What if she starts working here and she doesn't like the way we do things and tells her father to get another law firm?"

"Sure," Walt countered, "and what if you fall tomorrow and break both legs? What if the bottom drops out of the market? Anything *could* happen. But right now, if I hadn't interviewed Chuck's daughter, he'd be plenty upset. You asked me to handle this carefully, and I did. What more do you want?"

"Carefully?" You've got to be crazy!" Harold sputtered. "This means nothing but trouble. It's the riskiest thing I've ever heard of!"

■

Let's assume that you (Harold) are too upset with Walt's response to your request ("Treat this with kid gloves!") to successfully decode at this point. So start by defusing, then move on to reversing assumptions, and then to decoding. Remember, how would Harold view the situation?

EXERCISE:

Defuse Feelings

Your task: Fill in the blank columns, viewing Walt's response from Harold's perspective.

Benefits of meeting Harold's request as he intended	*Drawbacks of Walt's response*

Now, compare your answers with ours:

ANSWER SHEET:

Defuse Feelings

Benefits of Harold's request	*Drawbacks of Walt's response*
Ends sticky situation	Prolongs sticky situation
Limits the damage	Postpones the damage
Avoids future trouble	Invites future trouble
Minimizes antagonism of important client	Potential for antagonizing or losing client down the road
Keeps client's nose out of firm's affairs	Potential for client interference in firm's affairs

Now, *reverse assumptions* and get ready to decode. Assume that Walt's view is superior to yours (Harold's). Say to yourself, "Walt's a smart man—smarter than I am. What's he trying to tell me?"

EXERCISE:

Decode

Your task: Fill in the blanks, asking yourself the following questions about Walt's response. (Since you don't have Walt here to question, you'll have to figure out the answer to the second question from the dialogue you've read. Remember, in answering that question, think about what result Walt apparently anticipated from what he did.)

What's unexpected about the response?

How did Walt believe the response met the request?

Does the logic behind the response fall into a vertical or horizontal track? How?

Again, compare your answers with ours:

ANSWER SHEET:

Decode

What's unexpected about the response?

That Walt agreed to interview the client's daughter after being told to handle the situation with kid gloves.

How did Walt believe the response met the request?

1) Giving the daughter a chance avoided antagonizing client.
2) Call to client and agreement on no special favors headed off any fallout from a decision not to hire her.
3) The daughter may drop out on her own, and the firm would reap the benefit of having been gracious.

Does the logic behind the response fall into a vertical or horizontal track? How?

Vertical. Walt wanted to prevent immediate danger—offending the client by refusing to interview the daughter.

This exercise was based on a real life example. Harold, being horizontal, was anticipating the long-range results of interviewing the client's daughter. To him, the possible negative ramifications were so obvious that he was sure Walt would know what he meant by his shorthand request to treat the matter "with kid gloves," and he was baffled and enraged when Walt did what to him seemed just the opposite. As a result, he was negatively labeling Walt. He discovered by decoding (with our help) that Walt was actually fulfilling his request—from a vertical point of view. Walt was, in fact, treating the situation "with kid gloves" in terms of the short-term results he anticipated, which Harold didn't see.

Once Harold had calmed down and decoded, he found it much easier to see Walt's point of view. He realized that there *was* danger of upsetting the client if they chose not to interview his daughter. Harold also saw that there might be an advantage to opening the door to the daughter, in terms of good relations with the client. Harold had been concerned about possible damage down the road ("What happens if she wants us and we don't want her?"). But in their discussion following decoding, Walt alleviated Harold's anxiety in that regard: "If we don't want to hire her, I'll pinpoint a special talent she has, tell her that's unfortunately not the kind of talent we're looking for, and line up three interviews for her at other firms where her talent would fit in. She'll be pleased and so will Daddy."

When Harold saw that Walt could handle his concern in a way that would please the client, he was delighted. The smartness of Harold's thinking gave him assurance that they could counter any other difficulties that might later arise.

In the past, Harold had walked away from disputes like this one feeling insulted and outraged. This time, both men walked away smiling. By decoding, Harold had seen that Walt had a legitimate point of view; and by taking both views into account, the two of them were able to work out a mutually satisfying resolution. More important, Harold now understood that Walt's way of thinking was different from his, and he was able to use this knowledge to get better results in his ongoing dealings with his partner.

■

Did you find this decoding exercise easy or difficult? Did defusing feelings and reversing assumptions help? Of course, doing it vicariously, as you've just done, isn't quite the same as when your own feelings are involved in a real situation. So now, try it with someone you're upset with: your boss, your colleague, your spouse, your friend. We think you'll be amazed at how easily decoding falls into place once you remove the emotional interference that keeps you from seeing the other person's point of view. And, of course, always remember to verify.

TO SUM UP

We can't emphasize too strongly the importance of decoding, whether as a stand-alone procedure or as a first step in resolving a clash. The mere realization that there may be a difference in thinking styles, and that the other person is worth listening to, puts you way ahead of where you were.

The truth is, people often *are* brighter than you think. Blinded by your own thinking style, you may be blanking out other views, losing valuable information. Decoding allows you to *include* rather than to *exclude.*

Still, there are times when decoding isn't the answer. Sometimes you ask for a solution and get something that seems totally out of sync. You can't see how any intelligent person would believe that this solution resolves the problem! The next chapter focuses on the second part of our Communicoding formula—encoding—and how it can help you determine the value of these unsatisfying solutions.

9 ENCODE

Diverse and even contradictory problems can be found in the same dilemma—problems that lead to different and sometimes diametrically opposite lines of inquiry and attempted resolution.

—JACOB W. GETZELS, *Problem-Finding and Creativity in Higher Education*

Now that you've learned to decode, you know that foreign thinkers are usually much smarter than they first appear. In encoding, you'll discover that foreign thinkers are often more cooperative than they may seem, and their solutions—which may be diametrically opposite to the ones you expect—are often much more useful than they first appear. You'll learn that, because of Communicode differences, you are most likely misjudging many of the people you have to deal with—and losing out because of it.

THE NEED TO ENCODE: GAINING FOOTHOLDS IN THE FOREIGN LAND

You have a dilemma. You ask someone—a colleague, a subordinate, your spouse, a friend—to solve it. You expect a solution that meets your priorities: your expressed and most pressing objectives. What you get, instead, is something contrary to what you clearly said you wanted done.

At best, you feel stymied; at worst, betrayed. This party on whom you were counting to get you where you want to go has brought you to a dead end or gone in a different direction. It's as if you were mountain climbing and your guide, whom you were relying upon to point out the safest footholds, went off and left you clinging perilously to a cliff. The sensation of being stranded, stalled, let down, misled is a very important clue that you have most likely been relying upon a foreign thinker, someone whose signposts point in different directions than yours.

Most of us, when we go someplace in a foreign country, are willing to put ourselves in the hands of a guide—indeed, we often have little choice. A local person can be expected to know the way, maybe even a shortcut. We don't.

But when we set out for a destination in familiar territory, we generally have a good idea of how to get there. If our taxi heads in a different direction, our inclination is to suspect the driver of taking a roundabout route to run up the meter. We may even worry that the driver isn't taking us to our destination at all.

Thus, when we don't *realize* we're on alien ground and we receive a solution strikingly different from what we were looking for, we're first startled, then suspicious. We feel confident that we know the way. Why is the other party hindering our progress? Why is he taking the wrong route? Why is she pursuing *her* agenda rather than ours? What's in it for them? Are they misdirected, or are they taking us for a ride?

Such episodes often wind up in bitter accusations and altercations. But is it possible that the foreign "guide" has actually taken us where we want to go, and we don't realize it? Could it be that because the route looked strange, we didn't recognize the destination when we got there?

What a surprise *that* would be!

ENCODING: RECOGNIZING AN ALTERNATE ROUTE

Conventional wisdom visualizes a single route to a predetermined objective. Anyone who tries to take you a different way either doesn't know where you're going or, for some reason, is trying to keep you from getting there. Encoding assumes that the opposite thinker knows where you're going and may have found another, equally good or even better way to get there.

Kent was vice-president of an airline. He found himself receiving more and more frequent complaints about long delays in reclaiming checked baggage at one of the metropolitan airports. Deplaning passengers would arrive at the baggage carousel (a one-minute walk from the gate) and then would have to wait seven fretful minutes for their luggage to come down the chute. Meanwhile, they saw passengers from the same flight who had brought only carry-on luggage leaving the airport and getting a head start on their business.

Kent called in his chief of operations, Howard, whom he knew from past experience to be independent-minded and extremely competent. Kent outlined the situation and told Howard that he wanted the baggage delay problem solved quickly, as complaints were mounting.

Three days later, Howard's recommendation was on Kent's desk. It consisted of three typed lines:

MEMO

To: Kent
From: Howard

To eliminate the complaining:
- Use the baggage carousel farthest from the planes.
- Install mirrors next to the elevators.

Kent couldn't believe his eyes. He reread the memo again and again. He was beside himself. These Band-Aid treatments wouldn't solve the baggage delays! Howard was a bright guy. Why hadn't he done what he'd been asked to do?

When we ask someone for a solution, it's usually because we have confidence in that party's ability. So, when we get something completely different from what we expected, as Kent did, we're caught off guard. We find it hard to believe that this capable person has performed in such an inappropriate manner. Is it possible that we didn't make ourselves clear? To be fair, we may go back and make sure.

Kent phoned Howard. "Is this your idea of a joke?" said Kent, referring to the memo. "What did I ask you to do?"

"To solve the baggage delay problem as quickly as possible, so the passengers would stop complaining," said Howard.

"So you tell me to do it with mirrors!" said Kent icily. "How did a smart guy like you come up with such a half-baked solution?"

"Actually, I thought it was pretty clever—" Howard began.

"Clever, all right—clever enough to get it off your desk in a hurry," Kent snapped as he hung up the phone.

The encounter left Kent even angrier. He had given Howard the benefit of the doubt by making sure he understood what was wanted. "If he wasn't just trying to get rid of this in a hurry, he must be trying to needle me, get my goat," Kent fumed. What other explanation could there be for such slipshod work?

Was Howard really needling his boss or evading the issue? Could he perhaps be less capable than Kent had imagined? Or was the thinking behind his solution simply foreign to Kent?

Encoding offers an alternative explanation to the ones conventional wisdom can provide. Because Howard's suggestion of reassigning baggage carousels and hanging mirrors wouldn't change the time it took to unload baggage, Kent saw no value in that solution and therefore questioned Howard's motives in presenting it. Had Kent known how to encode, he might have discovered, to his surprise, that Howard's solution actually met his priorities—though in a different way than he had envisioned.

To encode is to uncover the gain in a solution that at first blush appears not to achieve your stated priorities. Literally, to encode is to convert information from one system of communication to another. Unless you can convert a foreign thinker's solution into your own code language, you can't perceive what you gain from it. The priorities it addresses appear to be different from yours.

Encoding may seem similar to decoding, but it's different in a very important way. In both situations, you've been hit with a surprise—a response or solution contrary to what you had in mind. The other party has heard what you wanted and has interpreted it differently than you intended. But in decoding, you're concerned only about understanding the logic behind the foreign response. In encoding, you're looking for the *usefulness* of the foreign solution. You must understand how the other party's solution serves your purposes. Until you do that, the foreign solution will not appear to give you anything that *you* truly value. Without encoding, the advantages of the foreign solution will remain concealed.

ENCODING: THE WORK AT HAND

- Find what's solved
- Verify the gain to you

In decoding, the Work at Hand begins with a step that most people tend to pass over: Find what's odd. Instead of identifying what's puzzling about the other party's response, they jump to mislabeling and think no more about it.

In encoding, the Work at Hand depends on a step that most people never get to: Find what's solved. Instead of looking for what the foreign solution *does* accomplish, they tend to remain stuck on what it *doesn't* do for them.

In encoding, the Work at Hand requires answers to the following questions:

1. *Which of the priorities you set are disappointingly missing from the other party's solution?* This one should be a snap! It's exactly what you're already stewing over. How does the solution fail to meet your priorities—the criteria you thought had been mutually understood? In our airport example, Kent believed that Howard's solution failed to eliminate the baggage delay; to Kent (horizontal), that would mean figuring out the source of the delay and adjusting the baggage handling procedures.

2. *How does the other party think the solution satisfies these priorities?* This key question is one that most people would never think to ask—or if they did, they'd ask it sarcastically, not really looking for an answer. As with decoding, it's essential to ask the *other party* this question, because the answer requires a leap into his or her mental processes. If, in fact, the other party thinks differently than you, it will be very difficult for you to understand how the solution satisfies your priorities. This information is extremely important to you because it tells you the usefulness of the foreign solution—a solution you almost certainly wouldn't have thought of yourself, but one that may serve your purposes just as well as, or perhaps better than, one you could come up with.

If, after getting the other party's answer to this question, you're still having trouble seeing the usefulness in his or her solution, you may need additional information from the other party. If you're a vertical thinker, request an example of how the solution would play out: "Can you take me through an example and show me how your idea would solve the problem?" If you're horizontal, request an example that displays the end result: "All right, suppose we solve the problem the way you've outlined. Can you give me an example that demonstrates the result you'd expect to receive?" (Later in this chapter, we present a chart that will assist you in finding the value in the solution when the other party's explanations and answers still don't do the trick.)

If Kent asked Howard the second question and probed his response as we've just suggested, Howard might explain that focusing on the complaints rather than on the baggage would be the quickest, most economical and doable way to deal with the problem. If the baggage was moved to the farthest carousel from the planes, the passengers would have to walk for six minutes to get to the carousel and would have to wait only two minutes for their bags. And if mirrors were placed by the elevators in the baggage area, people could comb their hair, fix their ties, and be distracted from the frustration of waiting. Although it would still take a total of eight minutes for the baggage to be unloaded, the time would seem shorter and the complaints would most likely abate.

Howard's answer might allow Kent to see for the first time that the problem could be defined as the passengers' *perception* that the time was excessive rather than the time it took for the baggage to arrive. Kent then might recognize that Howard wasn't merely applying Band-Aids or playing with illusions—he was, in fact, solving the problem by giving the passengers something to do other than fretting and worrying while the baggage was in transit from the plane to the carousel.

Although the transit time might be a bit longer than optimal, putting Howard's suggestions in place might obviate the need for a more complex, time-consuming, expensive change in the baggage handling system.

3. *Does the answer to question 2 fall into a vertical or horizontal track?* Armed with the answer to the second question, you now have the information you need in order to determine whether or not the unexpected solution arose from a foreign thinking style. Now that you understand how the solution met your priorities, think back to the characteristics of vertical and horizontal thought (outlined in Chapter 6) to determine which type of thinking you appear to be dealing with. Kent, for example, now might see that, to Howard, "eliminating the baggage delay problem" meant getting over the immediate hurdle: the passengers' complaints. The quick fix Howard suggested was a typically vertical approach.

When the three questions are applied to a situation, the value of the foreign solution is often readily apparent. Having completed encoding, Kent now might recognize that Howard's solution did, in fact, meet his expressed priorities—the need to speedily eliminate the complaints. Without encoding, Kent couldn't see the cleverness and creativity of Howard's solution. He had no handle on what it would do for him. He didn't recognize its usefulness in relation to his priorities. He didn't see it as opening another route he could take to reach his objective. He was confusing the dilemma that concerned him with the avenue of resolution that he, as a horizontal thinker, would have focused on.

With encoding, Kent could see the gain in Howard's solution—an alternative that he, being horizontal, might not readily have thought of. In fact, he had to admit that Howard's suggestions were clever indeed. They could be implemented far more quickly and inexpensively than a thorough study of the baggage handling procedures—and, in fact, could buy time in which to decide whether such an investigation was warranted.

Through encoding, then, you can gain from the use of the tools the foreign thinker has at his or her command. Without encoding, you lose that advantage.

WHEN TO ENCODE

As with Howard and Kent, the need to encode is rarely recognized before people have become inflamed and incensed. Sometimes they have even spent a great deal of time and energy trying to get the foreign thinker turned around in the "right" direction, and yet—because they don't understand the foreign code—another surprise hits them in the face. They feel tricked, undercut. Tempers flare, and antagonism builds.

What is likely to develop at this point is a real personality conflict. In fact, it's our contention that many ongoing personality clashes, both on the job and in personal life, are rooted in inability to appreciate foreign solutions and contributions.

Take the case of Dan and Marjorie. They've been married for a little less than a year and are planning a vacation together. Each has two weeks coming in February. Because it's already January, and Dan is on deadline for a major project, he has asked Marjorie to select the place and make the arrangements. After some discussion, they've agreed that she's to look for a nice, warm, relaxing spot—uncrowded, with some interesting things to explore, possibly a bit adventurous, but not too expensive. They want to be sure they both agree on the specifics, because Dan knows he'll be too busy to give the selection any further attention, and in the past they've had blow-ups over similar situations.

Now Dan has finally finished his project, and he asks Marjorie what she has done about the vacation. "Oh, Dan," she begins, "I found the greatest place—you'll love it. No one I know has ever heard of it. It's unspoiled, inexpensive, not a tourist trap. Of course, because it's off the beaten track, we'll have to change planes twice—but it'll be well worth it! I was lucky and got us the last two seats. I bought the tickets yesterday."

To Dan, harried from the constant pressure he's been under, "change planes twice" is all he has to hear. "I thought we were going to find a place to relax," he interrupts. "What is this, a vacation or an ordeal? Here we go again—you're not following through on what we agreed on. Can't you see how tired I am? With that schedule, we'll be thoroughly exhausted before we get there!"

Marjorie storms out of the room. "I do all the work and you criticize before you even hear where we're going! I *did* consider everything we agreed on! I gave it a lot of thought. Next time, *you* plan the vacation! Better yet, go alone!"

"Next time I will, if going with you means taking three planes!"

Dan hasn't even heard Marjorie's solution, and already they're at loggerheads! If things keep up this way, it wouldn't be surprising to find these two in the divorce court in a year or two. Indeed, "irreconcilable differences"—now the chief grounds for divorce—often stem from a buildup of small incidents like this one, in which husbands and wives like Dan and Marjorie can't see the value in each other's point of view.

On the business side, too, personality conflict—estimated to be the third most common explanation (following financial cutbacks and incompetency) for force-outs in corporate America—grows from repeated encounters in which one party puts down the other's contributions or questions the other's motives.

Consider these recent newspaper headlines, selected at random:

- EX-FANS GIVE [PETER] COOPER'S MONTGOMERY THE COLD SHOULDER: UNPREDICTABLE DEAL MAKER MAY BE ALONE IN UNDERSTANDING HIS VISION—Wall Street *Journal.*
- GONE WITH THE WIND: A RESPECTED EDITOR, AND NOW KEY STAFFERS DEPART ATLANTA IN SADNESS—Chicago *Tribune.*
- THE CLUMSY QUEST FOR IRVING BANK: BANK OF NEW YORK'S BID FOR IRVING, NOW ONE YEAR OLD, HAS BEEN DOGGED BY PERSONALITY CLASHES AND MISSED OPPORTUNITIES—New York *Times.*
- JAPAN LOOKS AT TRADE REFORMS: SINCERITY OF CALL ON COORDINATED TALKS IN QUESTION—Washington *Post.*

Of course, we don't know enough about these particular situations to conclude that encoding would provide a solution to these difficulties. But the headlines alone are enough to strongly suggest a need to investigate whether an encoding difficulty exists. Often, in such situations, a lack of trust and appreciation has built up over a long period of time. If encoding doesn't take place early enough, the eventual result is likely to be an irrevocable split.

To avoid these "hopeless" personality clashes, be alert to the following early warning signals that it's time to encode:

- *You immediately want to reject the other party's solution.* You can't believe it was meant to meet your priorities. Encoding can show you that it not only was *meant* to meet them but *does* meet them in a way you didn't expect.
- *You find yourself teaching the other party your way to solve the problem.* You explain and re-explain how your way is *the* way to handle it—to the point where you begin to ask yourself whether it wouldn't be easier, quicker, and less stressful just to do this "simple" task yourself. Encoding can help you to see the value in another way.
- *You find yourself suspicious of what the other party is up to or is trying to get away with.* As we mentioned earlier in this chapter, in situations that call for encoding, you generally believe the party you've asked to solve the problem is competent; therefore, when disappointed in the solution, you tend to question that party's motives. Instead of voicing or dwelling on such thoughts, encode.

Scornfulness, didactics, and suspicion are all indicators of a need to encode. By watching for these signals and encoding promptly, you can avoid a great deal of short-run frustration and long-run upheaval. You not only can ensure smoother relations and avoid painful ruptures with colleagues and loved ones, but you can gain from the solutions they have to offer, in ways you wouldn't have thought possible.

A HAPPY ENDING

Let's see how Dan used the first signal—his immediate rejection of Marjorie's vacation plans—as a cue to encode. After he had had a chance to cool down, he realized that Marjorie *had* done a lot of work in planning the vacation, and he ought to give her a chance to explain how she felt her plans met the priorities they had agreed on.

"Look, Marge," he began, "when you said 'change planes twice,' my brain just clicked off. I couldn't see how a trip that started off like that could possibly be relaxing. Let's start over. Why don't you tell me what place you have in mind and why you picked it?"

"Well, I collected as many brochures as I could from the travel agent and researched the ones that looked most appealing, keeping in mind that we wanted to combine some excitement with relaxation and moderate cost. I finally chose this island because it looked so beautiful and peaceful. Here—see for yourself." She showed him the brochure. "There are two miles of broad, sandy, deserted beaches. The island's just starting to be developed, so there's just one hotel. It looks fine, and the rates are quite reasonable. There are several short adventure trips available by car—the kind we enjoy. I know it's going to be a bit of a hassle to get to, but that's the price of all that splendid isolation. It's a question of balancing the inconvenience of the trip against what the place has to offer. I think we were lucky to find it! We can sleep on the plane, and we'll have days to recuperate in privacy on that gorgeous beach."

To Dan's surprise, as he looked through the brochure, he, too, found himself drawn to the pictures. He had to admit that if he had been planning the trip and the travel agent had mentioned changing planes twice, he (being vertical) would have immediately crossed this island off his list—and perhaps missed a great experience. Marjorie's horizontal selection process was more inclusive. She had explored as many options as possible and then weighed benefits and costs. Dan now saw that her choice did meet their original priorities, even though it was a choice he himself wouldn't have made.

Fortunately for our newlyweds, encoding revealed that a "personality clash," which might have escalated into serious conflict, actually disguised an easily resolved thinking style difference.

SAME PRIORITIES—DIFFERENT SOLUTIONS

In order to appreciate the usefulness of foreign solutions, you must understand that foreign thinkers will solve the side of the dilemma that you will tend to ignore. When presented with the same priorities, vertical and horizontal brains go in opposite directions. They head toward the aspect of the issue that keys into their natural thought processes. Thus foreign thinkers can provide you with solutions not readily available to you.

Miriam owned a small public relations firm. She was under deadline to complete three annual reports for different clients. All three reports were to include current on-site photographs. She had lined up the free-lance photographer she normally used for such assignments. Two days before the shoots were scheduled to begin, Miriam called to give the photographer last-minute instructions and was astonished to hear a recorded message indicating that he had moved.

"What are we going to do?" she said to Scott, her assistant. "Our photographer left us in the lurch. We have to get ourselves out of this jam. I'm tied up writing copy for these reports! It won't be easy to find someone who does quality work, is within our budget, and is available."

"I have some time today," said Scott. "I'll see what I can do."

The next morning, Scott reported that the problem was solved. "Great!" said Miriam. "But how did you find the right photographer so quickly?"

"I made a few calls. Three of the people I called seemed in line with the rates we've been paying, and two of them were available. I happened to have portfolios both of them had sent me some time back, so I picked the one whose work looked the closest to what we've been using."

Miriam was dumbfounded. "How could you have made this decision so haphazardly? Don't you realize these reports are for our three top clients? Didn't I tell you quality was important?"

"Sure," said Scott. "But we had only two days to find a photographer if we were going to meet the deadlines."

"What are you trying to do—do me in? Have you any idea how this guy's stuff stacks up against our competitors' art, or against other photographers in the area? Do you know what kind of equipment and film he uses? Do you know how expert he is in the darkroom? Did you get references from other firms he's worked for?"

Like Miriam and the other parties in our examples, when you receive a foreign solution, you'll inevitably find aspects missing—those most critical to your thinking style. Miriam, being horizontal, felt that Scott (vertical) hadn't given enough attention to quality. Dan, being vertical, felt that Marjorie (horizontal) had lost sight of the inconvenience of getting to the destination. In the airport example at the beginning of this chapter, Kent (horizontal) felt that Howard (vertical) had failed to go to the root of the baggage delays.

Actually, *the real value in foreign thinking is getting a solution that addresses aspects of the problem your brain would NOT head toward.* Miriam would not readily have found a satisfactory way to meet the shooting deadlines. Dan would have prematurely excluded a desirable destination. Kent would not have approached the baggage delay problem from the angle of the passengers' perceptions.

What's most important is that you begin to realize that your priorities can be met by an incomplete solution. Although something is missing from the foreign solution, encoding teaches you the value of what's there. In fact, the gain to you in the foreign solution is precisely that you receive what's missing from your *own* thinking.

The following chart graphically depicts this reciprocal relationship. It shows how the same priorities elicit different solutions from vertical and horizontal thinkers. The priorities shown on the chart are typical ones that tend to be important to most everyone. By following the broken lines on the chart, you'll be able to pinpoint what aspect is likely to be solved and what is likely to be missing when vertical and horizontal brains address these priorities. The chart will also help you find the gain to you in foreign solutions when your brain is having difficulty getting past what's missing.

In each section of the chart, the path taken by the vertical brain is shown by a single line; the path taken by the horizontal brain is shown by a double line. (The vertical solution is always shown on top and the horizontal solution on the bottom.) To use the chart:

1. Look at the priority being met.
2. Follow the appropriate path for your thinking style to find where your brain naturally goes—what's solved when you tackle a problem.
3. Continue following the same path in the same direction to find what's likely to be missing in your solution.
4. Follow the same path in the direction of the arrow. It will take you to what you receive thanks to the foreign thinker.

To repeat, *your gain is simply that the foreign solution addresses what's missing in yours.*

FIND YOUR GAIN: IDENTIFY WHAT'S SOLVED

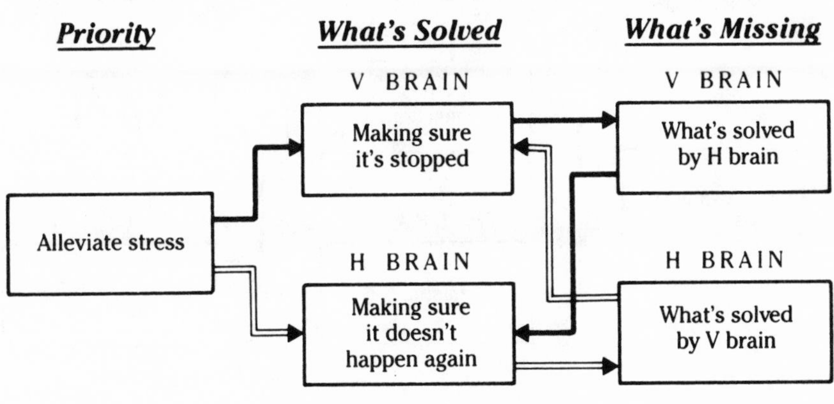

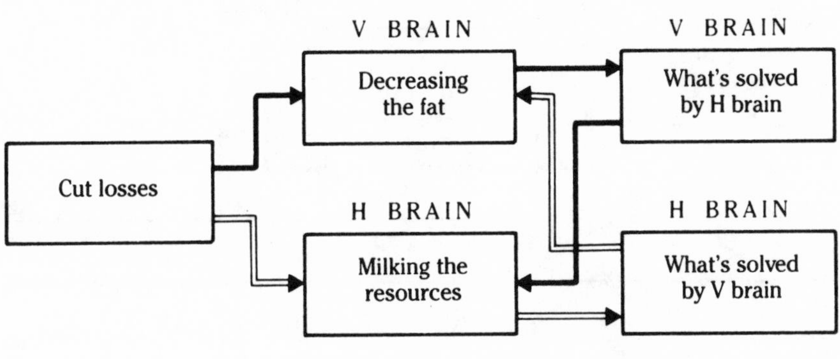

Key: ▬▬▬ V path
═══ H path

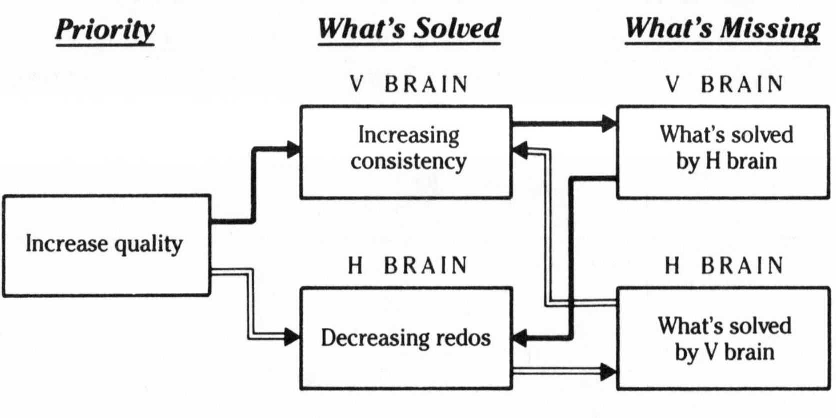

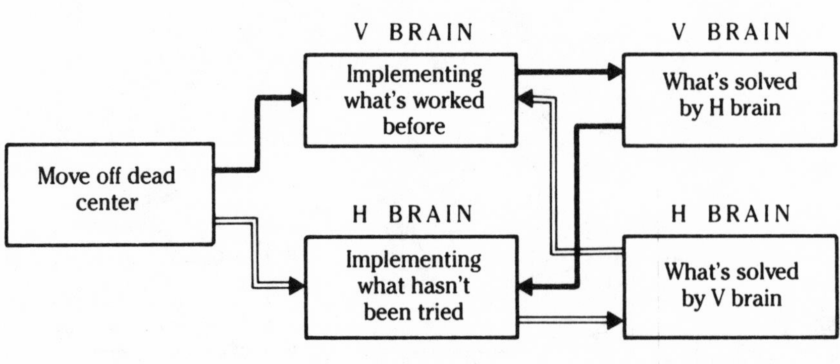

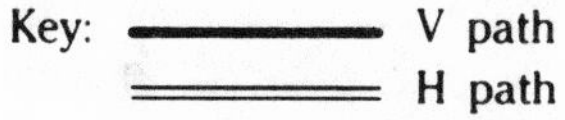
Key:
V path
H path

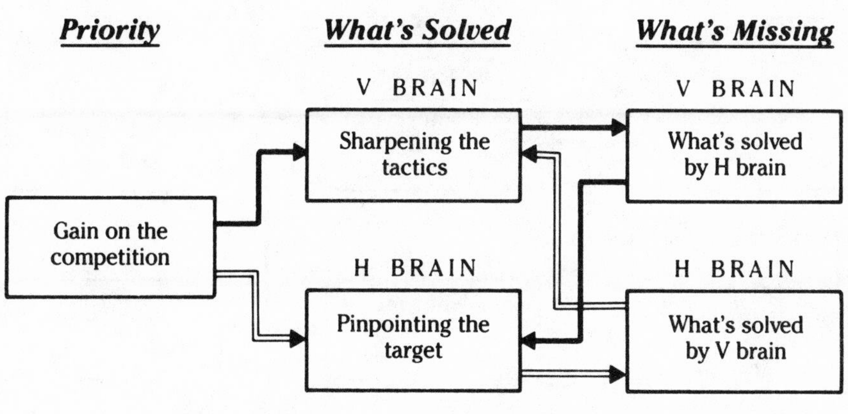
Priority
What's Solved
What's Missing
V BRAIN
Sharpening the tactics
V BRAIN
What's solved by H brain
Gain on the competition
H BRAIN
Pinpointing the target
H BRAIN
What's solved by V brain

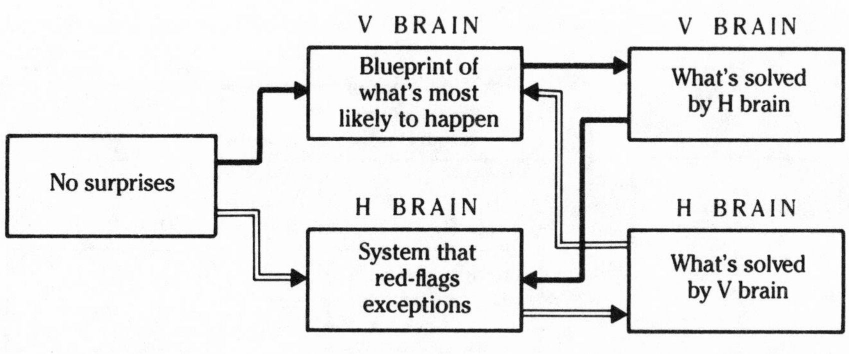
V BRAIN
Blueprint of what's most likely to happen
V BRAIN
What's solved by H brain
No surprises
H BRAIN
System that red-flags exceptions
H BRAIN
What's solved by V brain

Key: ▬▬▬ V path
═══ H path

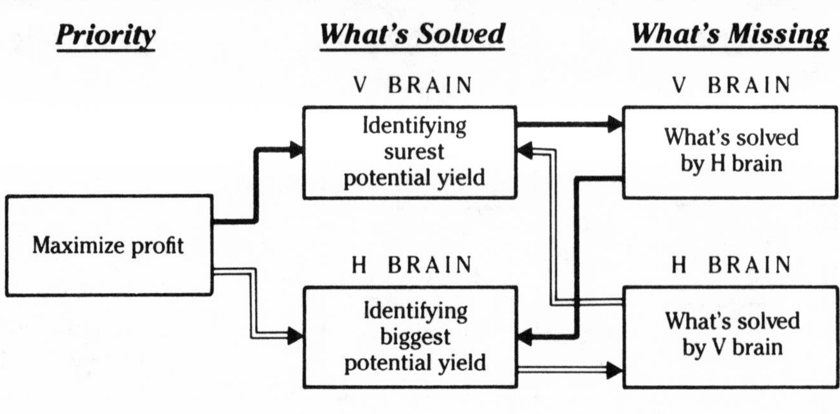

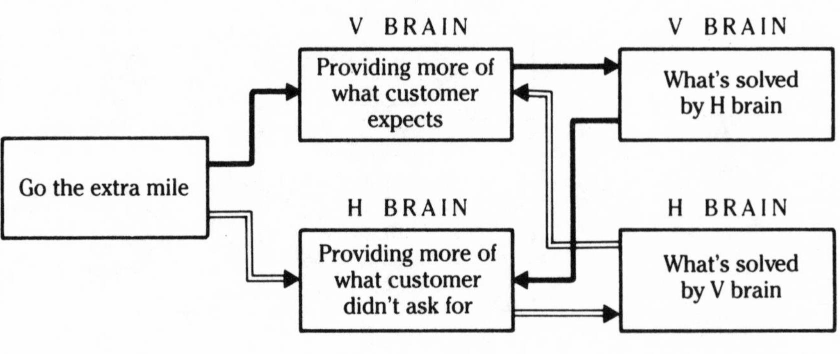

Key: ▬▬▬ V path
═══ H path

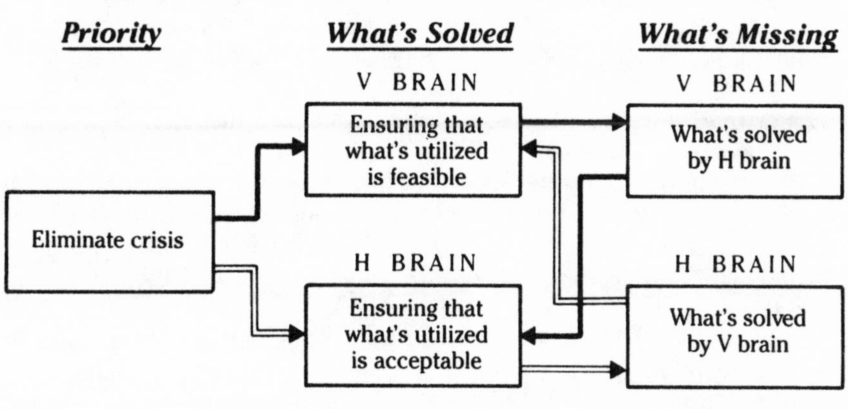

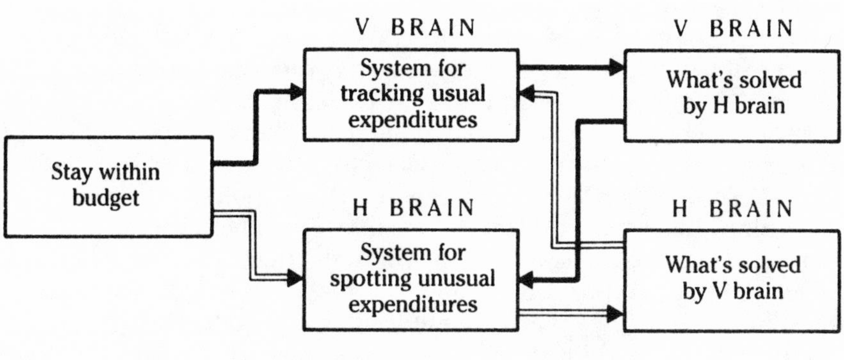

CHARTING THE GAIN

Let's see how, by using the chart, Miriam could find the value in the direction Scott's brain headed towards. As you'll recall, when we left our panic-stricken public relations executive, she was castigating her assistant for having been too hasty in choosing a substitute photographer.

Later that morning, after pinpointing what was disappointing to her about Scott's solution—his apparent failure to adequately assess the quality of the photographer's work—Miriam went over to his desk. "I'm sorry I flew off the handle," she said. "I know you tried to solve our problem. However, the way you went about it caught me by surprise. Perhaps you can explain to me more fully how you met the priorities I gave you."

Scott brightened. "Well, Miriam, I knew we had very little time to make up our minds. So I started by calling only photographers I had heard of. Either they had done work for one of our associates, or I had on hand various samples of their work. If they had been spoken of highly, or the work looked good, I called. The rest was a process of elimination. I first checked out availability and then rates. Obviously, it didn't matter how good they were if they couldn't deliver or if we lost money.

"At that point, I was left with only two choices. Luckily, I had samples of both of their work, so I didn't have to rely on someone else's say-so. I selected the one who seemed to measure up best."

By looking at our chart, Miriam could easily pick out Scott's priority. It was the same as hers: to alleviate the crisis. Under the "What's Solved" column, Miriam recognized Scott's solution as a vertical one: "ensuring that what's utilized is feasible." In other words, the photographer they used had to be available at the right time and at the right price. Her brain, on the other hand, automatically went to the horizontal solution: "ensuring that what's utilized is acceptable." While his first concern was feasibility, her first concern was retaining their accustomed standard of quality.

To Miriam's surprise, Scott's process made sense. She even had to admit to herself that in starting by assessing the quality of various photographers' work, she would probably have wasted precious time. Scott had a point: Even Ansel Adams would have been of no use to them if he was too expensive and couldn't meet the deadlines.

Furthermore, now that she had given Scott a chance to explain the process he used, she could see that he had, in fact, considered quality. It's just that he had given it a lower place among their agreed priorities than she would have.

Although Miriam now saw the gain in Scott's process of elimination, she still felt that the concerns she had about quality were worth pursuing. Limiting her choice to the two photographers Scott had located, she decided to call them back and ask a few specific questions about their experience, equipment, and developing procedures, to assess more thoroughly which of the two best met her standards.

What Miriam ended up doing, without being aware of it, was akin to a process we call Team Think, which we describe in Chapter 11. Simply stated, Team Think is a way of harnessing opposite thinking to develop more complete, creative solutions. It's only logical: Since something is missing from the output of each thinking style, why not put them together? How much more might you gain if you could purposefully employ the abilities of both thinking styles to solve problems and meet your priorities! Team Think, by combining opposite thinkers, produces ideas and solutions that neither party, no matter how high-powered and highly motivated, would easily—if ever—produce alone.

EXERCISE: WHAT'S MISSING

As you've seen, a solution can meet the stated priorities yet at the same time be incomplete. The purpose of this exercise is to give you practice in identifying how solutions do, in fact, meet priorities while still having something missing.

We've purposely chosen common, everyday situations to illustrate that point. The particular situations aren't important; we could easily have selected others. What's important to note is that *most* solutions have missing parts. But that doesn't mean they are worthless. The value is in *what's there,* rather than in what's *not* there.

In the first three columns of the following chart, we've described typical problems, the priorities established, and the solutions offered. The last two columns deal with how the priorities are met and what's missing from the solution. For each problem, we've left one of these last two columns blank. *Your task* is to read the chart and fill in the blanks. In some instances, you'll be determining how the solution meets the priorities; in other instances, you'll be determining what's missing—the issues that the solution doesn't address. In either case, be sure to check that the priorities are, in fact, met.

EXERCISE:

What's Solved?

Problem	*Priorities*	*Solution*	*How priorities met*	*What's missing*
Boss (H) asks employee (V) to devise new phone system to replace outdated one.	Must include specified features, be priced within budget, be installed by a certain date.	Employee recommends a system that meets all the specified criteria.	System does what's wanted, at right price, and can be installed in time.	
Patient (V) complains of soreness in lower back after surgery.	Relief from soreness and worry about outcome of surgery.	Doctor (H) assures patient that pain is normal and will subside.	Patient relieved that there are no unanticipated problems and soreness is temporary.	
Every time Muriel (H) asks Roger (V) to bring something home from work, he forgets.	Assurance that Roger will bring items home.	Roger asks Muriel to give him a reminder call five minutes before he's scheduled to leave.	If she calls him, odds of his remembering are increased.	
James (V) asks his wife (H) to make a special card for his out-of-state mother's 60th birthday.	Card to be unusual, memorable, and received on or before birthday.	Wife makes delicate lace three-dimensional card. Takes long time to make, can't be mailed—has to be boxed and Fed. Ex'd.		Advance provision for how card should be sent, to avoid playing catch-up at last minute.
Boss (H) asks personnel manager (V) to hire new comptroller.	MBA in finance, at least five years' experience in similar firm.	Personnel manager calls search firm, which sends someone over immediately. Applicant has great resume, makes good impression. Personnel manager hires her on the spot.	Boss gets new comptroller with credentials he asked for.	

Problem	*Priorities*	*Solution*	*How priorities met*	*What's missing*
Principal (V) wants teacher (H) to get students to write more comprehensive reports.	To upgrade quality of students' thinking.	Teacher gives class a talk on how ability to demonstrate reasoning is a key to future success.	Talk motivates students to improve reports.	
Boss (H) asks employee (V) to improve ineffective sales piece on company's products.	To impress potential customers.	Employee updates facts, rewrites descriptions of products.	An improved version of former sales piece.	
Band teacher (V) tells Christopher's mother (H) that he keeps missing practice because he left his instrument and music at home.	To have Christopher regularly come to band practice prepared.	Teacher devises a checklist for Christopher to use when leaving for school.		A way to address possible reasons (besides forgetfulness) for Christopher's missing practice.

ANSWER SHEET:

What's Solved?

Problem	*Priorities*	*Solution*	*How priorities met*	*What's missing*
Boss (H) asks employee (V) to devise new phone system to replace outdated one.	Must include specified features, be priced within budget, be installed by a certain date.	Employee recommends a system that meets all the specified criteria.	System does what's wanted, at right price, and can be installed in time.	A way to determine which system best meets criteria.
Patient (V) complains of soreness in lower back after surgery.	Relief from soreness and worry about outcome of surgery.	Doctor (H) assures patient that pain is normal and will subside.	Patient relieved that there are no unanticipated problems and soreness is temporary.	Immediate pain relief.
Every time Muriel (H) asks Roger (V) to bring something home from work, he forgets.	Assurance that Roger will bring items home.	Roger asks Muriel to give him a reminder call five minutes before he's scheduled to leave.	If she calls him, odds of his remembering are increased.	A way for *him* to keep track of requests without her reminding him.
James (V) asks his wife (H) to make a special card for his out-of-state mother's 60th birthday.	Card to be unusual, memorable, and received on or before birthday.	Wife makes delicate lace three-dimensional card. Takes long time to make, can't be mailed—has to be boxed and Fed. Ex'd.	Mother get beautiful card, on time, and will remember it.	Advance provision for how card should be sent, to avoid playing catch-up at last minute.
Boss (H) asks personnel manager (V) to hire new comptroller.	MBA in finance, at least five years' experience in similar firm.	Personnel manager calls search firm, which sends someone over immediately. Applicant has great resume, makes good impression. Personnel manager hires her on the spot.	Boss gets new comptroller with credentials he asked for.	Method for considering other applicants; might have found someone better.

Problem	*Priorities*	*Solution*	*How priorities met*	*What's missing*
Principal (V) wants teacher (H) to get students to write more comprehensive reports.	To upgrade quality of students' thinking.	Teacher gives class a talk on how ability to demonstrate reasoning is a key to future success.	Talk motivates students to improve reports.	Specific guidance on how to demonstrate reasoning in depth.
Boss (H) asks employee (V) to improve ineffective sales piece on company's products.	To impress potential customers.	Employee updates facts, rewrites descriptions of products.	An improved version of former sales piece.	Explanation of how company's products stay abreast of industry trends.
Band teacher (V) tells Christopher's mother (H) that he keeps missing practice because he left his instrument and music at home.	To have Christopher regularly come to band practice prepared.	Teacher devises a checklist for Christopher to use when leaving for school.	Checklist helps Christopher remember to take instrument and music.	A way to address possible reasons (besides forgetfulness) for Christopher's missing practice.

Did you notice how, in each situation, the solution—while it had something missing—did meet the priorities? Go back and ask yourself, in each case, whether the solution would be useful even without what's missing. We think you'll agree that in most instances, it would. So, next time you ask a foreign thinker to solve a problem and you immediately hone in on what's missing, think back to this exercise and ask yourself whether the foreign solution meets your priorities. If it does, what's missing may be irrelevant.

WHAT IF YOU STILL DON'T LIKE THE SOLUTION?

In most cases, we've found, encoding does enable people to see the gain in a foreign solution. However, it's possible that you can go through the encoding process and still feel dissatisfied—not just because something's missing, but because the solution really *doesn't* meet your priorities.

It may be that the other party *isn't* as competent or cooperative as you thought. More likely, what you may discover through encoding is that either a) you had a priority that was implied—that you need to make more explicit, or, b) your priorities are different from what you originally thought.

Carol had a dinner meeting coming up with an important client whom she particularly wanted to impress. She asked her assistant, Marcy, to run out at lunchtime and buy the client "a real nice gift." Marcy came back with a leather portfolio.

"That's beautiful," said Carol, "but how much did you spend on it?"

"About $100," said Marcy.

"What!" said Carol. "Our budget won't allow for such expensive gifts. Whatever were you thinking of?"

"Well, you told me to get something real nice—" Marcy began.

Encoding in this case wouldn't change Carol's mind about the extravagance of the gift. What it might do is to demonstrate her failure to explicitly state her priorities about cost. (After all, Marcy could deal only with the priorities Carol had expressed, not the implicit ones in the back of her mind.) Or encoding might awaken Carol to the fact that cost was a higher priority to her than she herself had realized. Thus, even if encoding doesn't have a "happy ending," much may be gained in terms of redefining or crystallizing priorities.

INTERFERENCES WITH ENCODING

Now that you know that someone who truly understands your priorities can meet them in an unexpected way, you're on notice to encode whenever you're tempted to brand a solution worthless. So what could possibly interfere with your mission to find the hidden value? The answer: Cynicism.

Like decoding, encoding is fairly easy to do—*if* you can get past your tendency to mistrust the other party's motives. If you can do that, you don't need to read the rest of this chapter.

However, most people have difficulty pushing their cynicism aside. When confronted with a solution that makes no sense in their thinking code, it's hard for them to believe that their priorities have been met. Even if they can see the logic in a foreign solution, they have trouble seeings its value to *them*.

For example, in the exercise you just did, Muriel may see Roger's logic in suggesting that she call him at the office to remind him to bring something home, but she may fail to see how she could possibly gain from that solution. Instead, she's likely to focus on the inconvenience of making the reminder calls and to assume that he's just trying to shift the burden of remembering onto her. Thus she won't recognize that the solution is well-intentioned and does meet her priorities—in fact, it may be the simplest way to ensure getting what she wants. She'll probably find it difficult to believe that a solution so foreign to her approach is meant to satisfy her. What will most likely be running through her mind—if not out of her mouth—are words like these: "Why is it such a chore for you to remember something I ask you to do? Your memory seems to work just fine when you're the one who wants to remember!"

When *your* thoughts are filled with mistrust and you find it difficult to encode, you're running into interference. Let's look at some typical ways your cynicism can divert you from the Work at Hand. Then we'll show you how to surmount these interferences and get back on track.

JUMPING TO WHAT'S MISSING

Okay, puzzle fans, admit it: In the exercise, didn't you have more fun finding what was missing in the solutions than identifying how they met the priorities? When a solution appears wrong, isn't your first tendency to determine what's been left out? You may delight in exposing all the variables the other party's solution omits—variables that "any smart brain" would have considered: "Yes, but, have you thought of . . ." "Shouldn't we take ____________ into account?"

What you probably don't realize is that your list of overlooked variables will include only those germane to your thinking code. You don't stop to wonder why someone else might be including different variables. You walk away feeling confident of your assessment—maybe even smug. You're certain that *your* variables are most essential; you haven't stopped to consider that something might possibly be missing from your own thought pattern as well. No matter how smug you feel, *you've* omitted an important piece of information: how the foreign solution meets your priorities.

Bert (vertical) asked Tom (horizontal) to develop an idea for increasing customer inquiries about a new product their company was about to launch. Tom developed an attractive direct mail piece, which instructed the reader to call for information regarding the new product and receive a free gift. Before Tom could even finish explaining the projected costs, the time involved, and other factors, Bert interrupted: "The switchboard can't handle that volume of calls, and there aren't enough inside people to answer all the questions we'll get."

What Bert failed to realize was that the very items he was identifying as missing showed that Tom's solution met his priority of increasing customer inquiries. If Bert could STOP, slow down, and encode, he might be able to recognize this. The two of them could then sit down and look at what problems might be involved in implementing the idea, and they could identify ways to fix the problems. Who knows? Their business might be booming sooner than either of them expected!

INVESTIGATING MOTIVES

You had a picture in your head of what a solution would look like. You were counting on that vision's being realized. You're jolted because the picture you envisioned is not what you received. You're confused, taken aback. Could this be sabotage?

When a solution doesn't appear to meet your priorities, you may conclude that the other party is deliberately changing or ignoring them. What other rational explanation can there be? After all, according to conventional wisdom, if the priorities are understood, the solution you get should resemble what you expected. If, to be fair, you check and find that the other party understood what you wanted, that's all the more reason to suspect some sort of power play. You quickly become convinced that the other party is meeting his or her priorities, not yours—"She must be trying to go around me, undermine my authority, impede my game plan." You walk away determined to thwart the saboteur: He's not going to do an end run around *me*!"

This type of thinking is convincing because the facts seem to support it. Sometimes the other party *is* out to get you. With same-brain thinkers, especially, sabotage may indeed be the likeliest explanation. But more often the true reason lies in thinking styles.

Henry, chief executive officer of a pharmaceutical manufacturing firm, asked Chuck, the firm's chief financial officer, to assist him with a problem he was having with the board. There was a feeling among some board members that certain budget allocations for new product research were causing profits to drop. Henry (horizontal) asked Chuck (vertical) to prepare a financial statement that would clearly show the growth the firm was experiencing despite these isolated losses. Chuck seemed eager to help, and Henry eagerly awaited his year-end financial statement.

A few hours before the board meeting, Chuck handed Henry the statement. As Henry scanned it, his face clouded. He saw no trend analysis, no comparisons with years past. How could growth possibly be demonstrated without reference to previous figures? Instead, the report was filled with charts ranking the firm among its competitors in such factors as current sales and return on investment. Henry felt he would look like a fool presenting this irrelevant material to the board. Finally he thundered: "I suspected you were looking for an opportunity to get me ousted as CEO, but I didn't think you'd be so clumsy about it!"

Henry was so convinced of Chuck's self-serving motives that he never bothered to ask Chuck to explain how his financial statement dealt with the company's growth. If he had, he would have been surprised to find that the statement showed a healthy overall growth for the current year despite losses in specific areas targeted for long-range development. Instead of a comparative year-to-year analysis, it concentrated on the extent to which the goals projected in this year's business plan had been realized.

ADDING PRIORITIES

Most people would agree that changing the rules in mid-game is unfair. Still, people do it all the time without realizing it.

Suppose you see that the other party *did* meet your priorities, but you're still not satisfied with the solution. Although you may see some value in it, you immediately nullify the value by *adding* to the original priorities. Your new criteria, of course, are of the sort that brains like yours naturally gravitate to but that the foreign thinker wouldn't have been likely to think of.

This happens so quickly that both parties barely notice. You're so taken aback that the other party could understand your priorities and still fail to address important aspects of the problem that you fail to recognize that these aspects weren't made explicit. You may have assumed they were obvious. Of course, since they were obvious only in your thinking code, these aspects were not addressed.

Adding priorities differs from *redefining* priorities, which was described as a potential positive outcome of encoding. When adding priorities, you fail to recognize that these criteria weren't originally stated. Instead of "Here are some additional points we should have considered . . . ," you hit the other party with "Why didn't you consider . . . ?" Thus, by adding new priorities retroactively, you negate the value of the solution.

The superintendent of an elementary school district assigned a committee of teachers and administrators the task of selecting a speaker to lead an in-service training workshop on techniques for teaching creative writing. The committee chose an out-of-state expert whose theories and methods were receiving wide attention in professional circles. The workshop appeared to be well-received, and the superintendent (horizontal) invited the committee chairman to report on it at a meeting of the school board.

At the board meeting, the committee chairman (vertical) detailed the way the committee had gone about selecting the speaker, outlined his qualifications, summarized some of the key points that had come out of the workshop, and reported on the staff's generally favorable reaction.

Instead of praising the committee's work, the superintendent and some horizontal board members began picking it apart: "What has been done to ensure follow-up?" "How do we know that the teachers will actually use these new techniques in the classroom?" "How can we justify the expenditure on a high-priced speaker unless we're developing a plan to ensure maximum usage?"

The committee chairman was bewildered. He had expected praise for a job well done and instead had received criticism. The superintendent and board members were disturbed that the committee had been so shortsighted as to engage an expensive speaker with no follow-through planned. Overlooked in the shuffle was the fact that the committee's expressly assigned task had been limited to selection of the speaker. The superintendent and board members assumed it was obvious that the committee's work should have included follow-up planning. But that was not obvious to the committee chairman or the members of the committee. By adding criteria after the fact, the superintendent and board members had negated the value of the committee's solution.

ELIMINATING INTERFERENCES

The cost of Jumping to What's Missing, Investigating Motives, and Adding Priorities is incalculable. It amounts to the loss of everything you could gain from opening your mind to the value of a foreign way of doing things.

As with decoding, the source of all these interferences is that you are unknowingly operating in a foreign land. Your conventional wisdom tells you that there's a right way to meet your priorities, and *this isn't it!* You're busy justifying your own position and putting down the foreign thinker; you never stop to think that the other party's solution may not only be the right one in his or her country, but may have something new and different to offer you.

We Americans have generously shared our expertise with people in less technologically developed countries. But many of us don't recognize that we, in turn, may have much to gain from studying foreign ways of solving problems. The pressure of severe economic competition is only beginning to force American business to face the fact that Japanese methods in some industries are more productive than ours.

As in decoding, your ability to accomplish the Work at Hand depends on separating your natural ethnocentric reactions from your assessment of the unexpected solution. Difficulty in doing this indicates that you need to slow down your brain, defuse your feelings, and reverse your assumptions.

To neutralize your reactions, defuse feelings:

Before you can get an unobstructed view of an idea that may emanate from a foreign brain, you need to clear your own brain of the negative reactions that are clouding your vision.

1. Make a list—the more the merrier—of everything that's missing from the other party's solution. Include all the factors that the other party overlooked or didn't consider.

2. Elaborate on all the problems you can think of that will ensue as a result of these missing pieces. Have fun—fill in all the horrific details you can think of.

3. Now list all the perverse personal benefits the other party will derive from his or her solution.

Are you breathing easier now? Okay—it's time to reverse your ethnocentric assumptions.

Reverse assumptions:

Right now you believe the other party is a nitwit or a self-serving saboteur. Start over. Forget your list of reasons why his or her solution isn't worth the time of day. Assume that there's a thinking style difference and that the other party is well-intentioned and is creatively attempting to solve your problem. In fact, assume that this foreign thinker is more creative than you. Assume that the other party has come up with a solution you wouldn't have been clever enough to think of—one that meets your priorities in a better way than anything you could have come up with.

If you were stuck in quicksand and someone came along with a derrick, would you reject it because you'd been hoping for a rope? Of course not. You'd eagerly ask what to do so you could take advantage of this superior means of rescue. You'd pay close attention to the instructions you were given, for you would know that not only your well-being but your very life depended on it.

Similarly, once you've reversed assumptions, you'll no longer see the foreign solution as an impediment. You'll be eager to find out how it can help you. You'll want the other party to explain the solution until its value becomes obvious to you. You'll ask clarifying questions to uncover this hidden value.

AND NOW TO ENCODE . . .

So now you're ready for the three questions:

1. *Which of the priorities you set are disappointingly missing from the other party's solution?* Having defused feelings and reversed assumptions, you should have a ready answer to this first question. You can move quickly to the second:

2. *How does the other party think the solution satisfies these priorities?* If you have trouble understanding the other party's explanation, turn back to the suggestions we've made earlier in this chapter and especially to the chart, "Find Your Gain." The chart also will help with Question 3:

3. *Does the answer to Question 2 fall into a vertical or horizontal track?* The answer to this question will probably confirm that you are, in fact, dealing with a foreign thinker, and it will help you understand the thinking behind that party's solution.

A SUMMARY EXERCISE IN ENCODING

Here's a case study in which Yvonne, a supervisor in a government agency investigating alleged unfair employment practices, asked a trusted staff member, Gordon, to "go the extra mile" in investigating an age discrimination complaint. Read the story carefully, putting yourself in Yvonne's place. Then we'll ask you to encode Gordon's solution.

■

The complaint Yvonne assigned Gordon to investigate came from a fifty-five-year-old man who claimed that he had been fired from his job as a machinist due to his age. The company insisted that age was not a factor in the dismissal—that the man had been fired because he couldn't get along with co-workers and customers. The claimant provided the agency with a list of fellow-employees who, he said, would back up his story.

Yvonne asked Gordon to determine whether or not the company's alleged reason for the firing was a pretext for age discrimination. "This is a sticky case," Yvonne warned Gordon. "A lot of eyes are on us. The complainant has friends in high places. Make sure you give him a fair deal—go the extra mile."

The difficulty Gordon saw in the case was that it hinged on subjective factors. Was the complainant "abrasive," as the company claimed? The answer could come only from the people who had worked with him. But would they talk freely? Or would fear of retribution from the company cloud their responses?

Gordon came up with what he thought was a clever strategy to get candid interviews. He decided to present himself as an executive recruiter seeking employment references for the complainant. Gordon thought the employees would be more willing to speak openly to a recruiter than to a government official. He discussed this approach with the staff attorney, who assured him that it was within legal bounds.

Gordon called all ten employees on the complainant's list. Every one of them, when asked for a "reference," praised the man's fine job performance. However, when asked about his personal qualities, each respondent without exception attested to his inability to get along with people.

Gordon turned in his report, confident that he had clearly established that the allegation of age discrimination was unfounded. To his surprise and chagrin, Yvonne was not at all pleased with his work.

"I told you to go the extra mile," she said. "How could you be fair to the complainant when you hoodwinked his witnesses? You should have disclosed the purpose of your calls. Your job was to be impartial, not to find a way to clear the company."

"How can you think I was biased against the complainant when every single person I talked to was on the list he gave me?" Gordon protested.

"That only made him look worse—getting his own people to talk against him. What you did was highly irregular. As you know, our normal procedure is to do more legwork, get lots of affadavits, talk to more people on all sides of the situation. If we start allowing such unorthodox procedures, we're setting a dangerous precedent within the department. Our procedures are deliberately uniform to guarantee that the complainant and the company both get a fair shake."

■

Let's assume that you (Yvonne) are too upset with Gordon's solution to successfully encode at this point. So start by defusing, then move on to reversing assumptions, and then to encoding. Remember, how would Yvonne view the situation?

EXERCISE:

Defuse Feelings

Your task: Fill in the blank columns, viewing Gordon's solution from Yvonne's perspective.

Factors Gordon overlooked	*Difficulties that will ensue*

Now, compare your answers with ours:

ANSWER SHEET:

Defuse Feelings

Factors Gordon overlooked	*Difficulties that will ensue*
"Recruiter" ruse suggested entrapment	Agency's reputation endangered
Complainant would feel duped	Complainant may go to higher-ups or media
Should have talked to more people	Other investigators may try unorthodox procedures
Didn't follow standard operating procedures	

Now, *reverse assumptions* and get ready to encode. Assume that Gordon's solution is superior to the one that you (Yvonne) had in mind. Say to yourself, "Gordon's a clever, creative guy. How might his solution meet my priorities?"

EXERCISE:

Encode

Your task: Fill in the blanks, asking yourself the following questions about Gordon's solution. (Since you don't have Gordon here to question, you'll have to figure out the answer to the second question from the dialogue you've read. Remember, in answering that question, think about what you [Yvonne] might gain from Gordon's solution. Use our "Find Your Gain" chart on pages 183–187 to help you with the third question.)

What priorities are disappointingly missing from Gordon's solution?

How did Gordon think his solution met those priorities?

Does the thinking behind the solution fall into a vertical or horizontal track? How?

Again, compare your answers with ours:

ANSWER SHEET:

Encode

What priorities are disappointingly missing from Gordon's solution?

Didn't go the extra mile—wasn't impartial—didn't disclose purpose of calls.

How did Gordon think his solution met those priorities?

Bent over backwards to be fair to complainant by interviewing all his suggested witnesses and devising a way to make them feel safe in telling the truth. Checked strategy with legal department.

Does the thinking behind the solution fall into a vertical or horizontal track? How?

Horizontal. Gordon provided more of what the "customer" (Yvonne) did not expect—a method to ensure honest answers from the witnesses. Her vertical way would have been to provide more of what was expected—that is, to follow standard operating procedures.

Yvonne herself didn't actually encode Gordon's solution. But she had a friend who had taken our Communicoding course and who helped Yvonne to see that Gordon's solution actually met her priorities. When Yvonne told the friend what he had done, the friend (before hearing the outcome) quickly responded, "Wasn't that a clever way of handling the situation? People would be much more likely to say positive things to a recruiter than to a government investigator—especially if they were afraid of repercussions from the company. Wasn't the complainant lucky to have someone like Gordon on the case?"

Yvonne was amazed at the difference between her reaction and her friend's. After discussing the merits of Gordon's solution, Yvonne felt that she had misjudged him. He had definitely used a foreign method, and it had thrown her. She, being vertical, had assumed that any departure from the ususal modus operandi was suspect.

Now Yvonne had to admit to herself that Gordon had, in fact, "gone the extra mile" for the agency. He had indeed tried to ensure that the complainant got a fair deal. Although his procedure was unorthodox and not advisable in every case, in this instance it had been effective.

TO SUM UP

The most essential thing to remember about encoding is that more often than not, despite appearances to the contrary, a foreign solution does meet your priorities. A solution that seems unsatisfying may actually produce more gain to you than anything you might have thought of yourself.

Different does not necessarily mean *inferior.* The more familiar you become with encoding, the more frequently you'll be able to translate *different* as *useful, creative.* Perhaps the next time you're confronted with a disappointing solution you'll say to yourself, "There's a hidden treasure here somewhere—let's see if I can find it!"

10 Recode

We may convince others by our arguments; but we can only persuade them by their own.

—JOSEPH JOUBERT, *Pensées*

- You are vice-president of operations at a mid-sized chemical engineering company. You've come away from a meeting of the senior management committee feeling totally stymied. "They keep saying that reversing the high turnover in the research department is a top priority," you tell your wife. "Yet every time I try to tell them why it's happening, they shut me up. It's so obvious that the trouble stems from the system for channeling the money to various projects, but when I raise that issue, they tell me to stop talking theory. I've demonstrated the linkage to budgetary allocations in every way I know how. Why can't they get the message?"
- You are a sales associate at a real estate firm. The telephone setup in the office is driving you out of your mind. "Yesterday a client told me that the phone rang twenty times before someone on the switchboard picked it up," you tell your colleague. "I've told the powers-that-be that our phone equipment is antiquated, but they say it's not worth the expenditure to update it. I don't for the life of me see how they can sit and strategize about the company's growth over the next five years when they have phones that don't work! But they act as if I'm the one who's crazy. It doesn't seem to matter what I say—they just don't get my point."

Recoding is about influence. It's about attaining influence with foreign thinkers—your boss, your colleagues, important intimates. It's about being valued as someone who gives good counsel, who is clever, sound, and wise.

In decoding and encoding, you were in the critic's seat and the spotlight was on the foreign thinker. In recoding, the roles are reversed. The focus is on you. You are being seen through the eyes of "foreigners" who, unaccountably, don't see things your way.

What can you do to impress these unreasonable parties? How can you get them to listen to you?

THE NEED TO RECODE: GAINING LEVERAGE IN A FOREIGN LAND

The need to recode begins with a rejection. Your idea has been dismissed out of hand. You expected instant approval and received instant discouragement. You are puzzled. The value of your contribution is obvious to *you.* You've added something that will obviously enhance the other party's stated objective; or you've subtracted something that would clearly have gotten in the way of achieving that objective. In fact, your contribution is so necessary to meet the stated end that you hesitate to mention its obvious benefits because to do so would seem embarrassingly like overstatement.

Yet, for some reason unknown to you, your view is simply brushed aside. What's obvious to you, it seems, is *not* obvious to the other party. How can this be?

Suppose you emigrated to a foreign land. Wouldn't you first have to become thoroughly conversant with the langauge and customs of that country before you could hope to achieve a position of influence, power, and prestige? How, then, can you expect to become a member of a foreign thinker's inner circle unless you learn to talk the way the other half thinks? Wouldn't it be surprising if you could?

RECODING: DEFYING CONVENTIONAL WISDOM

To get through to a foreign thinker, you must not only surmount your own logic but defy conventional wisdom. When your ideas appear to fall on deaf ears, conventional wisdom teaches that you literally may not have been heard or understood. After all, any fair-minded person couldn't help but see what's so obvious to you. So, being a fair-minded person yourself, before questioning the other party's competence or motives you give it another shot. You repeat your views. You restate them every which way. You clarify. You point out the costs of the other party's chosen path, as well as the benefits of yours, in a sincere effort to be constructive and helpful.

When you do this with a "compatriot"—someone who shares your thinking style—it generally works. The other party will most likely appreciate your calling attention to this vital information.

objective), plus a CRITICAL DIRECTIVE. The critical directive is the brain's guiding strategy for carrying out the priority. A critical directive is like a brainflash—an instant signal from your brain that tells you what to do. As soon as your brain hears a priority, such as "Stay within budget," the brain sends you the flash—like an electronic sign flashing in your head, directing you where to go.

Another way of thinking about the critical directive is as a rallying cry—a watchword for action. When a vertical brain hears, for example, "Cut your losses," the brain automatically cries out: "BOOM, BOOM, BOOM! DECREASE THE FAT, DECREASE THE FAT!" All of the thinker's forces are marshaled behind this cry. Everything the vertical does from that point on is aimed at decreasing the fat. The rallying cry is so loud that it filters out any extraneous information that might interrupt or interfere with fulfilling the critical directive.

The horizontal brain, upon hearing the same priority ("Cut your losses"), issues an equally loud and equally compelling cry: "BOOM, BOOM, BOOM! MILK YOUR RESOURCES, MILK YOUR RESOURCES!" All of the horizontal's forces rally around this cry. All efforts from that point on go toward milking the resources. The brain's signaled strategy blocks out any extraneous distractions.

Unlike priorities, which are usually explicit, critical directives are most often implicit. People usually see no need to state the directive they are following; they assume it will become obvious when they state the priority. Because an automatic association is made in their own minds (HEAR PRIORITY–FOLLOW DIRECTIVE), they assume that the same automatic association is made in everyone else's mind.

This assumption is only half-right. It's true that the association between priority and critical directive is automatic. What's *not* true is that there's only one automatic association that can be made. Actually, there are *two* possible automatic associations. Depending on thinking style, a particular priority evokes either a vertical or a horizontal brainflash or rallying cry.

The critical directive, then, is an invisible but controlling part of a thinker's agenda. There's nothing sinister about this; in fact, it's perfectly natural. Because people assume that their thinking style is universal, they assume that any reasonable person who was genuinely trying to meet the priority would follow their critical directive.

The chart, "What's the Agenda," exposes the vertical and horizontal directives for implementing several common priorities. When you read the chart, notice how distinctively different the vertical and horizontal directives are.

WHAT'S THE AGENDA?

This chart depicts vertical and horizontal agendas that include selected priorities. To figure out the other party's agenda, first identify the priority that has been established. Look for the priority in the middle column. Then read across to the left to find the corresponding critical directive for vertical thinkers and to the right for horizontal thinkers. The priority + the critical directive = the agenda.

V-AGENDA				
			H-AGENDA	
V-Critical Directive	+	***Priority***	+	***H-Critical Directive***
Make sure it's stopped	+	**Alleviate stress**	+	Don't repeat the same mistake
Decrease the fat	+	**Cut losses**	+	Milk the resources
Increase consistency	+	**Increase quality**	+	Decrease redos
Find path of least resistance	+	**Move off dead center**	+	Find path of biggest breakthrough
Sharpen the tactics	+	**Gain on competition**	+	Pinpoint the target
Blueprint what's most likely to happen	+	**No surprises**	+	Foresee potential fallout
Measure gain against potential risk	+	**Maximize profit**	+	Measure risk against potential gain
Provide more of what the customer expects	+	**Go the extra mile**	+	Provide more of what the customer didn't ask for
Isolate and contain	+	**Eliminate the crisis**	+	Convert to an opportunity
Maintain cash flow	+	**Stay within budget**	+	Balance cash distribution

RECODING: REGAINING LOST GROUND

What impression do you make when you violate the invisible half of an important party's agenda—when you meet the agreed priority in a way that interferes with that party's critical directive? Let's look at a hypothetical example.

A problem has arisen in a department, a problem that's producing great stress. The obvious priority is the first one on the chart: to alleviate stress. The department manager is vertical. Her brain is flashing the directive: "MAKE SURE IT'S STOPPED, MAKE SURE IT'S STOPPED!" So she assigns the problem to one of her top staffers. He jumps at the opportunity to clean up the situation and impress the boss. However, because this staffer happens to be horizontal, his brain is flashing a different directive: "DON'T REPEAT THE SAME MISTAKE, DON'T REPEAT THE SAME MISTAKE!"

Five hours later, the boss checks back with him, believing that he's had ample time to resolve the situation. She is stunned to find that instead of stopping it, he has (he proudly tells her) been investigating how and why it occurred!

The staffer, too, is dumbfounded. He has diligently followed his critical directive: not to repeat the mistake. Of course, in order to do that, he had to get to the source of the problem. Shouldn't the boss be pleased with what he's done?

No. By investigating how the problem started, he did not stop it. He contravened the boss' agenda and thus, in her view, wasted precious time. The staffer wanted to impress his boss with his analysis of the situation. Instead, he impressed her with his inability to deliver.

In situations like this one (as in the dispute between Tim and Cliff over the atrium room), as long as you continue to act or speak in a way that threatens the foreign agenda, your worth will be suspect. Influence results from *enhancing,* not endangering, the other party's agenda. But how can you enhance the foreign agenda if you don't fully understand what it is?

When your proposed solution has missed the mark, it's natural to assume that you may have misunderstood the other party's priorities. It's always wise to clarify the objective, as Tim did with Cliff ("I see what you're driving at . . .") But with foreign thinkers, you'll often find, like Tim, that you have understood the objective and still have displeased the other party.

Because people believe their critical directives are obvious, if you ask what the other party is trying to achieve, you'll probably get a shorthand answer that leads you to believe your idea meets the objective. What you won't learn is the *full* agenda and how your view threatens it. What you won't recognize is that *your* critical directive is leading you to meet the priority in a way contrary to the other party's critical directive, a way the other party considers dangerous.

Recoding teaches you to ask the right questions—questions that tell you why you're meeting resistance and how you can regain lost ground.

Recoding is the ability to articulate your view in terms the foreign thinker can appreciate. Before you can influence a foreign thinker, you must let yourself *be* influenced. The key to successful recoding is your ability to grasp the full foreign agenda and how your idea harms it. You have to be willing to hear how you have unknowingly hindered what the other party wants done. Unless you can feel the danger, believe in the harm, you can't influence the other party. Influence requires the removal of the danger. Once you understand how to do that, you'll be able to reshape your view to protect and promote the foreign agenda—and gain the leverage you want.

RECODING: THE WORK AT HAND

- Find what's endangered
- Verify the protection you're adding

The process of recoding differs from decoding and encoding in a very important way. Decoding and encoding tell you what to do when you've been disappointed in another party's thinking; thus you direct the first question to yourself. With recoding, the shoe is on the other foot: *you* are the one whose thinking has disappointed someone. The other party sees something as being lost, hindered, injured, or damaged if your suggestion is followed. Since it's *your* thinking that has been rejected, you must find out why the *other* party finds it wanting. So you direct the first question to the other party:

1. *How does your suggestion interfere with the other party's agenda?* Of course, you won't ask the question in those exact words. You must find a way to phrase your question so as to elicit the information you're looking for. You'll probably need to start by clarifying the explicit part of the agenda (the priority, or pressing objective) and then ask a series of follow-up questions, like peeling the layers of an onion, to get down to the implicit information you're after: the critical directive. For example, you might say: "So we agree that our priority is to eliminate the crisis. How will my idea prevent us from realizing the goal? What strategy did *you* have in mind?"

You may have to rephrase your questions a number of ways: "What do you see as lost by my idea? What harm do you envision as a result of my suggestion? Why is this issue so critical to you?" Even then, the other party's answers are not likely to explicitly reveal the full agenda. Remember, people think and talk in codes. Because they believe their critical directives are glaringly obvious, they normally don't put those directives into words. They simply can't believe others don't know. You'll have to do some detective work to uncover the critical directive—the vital information you need in order to reshape your thinking and gain influence.

You, by the same token, will have difficulty believing in the danger. Your first impulse will be to deny that you've caused harm. You'll want to hold on to your belief that your idea is purely beneficial. You'll have trouble accepting that another party's critical directive could be so different from yours. You must keep asking questions until you actually *believe* that your suggestion has unintentionally interfered with the other party's agenda. You must continue the inquiry until that agenda, and how it has been threatened, are OBVIOUS to you. That may not become fully evident until you complete Question 2.

2. *Is the other party's critical directive vertical or horizontal?* This question will enable you to zero in on the other party's critical directive. The chart, "What's the Agenda?" may help. Referring to the chart, first identify which of the listed priorities comes closest to the one that the two of you are trying to meet. Then, on the basis of the other party's answers to Question 1, decide which of the two critical directives for that priority—vertical or horizontal—that party appears to be guided by. If you've gotten this far with recoding, your answer to Question 2 will most likely confirm that you're dealing with a foreign thinker, and you'll now be able to see *clearly* how your idea harmed the foreign agenda.

This information is both eye-opening and crucial—it's the foundation upon which you're going to rebuild your influence. So you must be sure your information is accurate. Restate it to the other party to make sure you've got it right ("So you're saying that if we do it my way, the result will be harmful because . . .").

What if your situation doesn't match one of the priorities on the chart? You'll have to figure out the critical directive for yourself. At this point you should know what the priority is. Be sure you can state it clearly in words and that the other party agrees you've stated it accurately. Then ask yourself, based on the knowledge of Communicoding you've attained so far, whether the other party's strategy for carrying out the priority seems to be vertical or horizontal. Try to put that strategy—the critical directive—into words and compare it with your own. You'll be surprised, with practice, at how adept you'll become at making the invisible visible.

The following exercise will give you a chance to try before going on to Question 3.

EXERCISE: FIND THE CRITICAL DIRECTIVE (SEE THE FLASH, HEAR THE CRY)

In this exercise, we're going to eavesdrop on reactions that actually occurred at four business meetings. In each case, the parties involved were of different thinking styles.

Your task is to determine the critical directive of the reacting party.

1. Read the scenario.
2. Look at the chart, "What's the Agenda." Decide which priority the reaction addressed.
3. Look at the vertical and horizontal critical directives for that priority. Decide which directive the reacting party was following.
4. Fill in the priority and the critical directive at the bottom of each column. Then look at the answer sheet and compare your answers with ours.

EXERCISE:

Four Reactions at Business Meetings

V.P. to Department Manager	*Chairman to CEO*	*Manager to Staff*	*Partner to Partner*
"It's always the same story, told a thousand different ways. I don't know why you don't get it. The customer was notified that his charge privileges were discontinued. You had someone in the department check it out, saw the error, reinstated service, apologized, and that was the end of it. What makes you think this would happen only once? How many other customers got the same notice in error? It's your job to make sure it doesn't happen again."	"How are we going to get the bottom line above water when our overhead is so high? You knew when you were hired that you were to save a sinking ship. Yet all we get from you are proposals on how to better utilize staff. It seems unfathomable that in an organization of five hundred people, everyone is necessary—no matter how well utilized."	"The reason we have a policy manual is so that policies will be followed literally. Lately I've noticed a disregard for proper procedures, especially with respect to filling out forms, filing forms, and mailing forms to customers. I expect that all matters surrounding these forms be handled at all times exactly as they appear in the manual. A checker has been assigned to proof all forms before they are sent out."	"What do you mean, we can't afford to purchase a $35,000 piece of equipment? It's our next step toward growth. It will earn its keep. It will help us be most profitable. We could even lease it out and make more money. And—let's make sure it's top of the line."
Priority ________	Priority ________	Priority ________	Priority ________
Critical Directive ________	Critical Directive ________	Critical Directive ________	Critical Directive ________

ANSWER SHEET:
Four Reactions at Business Meetings

V.P. to Department Manager	*Chairman to CEO*	*Manager to Staff*	*Partner to Partner*
Priority: Alleviate stress *Critical Directive* (H): Don't repeat the same mistake	*Priority:* Cut losses *Critical Directive* (V): Decrease the fat	*Priority:* Increase quality *Critical Directive* (V): Increase consistency	*Priority:* Maximize profit *Critical Directive* (H): Measure risk against gain

Were you surprised at how easy it was to infer the appropriate critical directives? Next time you're hit with a negative reaction, can't figure out why, and don't know where to turn, think back to this exercise, identify the priority and the critical directive, and position yourself to gain influence.

■

NOW BACK TO THE WORK AT HAND . . .

Once you know which kind of thinker you're dealing with and have identified the other party's critical directive, you're ready to reshape your suggestion by asking yourself Question 3:

3. *What can you suggest that will safeguard the other party's agenda?* The ball is back in your court. It's up to you to show how your thinking can help rather than harm the foreign agenda. That will require some *rethinking* on your part.

Go back to the drawing board. On the basis of the answers to Questions 1 and 2, you're now armed with knowledge of both parts of the other party's agenda: the priority and the critical directive. You now know what the other party is afraid your suggestion will interfere with. Either you must be able to explain how your suggestion follows the foreign critical directive in a way that's not clear to the other party, or you must adapt your idea to meet that critical directive. You may need to explicitly state benefits or safeguards in your idea that you previously left unsaid because you thought they were obvious. Or you may need to modify or repackage your idea, following the guidelines of the other party's directive. You must be able to reshape your idea in such a way that you eliminate elements that do not follow the foreign directive, and accentuate or build upon elements that do. Once you've shown how you can protect what's critical to the other party, the cleverness of your thinking will readily emerge.

Ask yourself, "What do I foresee in the other party's idea that will prevent his or her agenda from being realized? What could go wrong? What factors do I anticipate—factors the foreigner didn't consider, reasons why the objective can't be achieved in the way he or she envisions?" Tell the other party what you foresee and how it will endanger the foreigner's agenda. Then explain what can be done to protect that agenda.

For example, to a vertical thinker whose priority is "stay within budget," you might point out an immediate cash flow problem the other party has overlooked: "I know maintaining a steady cash flow is critical to you; if we don't ___________, our cash on hand will be dangerously depleted." To a horizontal, you might point out cash allocation problems: "I know you're concerned about how we balance cash distribution. If we don't ___________, the allocations are quickly going to get out of kilter, and it will be difficult to regain our balance."

Finally, verify that you have added a safeguard. You might say, "Does this way of doing it satisfy your agenda?" or, "Do you feel more comfortable with this new solution?"

Now that we've outlined the concepts involved in recoding, let's look at three examples of how it can work in practice.

SUCCESSFUL RECODING: EXAMPLE 1

First, let's return to the standoff we described earlier in this chapter between Tim, the building contractor, and Cliff, the homeowner who wanted to build an atrium room.

After consulting with us, Tim accepted our suggestion that he needed to recode. Cliff's priority was clear: he wanted to maximize his profit, to get the most out of the home he was building and the beautiful view. Tim, too, wanted Cliff to maximize his profit, and he meant his suggestion of a deck to achieve that objective, but in what seemed to him a more practical, doable way. Since their priorities were the same, Cliff's emphatic rejection of Tim's suggestion indicated that the two men might be following different critical directives.

Although still mystified by Cliff's reaction, Tim began recoding by trying to find out just how his suggestion interfered with Cliff's agenda. By questioning Cliff, Tim discovered that what Cliff envisioned was an indoor place with an outdoor feeling—a place where he could relax amid a jungle of potted plants, enjoy the breeze, and watch the sunset. What was lost in Tim's idea was that a deck couldn't be used in inclement weather, nor would Cliff be able to relax and read at night in an outdoor atmosphere.

Tim saw now why his suggestion angered Cliff. But before he could reshape his idea to fit Cliff's agenda, he needed to precisely identify Cliff's critical directive, the invisible part of that agenda.

By looking at the chart, "What's the Agenda?" Tim concluded that Cliff was a horizontal thinker. When a horizontal seeks to maximize profit, his brain flashes, "MEASURE RISK AGAINST POTENTIAL GAIN! MEASURE RISK AGAINST POTENTIAL GAIN!" The emphasis is first on the gain that might be realized and then on the risk. Cliff looked at his back yard, the view of the trees, and thought, "How can I get the most gain from that? Simple! Have a year-round atrium room to enjoy these pleasures continually. Even if it does cost more money and delay completion of the house, the gain will be worth it."

However, when Tim's brain registered the priority, "Maximize profit," it flashed the vertical directive, "MEASURE GAIN AGAINST POTENTIAL RISK! MEASURE GAIN AGAINST POTENTIAL RISK!" His emphasis was just the reverse of Cliff's—it was first on risk rather than on gain. Consequently, he immediately jumped to what could go wrong in building an atrium room and suggested the deck as a safer option.

Once it was apparent that year-round communion with nature in an indoor-outdoor setting was critical to Cliff's agenda, Tim saw that his idea of a deck spoiled that vision. It negated Cliff's critical directive. Tim verified his newfound understanding by saying to Cliff, "So you feel that the gain you can get out of an atrium room is worth the risk of cost overruns and scheduling problems?"

With verification complete, Tim recognized that he must modify his original suggestion to follow Cliff's horizontal directive. But Tim also knew that he was in a position to point out factors Cliff didn't foresee, factors that might diminish his gain. He said to himself, "If Cliff wants to get the most gain, I have to inform him of why an atrium room may not do it for him and how I can *ensure* the gain he wants to realize while minimizing the drawbacks."

"Cliff," he said, "Your idea of relaxing in an easy chair, enjoying the view in any direction, in any kind of weather, sounds great. I can see why you'd enjoy being surrounded not only by trees outside but by potted plants inside. I realize now that my idea of a deck won't give you what you're looking for. But *you* may not realize some of the headaches an all-glass room will entail—problems that may prevent you from getting as much out of your room as you envision. For example, were you aware that, even with sun-reflecting glass, you'll need shades or blinds on both the ceiling and walls? These, of course, will interfere with the view. And even with the shades or blinds, and with astronomical heating and air-conditioning bills, the room may still end up unbearably cold in winter and beastly hot in summer. Furthermore, the glass roof will need frequent exterior cleaning to maintain the beauty of the view. Any upholstered furniture will quickly fade—unless, again, you keep the shades down or blinds closed. And what kind of comfort would you have without upholstered chairs?"

Tim didn't stop there. Now that he had Cliff's attention—now that it was clear the was trying to help Cliff follow his agenda—he presented a new alternative, this time fitting his own critical directive to Cliff's. "I've given the matter some more thought," Tim said, "and I believe I have another possibility. How about a heated porch with sliding glass panels all around? By having a regular roof, you'll greatly cut down on energy loss without really sacrificing much, since with an atrium roof you'd have to keep the shades pulled most of the time anyway. You can have a skylight in the center to give the feeling of a room flooded with light. You can keep your major furniture pieces a few feet away from the perimeter, to minimize fading. You'll still be able to enjoy the breeze in summer and your potted plants in winter. And because the porch will be more efficient to heat and cool, you'll probably end up spending more time in it than in an atrium room, which you might well have to close off for a large portion of the year. Not only will the porch give you year-round enjoyment—it'll be more economical to build and maintain. We can order the materials along with everything else, and it will put us only slightly behind schedule."

Cliff's reaction to Tim's new suggestion was far more positive than before. He now saw Tim not as an obstacle but as a collaborator, trying to help him achieve his objectives and protect what was critical to him.

Of course, it's possible that after Tim pointed out the loopholes in his original plan, Cliff might have chosen to go ahead with it anyway. But even in that case, Tim—by warning of dangers that might later materialize—would have gained credibility.

As you can see, in order to influence Cliff, Tim had to considerably modify his original suggestion. But that's not always necessary. Here are two examples in which, through recoding, foreign thinkers were persuaded to accept ideas with only slight modification.

SUCCESSFUL RECODING: EXAMPLE 2

Martin owned an auto parts distributorship. Alex, his vice-president, was constantly dreaming up ways to make the business more progressive.

One of Alex's ideas was to diversify. He saw large wholesalers beginning to spring up. They could buy huge quantities of parts and sell them at deep discounts, undercutting the market for companies like Martin's. "We're a small outfit," Alex argued. "We don't have the capability to compete with these mass market operations. In three to five years the big guys will eat us alive."

His solution was to branch out to a hardware line—items of a sort that their present retail customers carried. Using their present channels of distribution, they could make up for any losses with new sales.

To Alex, adding such a line was the obvious solution to a serious problem he saw coming.

But every time Alex brought up the subject of diversification (which he did at every opportunity), Martin became annoyed. "Our sales volume is up every year," he said. "There's no reason to believe we're in trouble on that score. And how can I discuss diversifying when I keep hearing that we're late with our billing and that shipments to our major customers aren't going out promptly? I keep telling you that I don't want any surprises, yet I'm still getting these disturbing reports. Why don't you figure out what to do about that rather than worry about what may happen five years from now?"

When Alex came to see us, he was totally frustrated. "My boss can't see any further than his nose. He's always saying he doesn't want surprises. Yet he harps on the tiniest imperfections while ignoring a real crisis that will face us not too far down the road."

How could Alex influence Martin to see what he saw so clearly? Were they receiving different flashes, hearing different rallying cries? If so, what unintentional harm was Alex causing Martin? To influence him, he had to find out.

In teaching Alex to recode, we suggested he begin by asking Martin what he saw as the harm in diversifying. Alex at first saw no point in asking the question: "What possible harm *could* there be?" Finally, though, he approached Martin like this: "I know you're sick and tired of hearing my idea, and I'm not going to bug you about it this time. I just want to ask you a question that will help me set my own thinking straight. What do you feel we have to lose by diversifying?"

"What do you mean, what do we have to lose? The question is, what do we have to gain? Nothing!"

"Well, it would help me if you could pinpoint the danger you see in diversification."

"Isn't it obvious?" Martin replied. "If we had a broader range of products, we'd have a colossal mess on our hands! It's bad enough to have billing and shipping delays when we're dealing with a single product line. With more, the glitches in our operation would be even more troublesome."

Alex now saw for the first time a clear link in his boss' mind between the diversification issue and what Alex until then had regarded as minor housekeeping problems. The harm that Martin perceived in Alex's proposal was that to diversify while day-to-day problems existed was almost guaranteed to invite immediate fallout. Alex had been aware that the operational problems were eating at Martin, but until that moment he hadn't seen how these problems were connected with his opposition to diversification.

Alex reflected on what Martin's answers told him about his boss' thinking style. Martin's critical directive, given his priority of "no surprises," was to blueprint what was most likely to happen. When thinking about diversification, he focused on immediate fallout, anticipating that the existing problems would snowball. His thinking clearly fell into a vertical track. Given the same priority, Alex's critical directive was to foresee potential fallout by anticipating trends in the industry. His analysis of how diversification could prevent a negative effect on sales was clearly horizontal.

Alex, to his amazement, further recognized that Martin was right. Diversifying obviously *was* dangerous at that point; it could very well bring unpleasant surprises. Instead of being a way to safeguard against problems down the road, it could actually multiply the problems they were already having, if done without taking care of current operational issues.

Now that he saw the harm in his suggestion, Alex restated to check his understanding: "Are you saying that we have to put our day-to-day operations back on track—that any attention we give to diversification will detract from our ability to solve the problems we have right now? That if we diversify before we clean up those problems, they'll only be duplicated in the other lines we take on?"

"That's it, exactly!" said Martin. "If we can't get our house in order now, we won't be in business five years from now."

Alex now realized that he had been unable to get his boss' attention up to that point because he had failed to see that these "housekeeping problems" had to be eliminated before they could consider diversification. "Martin," he said the next day, "I've been thinking about our conversation yesterday. We do need to tighten our operations. I'm going to develop a plan for speeding up the billing and eliminating the late shipments."

"Good! Now you're talking!" said Martin.

Only when this step was completed did Alex reapproach Martin about diversification. But first he reshaped his presentation to fit Martin's agenda.

"Martin," he said a few weeks later, after the new billing and shipment procedures were in place. "I know you want no surprises, so I thought I should call your attention to an order we just lost to one of the new mass distributors. This was one of our oldest and largest customers. He told me he hated to move his business elsewhere, but our prices just weren't competitive with the big guy's, and it didn't make economic sense to stay with us. I've made some quick calls to other customers, and I've heard similar rumblings. They want to know if we can offer bigger discounts on large orders. I've made a few concessions, but we do have to make a profit. Of course, these may be isolated instances; our sales figures are fine overall, and we certainly can survive with one lost account, some complaints, and some concessions. However, maybe we should look at the situation more closely to see whether the same thing is likely to happen with other customers."

This time, by blueprinting what was likely to happen, information critical to Martin's vertical brain, Alex was able to persuade Martin. Perhaps, Martin saw, he had omitted an important part of the picture. Putting all their eggs in one basket might be creating a significant risk. Diversification might ensure a smooth operation by insulating them from market volatility.

"It's true we're doing okay right now," said Alex. "But if there *are* current signs that we could lose business—and this particular case may be such a sign—it's important to pay attention."

Martin responded, "I guess if we are going to consider diversifying, it will be less disruptive to do it while we still have some lead time and some options open to us."

"So you do agree that we need to consider diversification now so as to make sure we keep our operation on an even keel?" asked Alex, verifying that recoding was complete.

"Yes," said Martin. "I see your point now. Glad you kept after me."

Alex was delighted. Recoding had turned him from a virtual pariah to a valued, respected adviser. Martin now gave him credit for his ability to anticipate a trend. All because Alex had learned to shift the focus from *his* agenda to his boss'.

SUCCESSFUL RECODING: EXAMPLE 3

Diane's daughter, Carol, graduated from college with honors. While living with her parents, she checked into several diverse fields: modeling, commercial leasing and real estate, and running a travel agency or day care center. In each case, she did a lot of research about the field, talked to top people she was able to contact through her family's connections, then cooled off and dropped the idea.

This had gone on for almost a year, and Diane, the mother, was worried. It seemed her daughter was making a career of choosing a career. More and more, their conversations deteriorated into squabbles over the length and apparent aimlessness of Carol's search. Yet, although Diane was becoming increasingly frustrated with Carol, she did believe the girl was trying.

Diane saw that Carol was very good at coming up with options, enjoyed researching them, and did it thoroughly. She was clever at figuring out ways to talk to important people and get information from them. She was looking for the right career, one that would fit her interests and utilize her abilities.

After some thought, Diane approached her daughter with a suggestion to help her move off dead center. Diane suggested that Carol join an executive search firm, where she could use the skills she had demonstrated in investigating careers.

The idea seemed so appropriate that Diane was sure it would appeal to Carol. But the girl's initial reaction was extremely negative.

Rather than defending the merits of her idea, Diane began to recode: "Carol, what do you think you'll lose by my suggestion?"

"I don't want to box myself into a start-and-stop career."

"What do you mean?" Diane probed. "What do you think will happen?"

"I've never done that kind of work. How do I know I'll like it? I don't want to have to jump to something else six months from now—or, even worse, just stay and feel trapped."

Diane (vertical) had taken our seminars and had identified her daughter as a horizontal thinker. Now she saw that Carol *did* want to move off dead center, but not by finding the path of least resistance. Her critical directive was to make the biggest breakthrough, find something that would not only be a job but also hold her interest and become a career. She was afraid of being pushed into taking a job for the sake of having something to do. She was anticipating how miserable she might be if she got stuck in the wrong place.

Now that Diane knew what Carol saw as endangered by her idea, she was able to speak her daughter's language. She proceeded to explain how her idea safeguarded Carol's critical directive in a way Carol wasn't anticipating. "You're right—you could get stuck. But you're stuck now. Practically a year has passed, and you haven't found something you want to do. Perhaps my suggestion can help you get unstuck. While you're searching for jobs for other people, you might find the right one for you."

Once Carol saw that her mother's suggestion safeguarded what was critical to her—that it provided the opportunity for a big breakthrough—she began listing other benefits she saw in it: "I could be getting paid for what I'm doing now for nothing. And who knows, I might enjoy that kind of work!"

Without recoding, relations between Diane and Carol might have become increasingly strained. With recoding, Diane gained influence with her daughter and got her to move off dead center.

WHEN TO RECODE

Now that you see how effective recoding can be, you're undoubtedly eager to try it. How do you know when to recode? The following signals should alert you:

- *You have received a disappointing reaction to your idea.* It has been dismissed or rejected out of hand. You've demonstrated its brilliance in every way you can think of, but somehow its luster is apparent only to you. Recoding can make your suggestion shine in the other party's eyes.

- *The other party has come up with a substitute for your solution.* It has been replaced with a "more valuable" one. No matter what you say, the other party can see nothing but costs in your solution and nothing but benefits in his or her alternative. Recoding can help you tilt the scales.
- *You keep repeating the same points over and over.* You're stressing the benefits of your agenda and the costs of the other party's. Instead of continuing that futile, self-defeating behavior, recode.

Rejection, replacement, and repetition are all signals that it's time to recode. By watching for these signals and recoding promptly, you can salvage your waning influence or even turn an unfavorable situation completely around.

If you can do that at this point, you don't need to read the rest of the chapter. But most likely you'll need help to avoid some common interferences.

INTERFERENCES WITH RECODING

Now that you realize that foreign flashes exist and that your ideas may harm a foreign agenda, why may it still be difficult to enlist your own thinking in the service of the foreign thinker's critical directive? What could possibly deter you from discovering what's important to this party you're so eager to impress? The answer: Pride.

It's only natural to be proud of your own way of thinking. The logic of that system has helped you, minimally, to survive and very possibly to be quite successful. How could anyone question its merit or fail to immediately recognize its cleverness? It's hard to accept that it is precisely this wonderful, logical system that's actually *standing in your way* in your efforts to impress the foreign thinker.

Let's look at three ways in which pride in your own thinking style can manifest itself and can stop you from gaining influence in the foreign land.

ADVOCATING YOUR OWN AGENDA

When someone dismisses your idea, it's only natural for you to become its advocate. You have worked on something, have put time and effort into it, and truly believe that the suggestion or solution you've come up with satisfies the other party's objective. It's difficult to put your reasoning aside. You're convinced that if only the other party realized how smart your thinking was, how wise your judgment, he or she couldn't help but see the light.

It's especially difficult to avoid falling into this trap because, with like thinkers, advocacy generally *does* work; the issues they see as critical are in line with yours. Just the opposite is true when you're dealing with a foreign thinker.

Marshall (vertical) has been a bookkeeper for many years. He prides himself on his efficient record-keeping system and the orderliness of his books. Recently he changed jobs; his new employer is a small packaging house. After his first month there, he and his boss, Ernest (horizontal), went over the books. To Marshall's consternation, Ernest was quite disturbed about Marshall's system. He said it left out several important variables. Before Ernest even had a chance to finish his thought, Marshall pulled out some samples of the company's old record-keeping forms and began building a case for the superiority of his system. Ernest remained unimpressed; all he could see were the variables he thought were missing.

Where did Marshall go wrong? By interrupting Ernest and trying to convince him of the improvements he, Marshall, had made in the firm's old system, he failed to get a handle on what was critical to Ernest. Perhaps the variables Ernest was concerned about actually were covered by Marshall's system or could have been included with some minor adaptations. But Marshall's need to sell his own agenda got in the way of his finding out. By focusing on what he saw as the advantages of his system, he never understood what Ernest saw as its drawbacks.

RELUCTANCE TO DISAPPOINT

Nobody likes to fail. Nobody, especially in a subordinate role, wants to believe that he or she has not met expectations. Recoding requires you to accept that you have, in fact, disappointed the other party.

You've probably worked hard on your suggestion and take pride in its worth. *Of course* you would prefer to keep rephrasing it, hoping to find a way to impress the other party, rather than admit that your contribution is wanting. Yet the more you try to impress, the greater the likelihood that you'll disappoint.

Jake (horizontal), vice-president of planning at a large community hospital, saw a need to strengthen the relationship between the hospital and the physicians at a nearby medical clinic, who were being aggressively wooed by a competing hospital. Since this clinic was strong in obstetrics and gynecology, Jake developed a proposal to set up a birthing room, with special training for nurses and prospective parents to be done by doctors from the clinic. The beauty of Jake's idea, as he saw it, was twofold. Not only would it virtually ensure that these particular babies would be delivered in his hospital, but it would build good will with the doctors at the clinic, so that they would be less likely to send other patients to the competing hospital.

'hen Christine brought the finished ad to Charles for approval, she ıdly pointed out the extra touches she had put in. She had tightened wording of the previous ad and had added some airbrushing to the But Charles was dissatisfied with the ad's impact. He wanted a ıtly bolder typestyle and a sprinkling of more current lingo. Chris- adjusted each item Charles brought up, to meet his specifications. 'hen they were finished, Charles stood up and walked Christine to door of his office. He smiled proudly, "Good thing I have a keen se of what the consumer needs to hear from us, or we'd be in big ıble."

hristine walked away, disgusted. "Keen sense, my foot!" she thought. ıat makes that ad effective is the cleverness of my copy and the skill ed in making his trivial changes!"

ecause Christine didn't respect the significance of the issues rles raised, she never tried to figure out why her original version sed the mark. She never understood that whereas, to her, going the 'a mile meant providing more of what the customer expects, to him eant providing more of what the customer didn't ask for. He wanted urprise the client with a new approach. To him, the small changes in style and word choice significantly altered the ad's impact.

lerely going along with the changes her boss prompted didn't gain istine the influence she needed. It resulted only in reinforcing rles' good opinion of himself and his perception of the need to ely scrutinize her work.

t best, if you follow Christine's route, you'll be viewed as a somewhat ful fixer who's dependent on the other party's guidance. At worst, 'll come off as lazy, sloppy, or unconscientious, putting Band-Aids solutions that need surgery. In either case, you won't be seen as a ler, and you won't make the inner circle.

ELIMINATING INTERFERENCES

he costs of Advocating Your Own Agenda, Reluctance To Disappoint, Disrespecting the Foreign Agenda are immense. Aside from the otional costs—frustration, friction, a sense of defeat—the bottom is that unless you truly understand and respect the critical impor- ce of the other party's agenda, you can't be seen as a colleague. leagues share the same vision, have the same concerns, and work ether toward realizing the same aims. You can achieve this col- ality with foreign thinkers only by learning to recode.

s with decoding and encoding, the source of all these interferences hat you're operating in a foreign land and don't realize it. Your ventional wisdom tells you that your idea is exactly what's needed each the objective or solve the problem, and you can't see why the er party is so obtuse as not to recognize this obvious fact.

Jake was sure that Richard (vertical), the hospit
would be impressed by his plans for eliminating a p
converting it to an opportunity. But Richard, intent
containing the crisis, anticipated an immediate proble
plan would undoubtedly solidify relationships with th
clinic in question, it would almost certainly antag
influential group of doctors at another clinic, whose t
be utilized under Jake's proposal. Richard was dumbf
had failed to consider this implication. He kept sha
disbelief. "This isn't practical. It may be good in theor
won't work. If we strengthen our relations with one gro
offend another in the process, we're no farther ahead.

Jake, surprised by Richard's reaction and adamant
to disappoint, kept reiterating the benefits of his
urgently Jake argued his point, the more Richard que
ment. Not only hadn't Jake seen the danger that app
Richard, but he refused to see it even when it was po

Jake, without accepting the fact that he had disap
couldn't delve into Richard's concerns. If he had, he m
way to take care of them. As it was, the impressiven
was apparent only to him.

DISRESPECTING THE FOREIGN AGEN

In this final interference, you actually do hear
concerns and, for the sake of harmony, you go alon
other party will applaud you for your openmindednes
immediately or after a long discussion of the issues,
because you believe it's easier to acquiesce than to
what the other party is saying, and you try to come u

Unfortunately, this method of gaining influence, t
with the best intentions, is virtually guaranteed to
remedy you come up with can't truly protect what th
as endangered. Why not? Because you've solved th
understanding the critical importance of the issu
wants addressed. Although you may believe you're a
for the other party's concerns, you are merely pacify
and thus *disrespecting* his or her agenda.

Christine (vertical) wrote and designed advertise
agency's major clients was a thrift institution. The a
this institution had pulled in business, and she ha
ments on their slick design.

The fourth time the institution planned to run
campaign, Charles, the head of the ad agency, told
rest on our laurels. I want to go the extra mile for th

Your ability to recode depends on putting aside, for the moment, what seems critical to you and recognizing what's critical to the other party. Difficulty in doing this indicates (as in decoding and encoding) that you need to slow down your brain, defuse your feelings, and reverse your assumptions.

Defuse feelings:

Right now you're feeling rejected, mistreated, put upon—and it's all the other party's fault. Why can't this pigheaded character see the obvious merits in your idea? Before you can free your mind to translate your thinking into terms that mean something to the other party, you need to discharge all that pent-up emotion.

1. Make a list—as long as possible—of all the reasons why your way is best, why it saves the day. Go ahead—toot your own horn as loudly as you like.

2. Now write down all the reasons why the other party can't see the merit in your suggestion or solution. List all the flaws in the other party's thinking or character that get in the way of acknowledging your worth.

3. Lastly, shoot holes in the other party's apparent concerns. List all the ways in which those concerns are irrelevant, unimportant, and unnecessary to the issue at hand.

Are you feeling better? Good! Now it's time to reverse assumptions.

Reverse assumptions:

Up to now, you've been convinced that the other party is either unable or unwilling to hear you. You've assumed that the key to success—the gateway through the brick wall—is to bring the other party around to your way of thinking.

Your task at this juncture is to reverse assumptions. Instead of assuming that the other party needs persuading, assume that the party that needs persuading is YOU. You have harmed the other party's agenda, and you DON'T GET IT. Through the other party's eyes, *you* are the one who looks like an impenetrable wall. He or she is trying to convince you that your idea is harmful, and you are resisting for all you're worth. Instead, you must let the other party through the wall. You must let him or her convince you of the danger.

AND NOW TO RECODE. . .

Now that you're ready to recode, let's summarize the steps:

1. *How does your suggestion interfere with the other party's agenda?* The answer to this question wil probably be a revelation to you. Now that you've defused feelings and reversed assumptions, you should be truly interested in hearing it. Remember, your goal is to find out the other party's agenda (priority plus critical directive) and how you have threatened it. Using the information gleaned from the answer to Question 1, ask yourself:

2. *Is the other party's critical directive vertical or horizontal?* The answer to this question will most likely confirm that you're dealing with a foreign thinker and will help you see what elements you need to stress in translating your idea into that party's Communicode—making it fit the other party's critical directive. Remember, you can use the chart, "What's the Agenda?" to assist you in identifying the other party's thinking style and critical directive.

3. *What can you suggest that will further safeguard the other party's agenda?* Here's where you modify or repackage your idea to fit the foreign agenda. Frame your presentation in a way that clearly shows how the factors you anticipate will help realize the other party's vision. Be sure to emphasize what's critical to the foreign agenda and what factors the other party hasn't seen that could harm it. Don't forget to verify that you have, in fact, found a way to safeguard that agenda.

A SUMMARY EXERCISE IN RECODING

This summary exercise will give you a chance to practice recoding. As you read the story, put yourself into Samuel's place. Imagine how he feels about the reception Florence gives to his idea. Think about how he can influence her. Then do the recoding exercise.

■

Florence Mendes was president of a family-owned French winemaking concern. The company had a reputation for producing a high-quality, high-profit cognac. But despite an aggressive marketing program, Florence had seen no increase in market share, and sales remained stagnant.

Enter Samuel Fox, marketing consultant. Samuel, who was known as a crackerjack New York marketing expert and had worked in the consumer packaged-goods industry, was hired in hopes of revitalizing the enterprise. Florence was banking on Samuel's knowledge and experience to expand sales and gain on the competition by establishing a foothold in the United States.

After three months, Samuel presented his plan. He had done extensive test-marketing and, based on his findings, offered the following recommendations:

> Expand distribution channels by selling the product in discount, drug, and convenience stores. Cut price and expand volume. Although profit margins would decline, gross revenues and overall profitability would increase. Projections are that this strategy will result in a 25 percent penetration of the U.S. market within two years.

Florence was horrified. "We're just beginning to create consumer appreciation for our product in the U.S.," she argued. "If we begin by discounting, where can we go? Instead of gaining on the competition, we'll erode our position."

"Discounting is the most efficient method to achieve a sharp increase in market share," Samuel countered. "It has worked for other products, and it'll work for Mendes cognac."

"Mendes cognac didn't achieve its niche through mass marketing," Florence replied proudly. "We have a special image—one of quality, prestige, luxury. We have a tradition of excellence, and we have gone to great lengths to maintain it. How can we sell a prestigious product in drug stores? How can we keep our present customers if we change the image? We won't get anywhere unless we make sure we aim at the right market."

"We have a great product and a good track record," Samuel agreed, "but the company isn't growing. We need to try something new. Isn't that why you brought me here?"

"Yes, but let's not throw out the baby with the bathwater," Florence replied. "Maybe we'll sell more cognac this year, but what happens next year and the year after? What we'll gain in new business, we'll lose in old."

Samuel insisted that increases in volume would far outweigh the profit reduction per unit. He had figures and charts to back up his projections. He went over them in great detail, carefully building his case. Florence was adamant: she would have none of it. For the next hour, arguments flew back and forth, each holding fast to his or her point of view.

Samuel left the meeting glum and shaken. He had used every fact and argument at his command and still had made absolutely no headway. How could Florence be so unreasonable? She couldn't point to a single hole in his presentation, yet she refused to buy it. What could he do to open her eyes?

■

Let's assume that you (Samuel) are too upset with Florence to successfully recode at this point. Start by defusing and then reverse assumptions. Remember, how would Samuel view the situation?

EXERCISE:

Defuse Feelings

Your task: Fill in the blank columns, viewing the situation from Samuel's perspective.

Merits of Samuel's idea	*Flaws in Florence's view of idea*	*Holes in Florence's concerns*

Now, compare your answers with ours:

ANSWER SHEET:

Defuse Feelings

Merits of Samuel's idea	*Flaws in Florence's view of idea*	*Holes in Florence's concerns*
Low prices will boost sales volume and ultimately profits	Old-line, old-hat; won't accept change in times	Concern with unique image is stuffy, less important in U.S. than in Europe
Product will become more competitive	No familiarity with U.S. market	Excellence of product not the issue; market share is
Quick reversal of downtrend likely	Simplistic view of discount operations	Discounting common in U.S. market; "everybody does it"

Now that you've defused your feelings, *reverse assumptions* and get ready to recode. Clearly, your (Samuel's) approach isn't working. You need to get a better handle on what's bothering Florence before you can hope to influence her. Say to yourself, "Florence is trying to convince me of something, and I've been too stubborn to listen. I need to let her persuade me."

EXERCISE:

Recode

Your task: Fill in the blanks, asking the following questions. Since you don't have Florence here, you'll have to infer her agenda from what she said. (For help, first find Florence's priority on our chart, "What's the Agenda?" Then use the chart to determine her critical directive. Remember, agenda = priority + critical directive.)

What is Florence's agenda and how does Samuel's suggestion interfere with it?

Agenda:

Harm:

Do the issues Florence is concerned about fall into a vertical or horizontal track? Why?

What can Samuel suggest that will further safeguard Florence's agenda?

Now, compare your answers with ours:

ANSWER SHEET:

Recode

What is Florence's agenda and how does Samuel's suggestion interfere with it?

Agenda: Florence's priority is to gain on the competition; her critical directive is "Pinpoint the target." Her full agenda is to target the high end of the U.S. market by offering a prestige, quality product that will be seen as more desirable than its competitors.

Harm: Florence is concerned that discounting will aim at the wrong target. It will undermine the product's prestigious image and thereby adversely affect market share, both in the new U.S. market and the existing European one, resulting in irreversible erosion of the customer base.

Do the issues Florence is concerned about fall into a vertical or horizontal track?

Horizontal. She is concerned that the tactics being suggested—namely, price-cutting—may turn off the high end market. Thus an initial spurt in sales might be followed by an overall reduction in profitability. These concerns fit the horizontal critical directive, "Pinpoint the target."

What can Samuel suggest that will further safeguard Florence's agenda?

1) European and U.S. markets are largely independent; image in U.S. will minimally affect present customers.
2) Starting from zero in U.S.—no place to go but up; can't lose what you don't have.
3) Can penetrate market with lower-line cognac and then bring in higher-priced line.
4) Can limit discount to special introductory promotional period.

Samuel, being vertical, was initially so caught up in his own critical directive—"Sharpen the tactics" to expand market share—that he didn't read between the lines of Florence's reaction. He saw her concern about "image" as old-line European stuffiness, a desire to hold onto a traditional way of doing business simply for tradition's sake. He didn't see how his plan could possibly injure anything of vital importance. To him, the bottom line was a simple matter of balancing price and volume; when one went down, the other would go up.

Florence, being horizontal, looked beyond the immediate balance sheet. She perceived discounting as a threat to the image that had made the product successful. She felt it would take away from what her company had always stood for. She feared that existing customers would find the cognac less attractive when it was seen as a discount item and that she would be unable to replace this stable, loyal customer base. She further foresaw that the product would then lose much of its appeal to the low-price market. Price-conscious customers would initially buy it because its reputation would make it seem a bargain. But, as Florence explained when Samuel finally drew out her concerns, "once price drops, the quality of our cognac will be suspect." All in all, Florence felt strongly that Samuel's method would not reach the market she felt they should be aiming for.

Samuel had to agree that the company had enjoyed its past success by aiming at an affluent market. He admitted that discounting, if approached incorrectly, might harm the product's image and sales and lose old-line customers. But he also pointed out factors, critical to Florence's horizontal thinking, of which she may have been unaware. He explained that her worry about the impact of U.S. discounting on the European market might be ill-founded because the two markets tend to function independently of each other, and the image of a product in the U.S. could be unrelated to its image in Europe. With regard to the U.S. market, since the firm had no market share as yet, there was no need to worry about losing customers there. The U.S. was virgin territory, in which they could create an image and market.

Samuel then proposed a couple of ways to follow Florence's critical directive of pinpointing the right target and still sharpen the tactics by going the discount route. First, he suggested limiting the discounts to a special introductory promotional period. Florence would be consulted on the ads to make sure they conformed to the image she wanted to preserve. Second, he pointed out that some manufacturers whose products were introduced as low-budget items had been able to develop a high-quality image and add higher-priced models. The Honda automobile was one example. Lower initial prices had allowed Honda to demonstrate product quality to a large volume of customers who might not otherwise have purchased the automobile. Perhaps a Mendes brand cognac could be introduced in the same way.

Florence was impressed not only by Samuel's specific adjustments of his proposal but by his genuine interest in her concerns and his willingness to modify his thinking accordingly. Next time an important problem arose, you can be sure that Samuel was the one Florence turned to first for advice.

■

Did you find it difficult to do this exercise? As we warned you, recoding is hard to practice on paper because you really need the other party to interact with. Now that you have a sense of how to do it, why not try it with someone you've had trouble influencing, either at work or elsewhere? Remember, the other party's critical directive will probably seem to him or her to be too obvious to mention. So be persistent: Be prepared to dig with several follow-up questions to find out what the full foreign agenda is and how your idea harms it. Then show how you can safeguard that agenda in ways the foreign thinker did not foresee.

TO SUM UP

Recoding—like decoding and encoding—empowers you to turn thinking style differences to your advantage. It converts mishaps into opportunities. It takes you off the hot seat and puts you in the driver's seat. By revealing what's critical to the other party, it enables you to overcome rebuffs, gain leverage, and turn misfires into bull's-eyes.

Decoding, encoding, and recoding offer you a powerful set of tools. With them, you can get the results you desire, the solutions you need, and the influence you deserve. Even more exciting, once you've learned how to speak a foreign thinker's language, you can join forces. By teaming up, you can accomplish far more and far better than either of you could do alone. The next chapter will tell you how.

11 TEAM THINK

There's always an easy solution to every human problem—neat, plausible, and wrong.

—H. L. MENCKEN (vertical wisdom)

Sometimes it is more important to discover what one cannot do, than what one can do.

—LIN YUTANG (horizontal wisdom)

Can you face a foreign thinker without flinching? Decipher the logic or value of an off-base response? Salvage the situation when you feel your influence slipping?

Congratulations! You're getting the hang of Communicoding.

Now that you're becoming comfortable with your natural strengths and weaknesses and can recognize what foreign thinkers have to offer, what if you could consistently turn thinking style differences to advantage? Deliberately seek out opposite thinking to gain a new angle on a problem, a boost to a higher level of productivity, a clearer view of a potential breakthrough?

Team Think* is a system that maximizes brainpower by melding the complementary abilities of both thinking styles. Team Think guides and focuses the interaction of vertical and horizontal thinkers in all phases of problem-solving, strategizing, and decision-making. Team Think participants, working in pairs or larger groups, rapidly produce startling, satisfying results.

Our first Team Think seminar was held in 1985. Since then, the Team Think formula has been refined and utilized by business people around the country. This chapter will give you a taste of Team Think.

*TEAM THINK is a registered trademark of the Marsten Institute.

HOW OPPOSITE THINKING SAVED THE WHALES

In October 1988, the plight of three California gray whales—trapped off the Alaskan coast by the early onset of bitter cold winter and a massive, encroaching Arctic ice pack—captured world attention. An international rescue operation ultimately involved one hundred people and cost $1 million. You may remember the widespread relief when two of the whales were finally freed. What you may not realize is that this happy ending was the result of a combination of vertical and horizontal problem-solving approaches.

For two weeks, volunteer Eskimo whalers had labored continuously with chain saws, pickaxes, and steel bars to keep open two small breathing holes in the frozen Arctic surface while rescue authorities sought a way to free the gasping whales. U.S. Air Force helicopters were attempting to tow a massive hover barge from Prudhoe Bay, two hundred miles away, to the spot where the whales were trapped. The intent was to use the barge to break a pathway in the two-foot-thick ice to enable the whales to reach a warm-water channel leading to the open waters of the Chukchi Sea. But as the heavy barge inched toward the scene, the effort to keep the air holes open was taking a tremendous amount of time and manpower. One whale, apparently weakened by pneumonia, disappeared under the ice. The other two also were stressed, and it was increasingly doubtful whether they could hold out long enough for the icebreaking equipment to reach them.

Two Minnesota men, recognizing the imminent danger, flew in with six underwater ice melters normally used to free boats in frozen marinas. The supervisors of the rescue operation had politely declined their help, but these two men came anyway, at their own expense. They were certain that the Eskimos were working too hard, and that there was an easier way to keep the breathing holes open and large enough until the whales could be rescued.

The deicers, churning up warm water from beneath the surface, quickly cleared away ice and slush from the air holes. Within minutes, the whales surfaced. Within twenty-four hours, the holes were three or four times as large as before. What's more, they could now be *kept* open. The deicers had accomplished in a matter of hours far more than the rescue workers had taken days to do by hand.

What the Minnesota men provided was a more efficient solution to the immediate (vertical) problem: how to keep the whales breathing. Their small deicers couldn't address the underlying (horizonal) problem: how to get the mammals out of the ice pack and into warm water. But the deicers did buy time—the whales had a larger area to breathe in, and their respiration stabilized. And, in fact, the final solution built on the idea of enlarging the breathing holes. After failing to move the barge in, rescue workers eventually used helicopters and battering rams to cut a series of surfacing holes. They coaxed the whales from one hole to the next until two Soviet icebreakers finally arrived to smash the last barrier to open water. Thus the two thinking styles, working in tandem, saved the day.

TEAM THINK AS A DELIBERATE ACT

The rescue of the whales was, in a sense, Team Think by default: an inadvertent, fortunate fusion of vertical and horizontal thinking. Initially, the people in charge of planning and executing the operation were putting virtually all their eggs in a horizontal basket. The rescuers were so preoccupied with how to clear a path from the ice pack to open waters that they were blind to the need to allocate more attention and resources to the immediate problem of keeping the air holes open long enough to keep the whales alive. They saw no reason to consider the offer of the deicers, since it was impracticable to use these small machines to break up the five miles of ice between the mammals and the channel to open sea. Luckily, the initiative and perseverance of the Minnesotans prevented a dilemma from turning into a disaster.

Look at the results that were accomplished by an accidental mating of thinking styles! What if the rescuers had *deliberately* blended the two kinds of thinking? Might they have found a more expeditious way of freeing the whales, and perhaps saved the third one as well?

Can we afford to rely on hit-or-miss methods? How many more disasters, large and small, might be averted by intentional application of both horizontal and vertical skills! How many explosive discoveries and inventions might be promoted by methodically linking the two kinds of thinking! Are we ready to gain fresh perspectives on the urgent problems challenging American business today?

THE NEED FOR TEAM THINK: DESIGNING FRESH PERSPECTIVES WITH FOREIGN THINKERS

Your company or your industry is riding a current of change—expansion too rapid to comfortably absorb. Or you may be stagnating without even knowing it, left behind in the eddies and backwaters. You may feel overwhelmed and overdriven or exhausted and drained, waiting for a merger or acquisition to play itself out. Whether you're moving too fast or hardly at all, events are controlling you. In either case, the situation, the players, the times are stressed. The circumstances require something different. As Roger B. Smith, chairman of General Motors, has said, we need to find "15-cent solutions to million-dollar problems." But how?

In the face of a breaking wave of global competition, the headlines of leading business publications clamor for increased creativity and collaboration. But can our business leaders supply the answers the situation requires within the time limits the situation demands? Do they possess the strategies to produce creative, collaborative solutions that will enable American business to stay afloat during the crucial catch-up phase? Can they productively manage employees who (according to projections) will, in the 1990s, be working in unsupervised, self-managing teams, performing flexible, shared functions?

Teamwork is a recurring buzzword. Everyone lauds it, but few know how to do it or why it's beneficial. Most companies talk team but reward individual star performers. As Robert W. Keidel, senior consultant at the Wharton Center for Applied Research, has observed, companies typically try to "increase" teamwork by adding it onto existing management structures. Instead of building a teamwork *system* into the core of organizational functioning, they view teamwork as a way to improve communications and good will.

This is a flawed notion of teamwork. As Professor Abraham Zaleznik of the Harvard Business School points out, "getting people to cooperate is not the executive's real work." Effective teamwork is not an end in itself but a means to do the real work of American business. What's needed is a way to utilize teamwork more creatively to tackle the tasks facing American business today.

Like teamwork, everyone wants creativity but few know how to get it. Business talks creativity; but again, it's treated as an add-on—a desirable extra. In actuality, an infusion of creativity requires fundamental changes in corporate culture.

American business has unknowingly set up conditions that undermine creative thinking. The accepted norm is to demand long hours, quick decisions, and positive results from fast-trackers fearful of losing momentum and vitality. The industry leader who can take the heat while remaining on the go has been the enviable model portrayed to up-and-comers.

Research is now identifying those very conditions—pressure and fatigue—as killers of creativity. Dr. James A. Horne, a British psychophysiologist, found that loss of just one night's sleep significantly curtails spontaneity, flexibility and originality—the abilities to shift perspective and escape conventional thought patterns.

Can we utilize teams to more easily achieve the creative results we so sorely need? What's the best way to merge the thinking of individual team members so as to augment their creative potential? How can we ensure that the right questions are asked and the right problems raised to dramatically elevate the creative process? Can we charge mental batteries by consciously connecting opposite brains?

Welcome to the joys of Team Think!

TEAM THINK: A NEW KIND OF TEAMWORK

Our contention is that creative collaboration must be built into the very guts and sinews of an organization, and that *effective teamwork must be designed around the way people think.* We see teams of economists, financiers, and investment specialists. We see teams of physicists, geologists, and biologists. We see teams of computer, marketing, and finance people. What isn't recognized is the need to team up "experts" in vertical and horizontal thinking.

A top investment brokerage house underwent a period of intense stress. Morale and productivity were at a low ebb, and turnover was high. Profits had begun to decline, and management feared that the downward trend would not be reversed unless these companywide problems could be solved. Meetings with outside consultants and staff representatives yielded only minimal, short-term improvement.

Management for some time had seen a need for new blood. But management did not recognize that the *type* of new blood needed was opposite thinking. When appropriate "blood types" happened to be hired, they had difficulty assimilating into the culture. Their ideas were challenged, discouraged, or dismissed. Team Think not only demonstrated the value of this transfusion of foreign thinking but assisted in revitalizing the organization. The result: new initiatives, higher morale, and increased productivity.

Team Think is a system to harness the two thinking styles to produce more efficient, creative, quality results. As you saw in recoding, vertical and horizontal brains automatically and naturally head toward different aspects of an issue. They have different critical directives and foresee different kinds of difficulties. Consequently, they become expert at asking questions and anticipating problems in the particular areas critical to their thinking styles. Since the key to smart solutions is the range of questions raised and problems exposed, what could be more logical than to pair these two kinds of experts to ensure that all crucial questions are answered and all critical problems addressed?

Although Team Think is beneficial in every arena of human endeavor from medicine to marriage, its efficacy is most dramatically evident in business, where every moment and every dollar count. Team Think accelerates accomplishment, expands efficiency, and capitalizes on capabilities by integrating vertical and horizontal input in a considered, coherent way. It enables both kinds of thinkers to get further faster and with less effort.

Collaboration is based on *ease.* Each team member supplies the fruits of his or her natural abilities while exploiting the natural, easy contributions of others. Thus, given the same time allotment, vertical-horizontal teams spawn ideas and alternatives that neither type of player, no matter how high-powered, could readily (if ever) generate alone. Yet team members report that they are more keenly aware of their individual contributions than when they operated solo!

Ideally, Team Think operates in a business setting in which all players have been trained in the method. Team members—whether members of a department, committee, or task force—know each other's thinking styles. They each know what's easy for them and what's difficult, and they are aware of the rewards they can reap from harvesting foreign thought. They know precisely when and how to tap vertical and horizontal input. They know how to nurture and blend both kinds of brainpower for optimal efficiency.

We recommend teams of four to eight people, composed of equal numbers of vertical and horizontal thinkers. Teammates of the same thinking style stimulate each other, and opposite thinkers feed off one another, ensuring that all conceivable bases are covered.

Continual interplay between the two kinds of thinkers forestalls trouble and speeds solutions. Issues are consistently dealt with before they arise, avoiding surprises and saving time, money, and effort. Horizontal thinkers working alone often run into unexpected execution snags. Vertical thinkers tend to receive unwelcome repercussions. Working together, the two kinds of thinkers can cue each other to head off these hazards. They can red-flag at an early stage potential errors and omissions that one or the other probably would have overlooked until much further along.

A major oil company was seeking innovative ways to locate potential oil drilling sites. Huge expenditures were involved. Top executives were dissatisfied with the recommendations they were getting from their teams of specialists but couldn't figure out why. They kept sending the recommendations back for reconsideration. The process was time-consuming, costly, and debilitating, and the final results were disappointing.

The managers were amazed to discover the crux of the problem: the recommendations were distinctly vertical or horizontal. Each was missing critical components of the other thinking style, and each time they were sent back, the result was more of the same. Team Think seminars enabled team members to produce far more complete recommendations with far less expenditure of time and effort.

Since the purpose of this book is to arm you with skills you can use in dealing with others who are unfamiliar with thinking style differences, you may not be in a position to utilize the full scope and design of Team Think. But you needn't forgo the advantages of opposite thinking. Just because others don't know the method doesn't mean you can't do it. For the remainder of this chapter, we're going to narrow our focus to Team Think techniques you can use whether or not the parties you're dealing with have taken our seminars or read this book. Techniques you can use in situations in which you, your department, or your company are stuck—using the same old ineffectual techniques, spinning round and round like a record with the needle caught in the same groove.

TEAM THINK: DEFYING CONVENTIONAL WISDOM

You're burning the midnight oil, you're gulping coffee and fighting sleep. You just can't make the pieces of your project come together. Something is eluding you. Your thinking is blocked. You're going around in circles. You're suffering from STAGNATION.

At such moments (and we've all experienced them), you begin to feel there's something wrong with you and the way you think. But it doesn't occur to you that you need input from an opposite thinker. Instead, you pour more coffee and redouble your efforts.

What you're doing, whether you realize it or not, is trusting to conventional wisdom: the historic American credo that obstacles are there to be surmounted—that where there's a will, there's a way. The United States is a nation of immigrants. Our forebears coming to this land of opportunity quickly learned that the streets were not paved with gold—that to survive and succeed, they must expect to overcome adversity. Struggle became a way of life: whether against the forces of nature, against adverse conditions, or against adversaries vying for jobs or markets. Those newcomers who made it *to* this country and who made it *in* this country learned from experience to believe in the efficacy of effort. They instilled in their children and their children's children the unquestioned belief that hard work and dogged drive would see them through.

This belief that gain comes from struggle became ingrained in our societal structure. In our economic system, individual enterprise was the source of profit; in our legal system, the clash of adversaries was the source of truth. And the conventional wisdom has paid off. The United States has been the most powerful, most productive nation on earth. As a group, we are one of the most prosperous, most privileged peoples in history.

However, the price of our success has been an excessive expenditure of time, money, and effort—commodities that are increasingly becoming short in supply. As syndicated columnist William Pfaff has written, "The United States can no longer afford an ideology of doing everything wastefully. Elegant solutions count: The country badly needs them." In the face of international competition, is it sensible to dissipate energy vying with each other? With a flood of litigation clogging our courts, is it realistic to insist on the efficacy of adversarial methods?

Adversarial methods are wasteful because they are isolating. They deprive you of what opposite thinking can offer. When you hit a brick wall, your expectation of having to struggle alone makes you *stick to it, do more,* and *work harder.* Like the Eskimo whale rescuers, you keep pushing yourself to dig more diligently.

We're not saying that persistence, activity, and effort never pay off. But (as you can see in the accompanying chart) in situations that require opposite thinking, strategies based on perseverance are likely to fail. The harder you strain, the more you prolong your stagnation. Furthermore, as you tire, you're less able to utilize acquired abilities—the kind you need to get past the block.

As you learned in encoding, foreign solutions are valuable precisely because they provide what's missing from your own. Stagnation is due to an overload of one type of thinking. Only certain questions are being asked—those germane to the thinking style of the dominant players. These players (like those in charge of the whale rescue) are ignoring, downplaying, or not utilizing opposite thinkers. They are sticking to a particular course, headed for a dead end.

At such a juncture, an opposite thinker can show you the quickest, most effortless way out by raising questions that reveal obstacles you don't see. Like a sponge, the foreign expert will quickly and easily soak up information relevant to his or her critical directive and, with the same degree of ease, expose the essential issues you haven't addressed and the salient problems you haven't considered.

So, when you're stuck, what could be wiser than to defy conventional wisdom! It's time to turn to someone who can plug the holes in your thinking by including variables your natural style overlooks. Someone

CONVENTIONAL WISDOM: STRATEGIES THAT FAIL

Strategy	*Why You Think It Should Work*	*Why It Can't Work*
Stick to it	Not enough time spent on project to date.	Spending too much time already. More expenditure of time and energy will only lead to fatigue, frustration, and diminished ability to think clearly.
Do more	Not enough thought or action applied to project to date.	Stepping up activity is pointless—will not illuminate what led to stagnation. More of the same will only lead to more ineffectual results.
Work harder	Not enough effort expended on project to date.	Working too hard already. More pressure to perform will only add stress and impede clear thinking.

whose opposite thinking will stimulate your creativity. Someone with whom you can produce solutions you never thought you were capable of.

But how, exactly, do you go about it? Let's look at Team Think in action.

A TEAM THINK SUCCESS STORY

A fifty-year-old sign manufacturing firm for the first time in its history was losing market share. The past fiscal year had shown a 15 percent drop. The marketing department was asked to reinvigorate the company's marketing plan in an effort to regain ground.

Valerie, vice-president of marketing, met with various members of her staff and other key people at the firm. They explored options and developed a strategy to reverse the trend. They reviewed the existing sales approach, arranged for advanced training courses for the sales force, updated and redesigned collateral materials, and worked with the advertising agency to get a new campaign underway. After nine months the downtrend had been halted but showed no signs of reversal. Members of the marketing, sales, and advertising departments had no more ideas. They knew they were stumped.

Familiar with Communicoding and Team Think, Valerie knew that she was a vertical thinker and that her department overly favored vertical approaches. She suspected that the strategies being pursued were strongly vertical in character. She speculated that if the company was to gain on the competition, horizontal input might be needed. So she solicited the help of Alexander, manager of quality control. Although their job functions didn't normally connect, she recalled that at management meetings he often came up with ideas that she recognized as horizontal.

"Electronic signage is the answer," Alexander told her. "It's definitely the wave of the future. Signs will no longer be manipulated manually. This company needs to catch on, or we'll be out of the running. I'll bet someone in the new products department could be useful."

Valerie organized a committee whose members included Alexander and representatives from the marketing and new products departments. At the first meeting she and other vertical thinkers on the committee expressed willingness to consider a limited thrust into electronic signage. "But let's not go off the deep end," she cautioned. "Let's introduce one product line and see how we do."

Since financial institutions constituted the firm's largest single market, the product chosen was an electronic board displaying interest rates that could be updated at the touch of a button. In order to be initially competitive with the mechanical rateboards currently in use, the marketing people estimated that the price would have to be in the $600 range.

"Let's not limit our vision right off the bat," Alexander counseled. "Let's make a wish list of the features that might give our rateboards the edge over our competitors'. Then we'll see what costs we come up with."

After doing careful research, the new products department representatives on the committee presented a proposal for a highly-styled information booth with remote control, an electronic moving sign, and a video screen with graphics advertising bank services. Total cost: $2,900. And, as an alternative, a somewhat stripped-down version for $1,400.

"Those models are attractive," Valerie admitted, "but more costly than what I had in mind. Based on my department's market research, the electronic rateboard will be a go, but we need a simple $600 version."

Alexander asked, "What features will be key to market acceptance?"

"Unquestionably, the remote control," said a representative of the new products department who was a vertical thinker. "I'd suggest eliminating the TV screen and the other marketing features. That should bring the cost under $800."

"Fine," said Valerie. "And let's do a limited test marketing of the more expensive models. If it looks as if they'll fly, we may be able to offer all three."

The next step was to lay out the project for senior management. A task force of vertical and horizontal thinkers was formed to consider the feasibility of retooling and other long-range planning issues. After much ironing out of problems, the task force recommended a small-scale venture into electronic signage, and management endorsed the proposal.

The company ended up with a three-model rateboard line that proved its appeal to every bank and every budget: a simple, strictly informational display for small banks; a mid-priced version with moving message sign for larger banks looking for a selling vehicle; and a highly-styled marketing message center for design installations in major financial institutions.

What occurred here was a classic example of Team Think. Valerie and her marketing people were stuck; they needed to find a new direction. Horizontal input, targeting the direction in which the industry was moving, brought up issues that vertical and horizontal thinkers, working together, successfully resolved. The team product—the three-model rateboard program—provided a much farther-reaching solution than any of the players would be likely to have dreamed up alone.

TEAM THINK: THE WORK AT HAND FOR STAGNANT SITUATIONS

- Find what's added
- Verify the blend

You're stuck. Like Valerie, you've sought out an opposite thinker, explained your dilemma, and asked for a recommendation. Now what?

The Work at Hand begins with examining what the foreign solution provides: what it adds (or subtracts). How did the other party arrive at this idea? How will it help you get unstuck? What critical directive does it follow and why? How does this critical directive differ from your own? As you proceed with Team Think, you'll ask yourself: What dangers is this party foreseeing, and how does the recommendation protect against them? What dangers am *I* foreseeing, and how does my recommendation protect against them? How can we blend our recommendations in a way that gives us the best of both agendas?

The answers to all these questions will emerge as you consider the three central ones that make up the Work at Hand.

1. *What will the foreign agenda provide?* Our chart, "Vertical and Horizontal Routes," which follows, may help you size up the foreign recommendation and discern the foreign agenda. The chart traces the paths the two kinds of thinkers take to meet the same priorities. First find the priority that most closely resembles the one you and your partner have mutually agreed upon. Are you seeking to eliminate stress? Maximize profit? Stay within budget? Follow the path of your partner's thinking style to identify the critical directive for that priority. Continue following the same path to identify what the other party provides by following that directive. (You'll get to the last row of the chart, "What's Protected," when you answer Question 3.) As in recoding, if the appropriate priority isn't on the chart, try to figure out the foreign agenda based on what you have learned about vertical and horizontal thinking.

Remember, upon hearing the priority, the brain automatically flashes the critical directive—the vertical or horizontal strategy for meeting that priority. The flash signals the thinker to expend all available effort to execute this strategy. The strategy leads to what's provided. Because each thinking style provides what's missing from the opposite thinker's solution, a blend of what both thinkers provide will ensure that all aspects of the problem are addressed.

VERTICAL AND HORIZONTAL ROUTES

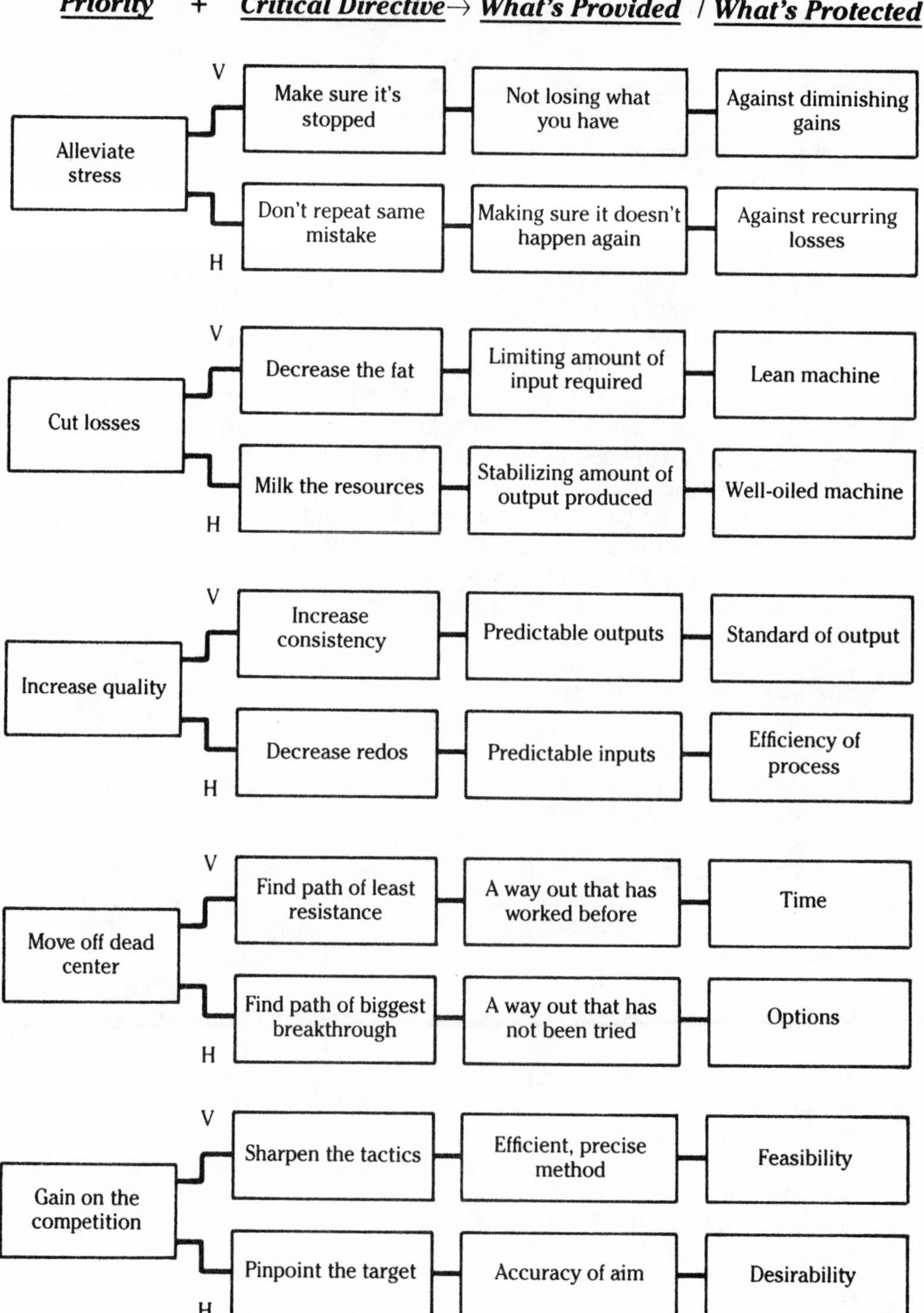

Priority	Route	Critical Directive	→ What's Provided	/ What's Protected
Alleviate stress	V	Make sure it's stopped	Not losing what you have	Against diminishing gains
	H	Don't repeat same mistake	Making sure it doesn't happen again	Against recurring losses
Cut losses	V	Decrease the fat	Limiting amount of input required	Lean machine
	H	Milk the resources	Stabilizing amount of output produced	Well-oiled machine
Increase quality	V	Increase consistency	Predictable outputs	Standard of output
	H	Decrease redos	Predictable inputs	Efficiency of process
Move off dead center	V	Find path of least resistance	A way out that has worked before	Time
	H	Find path of biggest breakthrough	A way out that has not been tried	Options
Gain on the competition	V	Sharpen the tactics	Efficient, precise method	Feasibility
	H	Pinpoint the target	Accuracy of aim	Desirability

Priority + ***Critical Directive*** → ***What's Provided*** / ***What's Protected***

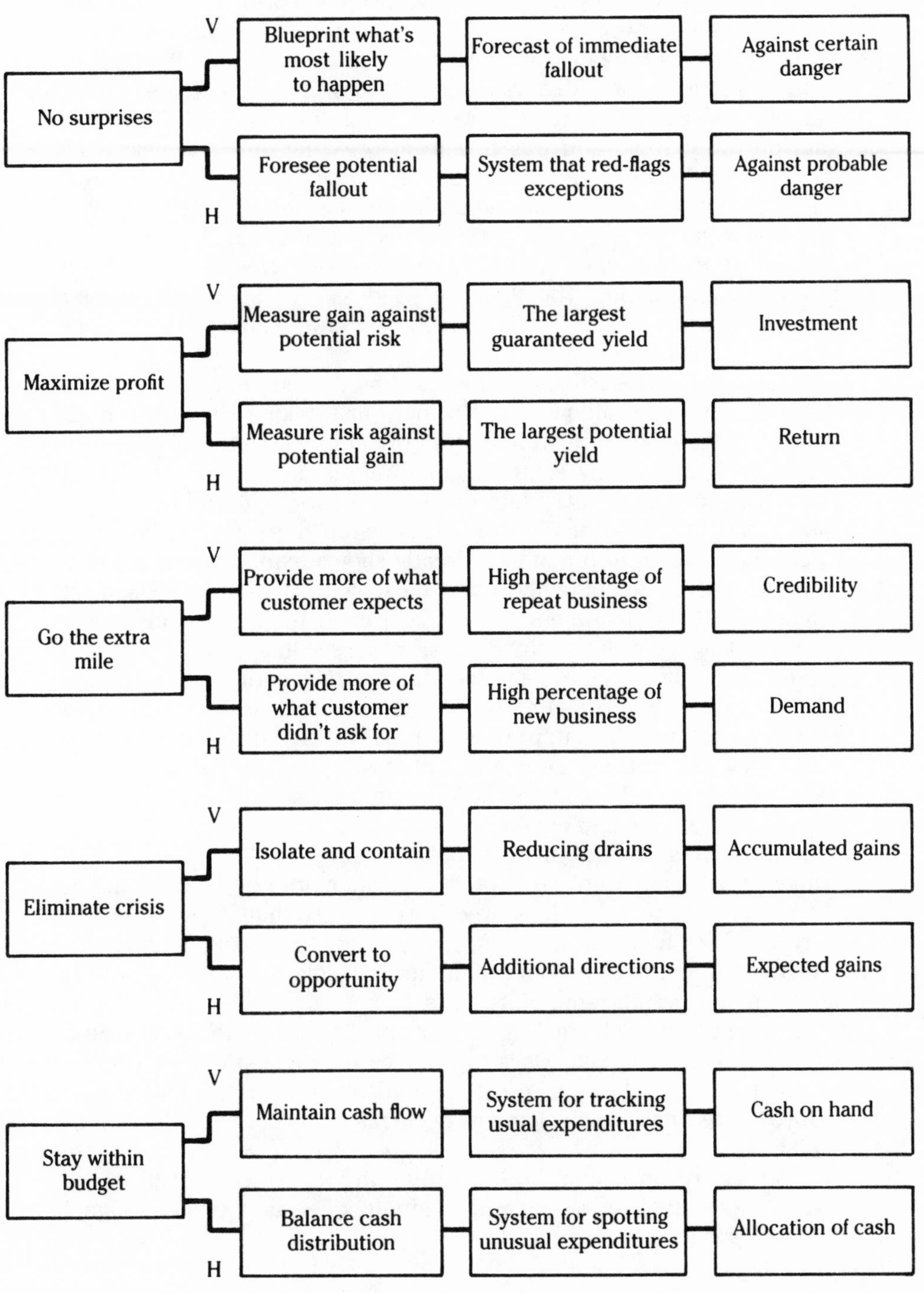

To illustrate how to use the chart, let's think back to our example about the sign company that was in a slump. The company's priority was to gain on the competition. By looking up that priority on the chart, you can see that Alexander's recommendation of going into electronic signage followed the horizontal critical directive, "Pinpoint the target." What this strategy provided was "accurate aim." He correctly perceived that electronic signage was the wave of the future and that the way to gain on the competition was to aim at breaking into this new field. Could vertical thinkers have provided the same recommendation? Yes, but after investing more time and probably considerable trial and error.

2. *What will your agenda provide?* Hearing and examining the foreign recommendation will probably give you some clues to what's been blocking your thinking. The other party's ideas will undoubtedly trigger new ideas in your head. You'll undoubtedly have a suggestion of your own, or a modification of the other party's.

Now take your idea through the chart as you did with the opposite thinker's. This time follow the path for your thinking style. How does your recommendation provide what's critical to your agenda?

In our sign company example, after Valerie and the other vertical committee members heard Alexander's idea about electronic signage, they came up with the idea of focusing on a single product line (electronic rateboards) that had already shown market strength. They also focused on keeping the price close to that of the mechanical rateboards their customers were accustomed to. By looking at the chart, "Vertical and Horizontal Routes," you'll see that in seeking to gain on the competition, Valerie and the other vertical committee members were following the critical directive, "Sharpen the tactics." What they provided was an "efficient, precise method" of maximizing the chances of gain and minimizing the chances of loss. Could horizontal thinkers have provided such a method? Yes, but again, with much greater expenditure of time and energy.

3. *How can what each provides be integrated to maximize efficiency?* Sometimes a Team Think solution is simply a matter of doing both. But more often than not, the cross-breeding of the two thinking styles yields a hybrid that's new and different. Rather than A+B=AB, Team Think integrates A and B to produce C. In Team Think, the whole is almost always more than the sum of its parts.

The real beauty of Team Think is that you get to leave things out. Find shortcuts. Faster, simpler ways to produce the highest quality results. How can you blend opposite recommendations most efficiently? How can you determine which elements of each to incorporate and which to omit?

A vertical or horizontal brain, in following its critical directive—its strategy for action—foresees and encounters certain types of dangers and continually develops appropriate, effective means of protection. Thus each kind of brain is specially equipped by inclination and experience to recognize and deal with different kinds of dangers. Once each party's thinking is out on the table—clearly exposed and verified—the interaction has a galvanizing effect. Each thinker's contribution elicits refinements from the other, elevating the ideas to an increasingly sophisticated level until a blended solution begins to emerge. This process continues until it becomes apparent that both views have been efficiently integrated. The end result will be the fastest route to a solution that ensures maximum protection against the broadest range of harm.

Now, to help you identify the key elements to blend, check the third and fourth columns of the chart, "Vertical and Horizontal Routes." Start with the other party's recommendation. Compare it with the chart. What does the foreign agenda provide? What does it protect? How, specifically, does the other party's recommendation make this provision and offer this protection? Ask the foreign thinker what dangers he or she was seeking to eliminate and how. (Remember, foreign thinkers are experts at raising problems you don't think of.) Now do the same thing for your recommendation. Look at the chart. Specifically, what does your agenda provide and protect? What dangers were you trying to eliminate and how?

Once the dangers that both thinking styles anticipate are brought to the surface, the fun begins. By putting your heads together, you can decide on the most efficient way to eliminate all conceivable danger and guarantee maximum protection: the best order, the least duplication of effort. You'll be amazed at how clever you become together! As you become skilled in Team Think, the process becomes exhilarating. Instead of dismissing foreign thinkers as doomsayers, you'll actually begin to look forward to hearing the hidden dangers they foresee.

In our sign company example, the verticals were protecting feasibility: "We can't afford to retool the whole plant, so let's start with a product we know can be sold at a price people will pay." The danger they saw was that of overextending—committing major resources to a wide array of unproven products. Alexander and the other horizontals were protecting desirability: "Let's make a wish list of all the features that would make our product more desirable than the competition's." The danger they saw was that they might be left behind in the race toward progress.

Through Team Think, the verticals helped the horizontals more *easily* protect desirability by narrowing the target. Instead of spending weeks or months investigating the whole gamut of electronic signage, they quickly picked one item—rateboards—with the surest market appeal and concentrated on getting the price down. The horizontals helped the verticals more *easily* protect feasibility by designing not one but three rateboards. Instead of going into production with only one model, of limited capabilities, and then having to play catchup with market demand, they achieved economies of time and scale by tooling up to produce three related models readily saleable to different markets. Thus feasibility *and* desirability were efficiently protected in the final solution: a triple-tiered, triple-threat product line.

WHEN TO TEAM THINK

Many times, as in the situations we've described in this chapter, the need to Team Think doesn't become apparent until stagnation sets in. Your thinking (or that of your department or committee) is blocked; conventional wisdom isn't working. You've hung in there, kept moving, and worked as hard as you possibly can. If this is the fix you're in, chances are that the input of one or more opposite brains is *mandatory* to get you unstuck.

Look for the following signals. They will alert you to put Team Think in motion.

- *You are easily and frequently distracted from your task.* You find it difficult to concentrate. You can't seem to stay focused. Team Think, by injecting a new element, a new point of view, will help you refocus.
- *You are endlessly reviewing already-obtained facts, without making progress.* You've read the same page over and over. But where is the answer? Team Think will redirect your attention to something fresh and different.
- *You are spending extensive time on projects you know should require less time.* Although you consider yourself a reasonably fast worker, the time you're spending on this project seems interminable. Team Think will provide the quickest, most direct route to the best solution.

Distraction, wheel-spinning, and foot-dragging are signs of stagnation—signs that you need the fresh insights foreign thought can provide.

Not every project, of course, requires the conscious collaboration of vertical and horizontal thinkers. Many solutions can sufficiently satisfy priorities by utilizing one thinking style or the other. Team Think is most essential when a project involves spending a great deal of money and the outcome will significantly impact the company in both the near and far term. At these times, don't wait for stagnation to set in. You'll get further faster and with less strain by employing Team Think techniques at the outset.

One of our client companies, which provided seasonable services through a unique marketing strategy, was a huge success in its first two years, quadrupling projected revenues. Around the beginning of the second year, the vertical partner saw that the largest guaranteed yield might lie in branching out to other cities. The horizontal partner agreed but was concerned that such a move be done in a way that would achieve the largest potential return on the dollar.

They held a series of discussions, in which the vertical partner focused on such issues as when to make the move, whom to hire, and how much to spend, while the horizontal partner centered on such questions as how to unify the image and methodology of the various branches so as to preserve the uniqueness that was the secret of the company's success. Eventually they worked out a plan that met the concerns of both. In the company's third year, after the opening of the first branch office, the profit margin remained level, including all expenditures for the new office; and projected revenues for Year Four showed a whopping 25 percent increase. Thus Team Think, by efficiently combining the abilities and agendas of the horizontal and vertical partners, ensured top dollar on their investment.

INTERFERENCES WITH TEAM THINK

Now that it's clear that putting heads together with opposite thinkers can truly pay off, what could possibly get in the way of utilizing this fantastic resource? The answer: Self-reliance.

In many business applications of Team Think (as in most of the examples in this chapter), it's not just an individual but a department or even a whole company that's stuck. However, as with anything else, in order to put Team Think into play it takes someone to get the ball rolling. Teamwork begins with the individual. If Team Think isn't working (or isn't even being tried), we must look to the interferences that keep individuals from effectively utilizing opposite thinking—attitudes that will undermine any departmental or companywide attempt at creative collaboration.

Team Think can be fairly easy if you can squelch the suspicion that you're cheating by not DOING IT ALL. A legacy of the adversarial tradition is the notion that picking someone's brain is the lazy way out. Obviously such a belief will keep you and others in your company from taking full advantage of Team Think.

Let's look at three specific ways in which you or others in your company may be diverting yourselves from the Work at Hand.

BELIEVING MOTION IS MOVEMENT

How many times have you said to yourself, "Doing something is better than doing nothing"? How often do you flit from one activity to another with barely time to catch your breath and check your watch?

The belief that motion is movement can be highly deceptive. Suppose you're working diligently on a project. Your deadline is three days off, there are mounds of paper in front of you, and you're stuck. You tell yourself to keep moving—any break in the flow will slow you down. You come up with answers you're not totally satisfied with, but you go on. You know that the shortest route between two points is a straight line. What you don't consider is that straight lines can become dead ends. A detour toward opposite thinking often proves to be the shorter way to go.

John (vertical) was camping out with his brother, Mike (horizontal). John was hunting and Mike was fishing when an unexpected downpour struck. John got back to the campsite first. He was wet and very cold, and he knew Mike would be, too. His immediate impulse was to get a fire going. The damp kindling wouldn't catch, so he tried dousing the wood with the gas normally used for lighting the stove. But in his anxiety to keep moving and get the fire lit, he never checked to see whether there was another bottle of fuel. He tried three times to light the kindling. Each time, he used about one-third of the bottle of fuel, and each time the wood burned for about three minutes.

When Mike returned, he found no fire and no fuel. "I can't believe this!" he said. "Why didn't you use some of the fuel to light the stove? We could have dried out some of the kindling. Now we have only two choices: leave right away or stay here and freeze."

Thus John's well-intentioned haste to light the fire proved counterproductive. If he had slowed himself down, he might have preserved more options. As it was, his compulsion to get the job done *prevented* it from getting done.

RELUCTANCE TO CRY "UNCLE!"

No one likes to admit defeat, give up, stop trying—it's not the American way. If you're a certified, true-blue believer in ways that don't work, you'll go to any length to avoid throwing in the towel. Your unwillingness to cry "Uncle!" will keep you on a familiar, unfruitful, frustrating path. You'll stay up all night. You'll blame others, blame circumstances, blame environmental factors. And you'll convince yourself that these rationalizations are true.

Sarah (horizontal) was a crackerjack puzzle-solver. She prided herself on being able to solve any and all brainteasers quickly and easily. One day she spotted what she was sure was a misprint in the teaser in the newspaper. So confident was she of her prowess that she called the editorial office to report the mistake. To her surprise, she was told that there was no error—the puzzle was correct as printed.

How could that be? Sarah decided that the person who answered the phone had been too lazy to check. "He just said that to get rid of me," she told herself.

Perhaps Sarah was right, and the puzzle was printed wrong. Or could it be that the solution required vertical input? Being unable to admit defeat, Sarah will never find out.

This may seem like a trivial example, and Sarah may seem like an easy person to write off. But reluctance to cry "Uncle!" occurs more frequently than you may be aware. How often do you or people you work with refuse to admit mistakes, blame anyone and anything but themselves—and at what cost?

"PEOPLE IMPEDE MY PROGRESS"

You know you're stuck. You're spinning your wheels. You're seriously considering sending out an SOS. You've even identified a foreign thinker who may be able to help.

You weigh the pros and cons. You realize that foreign input could be valuable. But then you think about the hassle of getting it. First you'll have to bring the other party up to speed, answer questions, make explanations. Then you'll have to sift through a bunch of offbeat notions to separate out the useful kernels. Will the end result be worth it? Or will it just mean more delay?

One of our vertical clients who happens to have a horizontal partner told us that he found it easier to go ahead and make decisions without consulting his partner, even though his partner often foresaw problems he himself didn't anticipate. "Jack asks so many questions and goes off on so many tangents," he explained, "that it's easier not to bring him in. I'd rather risk making a mess and having to clean it up later."

After trying Team Think, our client's attitude did a 180-degree turn. "Now that I understand how Jack thinks, I'm amazed at how helpful he can be. His questions point to hitches I hadn't noticed, and there's usefulness in the 'tangents' he pursues. Now I can see how I've slowed us down in the past by not involving Jack earlier."

ELIMINATING INTERFERENCES

The costs of Believing Motion Is Movement, Reluctance To Cry "Uncle!" and "People Impede My Progress" are incalculable, and the biggest loser is *you.* As you learned in Chapter 3, DOING IT ALL often carries steep penalties, the most significant being the underutilization of natural abilities. The Work at Hand requires that you begin to define *self-reliance* as increasing your dependence on your natural abilities, instead of relying on yourself to DO IT ALL.

As you gain success in employing Team Think, you should begin to feel more comfortable about turning to someone whose natural abilities complement yours. Difficulty in doing this means that you need to slow down your brain, defuse feelings, and reverse assumptions.

Defuse feelings:

Defusing feelings in Team Think is different from defusing feelings in decoding, encoding, and recoding in that you haven't yet heard the other party's solution. Your resistance is not only to a foreign thinker's ideas but to the very idea of going to that party—or anyone else—for help. Perhaps your previous contacts with the foreigner make you hesitant to seek out his or her assistance. Is it really worth the trouble? Isn't it simpler just to handle the situation yourself? Shouldn't you be able to do that anyway?

Before you can Team Think, you need to get those feelings out of your system.

1. Write down all the benefits you can see in doing the project solely your way or solving the problem on your own.

2. Write down all the drawbacks of incorporating opposite thinking.

3. Go ahead—have fun! Write down in detail your rationale for going it alone: your cherished-from-childhood conviction that you can do anything if you put your mind (not two minds!) to it.

All right. Now it's time to reverse assumptions and approach the other party.

Reverse assumptions:

If you're like most Americans, you probably believe in the efficacy of the adversarial process. You assume that individual effort is the source of productivity; that gain flows from struggle; that truth is revealed through the clash of ideas. You believe that your job is to point out what's wrong with the other party's ideas and the other party's job is to point out what's wrong with yours; that if you keep hammering away at each other, the best solution, the most creative idea, will win out. As in a court of law, the prosecutor and the defense attorney, by poking enough holes in each other's arguments, will help the jury decide which case has the most merit (by virtue of having the least holes).

The basic premise of Communicoding is a rejection of this adversarial model. We've shown throughout this book that it's *to your interest* to avoid or resolve thinking style clashes and to recognize the value in the opposite thinker's views. But old mental habits are hard to shake. So it's likely that, in order to successfully Team Think, you'll have to consciously reverse your assumptions. Instead of looking for what's wrong with the foreign solution, you'll have to make yourself look for what's right about it. And the other party will have to look for what's

Let's walk through the process step by step. We'll give you sample answers for comparison at each step of the way. Of course, there are no "right" answers to this exercise. There are many possible answers when you Team Think. (When you *don't* Team Think, there's only one possible answer: yours!) When you bring the strengths of both vertical and horizontal thinking to bear, the possibilities are bounded only by your creativity and that of your teammates. Our answers, then, are merely illustrative—an example of Team Think in operation. It could be that the answers you and your partner will come up with will be far better!

Step 1: Identify the Priority

First, look at the dilemma depicted in the scenario and agree on what priority you're addressing. Then check your answer against ours.

Your answer: Priority is ______________________________

Our answer: Priority is "Eliminate the crisis."

Step 2: Make Separate Recommendations

Now, without input from each other, come up with your individual recommended solutions. Write them on the following chart. You'll have two solutions: one from the vertical thinker and one from the horizontal.

Recommendations

Vertical recommendation	*Horizontal recommendation*

Now compare your recommendations with ours:

SAMPLE ANSWER SHEET:

Recommendations

Vertical recommendation	*Horizontal recommendation*
We need to maintain current coverage levels on items our employees really care about but find ways to cut corners or reduce coverage on marginal or little-used items. For example: ■ Leave hospital and physician coverage unchanged but require pre-admission evaluation; exclude weekend admissions ■ Reduce high prescription claims by using a mail order prescription service ■ Reduce coverage for skilled nursing to 17 days; 50% for days 18 to 21 ■ Reduce hospital charges by instituting a hospice program for terminally ill We could also compare HMO coverage to our needs and check other carriers' premiums.	We need to find a different vehicle for medical insurance. We could check into another carrier that specializes in our industry. Maybe there's a possibility of going in on an insurance policy with another retail chain. HMOs and PPOs are other potential vehicles. But going the self-insurance route would probably be best. By bypassing a carrier, we'd immediately begin to save money. If self-insured, we could pick and choose coverages based on our employees' needs rather than what the carriers offer; for example, we could add eye care and/or dental coverage. And funds set aside for risk management could become a part of our investment plan.

Step 3: What's Provided? What's Protected?

Next, review your recommended solutions (or, if you prefer, the vertical and horizontal suggestions we outlined on the preceding sample answer sheet). Decide what each of the two recommendations provides and what each protects. Write the answers on the chart below.

What V and H Provide and Protect

	Provides	*Protects*
Vertical Recommendation	Reduce drains: (How?)	Accumulated gains: (What?)
Horizontal Recommendation	Additional directions: (How?)	Expected gains: (What?)

If you used our sample recommended solutions to do this step, compare your answers with ours. Then turn back to the sample vertical and horizontal recommendations to see how they offer the provisions and protections summarized below.

SAMPLE ANSWER SHEET:

What V and H Provide and Protect

	Provides	*Protects*
Vertical Recommendation	Reduce drains: (How?) Maintains desired coverage at stable or lower cost by reducing or eliminating less desired or used features	Accumulated gains: (What?) Benefits that employees most value and use (i.e., hospital and physician coverage)
Horizontal Recommendation	Additional directions: (How?) Offers flexible coverage at stable or lower cost by eliminating carrier	Expected gains: (What?) Benefits expected from eliminating middleman (carrier): flexibility, potential cost savings, self-directed risk management

Step 4: Combine Recommendations

Now combine the vertical and horizontal recommendations, taking into consideration what each provides and protects. The result will be a Team Think solution. Write your answer down and compare it with ours.

Your Team Think Solution

SAMPLE ANSWER SHEET:

Our Team Think Solution

Self-insure with coverage tailored to items employees care about most and use most. Ability to cut back on selected items to reduce costs. Add desired coverages such as eye care and dental treatment.

Step 5: Blend for Maximum Efficiency

The solution you arrive at by combining the vertical and horizontal recommendations may be good enough. But more likely, as you further discuss your Team Think solution, each party will be able to further perfect the solution by identifying what's still missing or what's extraneous in light of his or her critical directive. The result: the final Team Think solution.

Write down your final Team Think solution (reached by refining either *your* initial Team Think solution or *ours*). Then look at our final Team Think solution for comparison.

Your Final Team Think Solution

SAMPLE ANSWER SHEET:

Our Final Team Think Solution

After discussing the sample solution outlined above, vertical thinkers (concerned about protecting the company's accumulated gains) might point out that self-insurance would leave the company open to unacceptable risks in view of the recent claims history. Horizontal thinkers then might come up with another new direction: asking employees to contribute a small proportion of the cost in order to underwrite the desired new and existing coverages. If costs rose, employees would be assessed to cover them. This refinement would provide a mechanism for controlling the company's risk as well as an incentive for employees to avoid unnecessary claims. Verticals in turn might further refine the idea of a contributory premium by suggesting a sliding scale based on salary and claims history. To keep the union from balking at a contributory plan, horizontals might add a health incentive plan offering year-end rebates for employees with low or no claims.

Thus, the final Team Think solution: Self-insure with coverage tailored to items employees care about most and use most. Ability to cut back on selected items to reduce costs. Institute contributory premiums keyed to salary and claims history. Add desired coverages such as eye care and dental treatment, and a health incentive plan.

For a summary of the entire process, see the accompanying chart.

MASTER ANSWER SHEET:

Solving the Medical Insurance Dilemma

Priority	*V solution*	*H solution*	*What V solution provides & protects*	*What H solution provides & protects*	*Team Think solution*	*What Team Think solution provides & protects*
Eliminate crisis	Keep most desired & most used coverages, limit or reduce others	Self-insurance, flexible benefits; add to some coverages	Maintain desired coverage at stable or lower cost; protect benefits employees most desire and use	Offer flexible coverage at stable or lower cost; protect benefits expected from elimination of carrier	Self-insurance with flexible coverage, retaining most desired benefits; contributory premium keyed to salary and claims experience; some expanded coverages and health incentive plan	Maintains most desired and utilized coverages and offers flexible added coverages at stable or lower cost. Protects expected gains from elimination of carrier; protects accumulated gains by keeping benefits employees most value and use

Now that you've experienced Team Think, why not try it again—this time with a real problem on which you're genuinely stuck. Something in the department where you work, something on which you and your staff are blocked, or a companywide issue that seems to recur again and again. A problem that is continually identified but on which no progress is made.

Since this really *is* your problem, you may find it necessary to defuse your feelings before teaming up. If not, skip the next chart and go to it!

EXERCISE:

Defuse Feelings

Your task: Fill in the blank columns.

Benefits of thinking problem through by yourself	*Drawbacks of seeking opposite thinker's help*

Here are some possible answers. Are they similar to yours?

TYPICAL ANSWER SHEET:

Defuse Feelings

Benefits of thinking problem through by yourself	*Drawbacks of seeking opposite thinker's help*
Have done the homework, am on top of the problem	Having to bring partner up to speed will slow me down
Can impress the boss, be a star	Partner may steal my ideas or come up with suggestions that won't work

Now that you've defused your feelings, reverse your assumptions. Assume that seeking out a foreign thinker will help you get unstuck, rather than slow you down—that a solution you reach together will be far superior to any you could achieve on your own.

Now pick a partner of the opposite thinking style. Work together to find a solution to that "intractable" problem. Fill in the accompanying chart. Then, if you wish, go to another pair of opposite thinkers for more input.

EXERCISE:

Solving Your Own Dilemma

Priority	*Your solution*	*Opposite thinker's solution*	*What your solution provides/ protects*	*What opposite solution provides/ protects*	*Team Think solution*	*What Team Think solution provides/ protects*

Were you surprised at the quality of the solution you and your partner(s) were able to achieve? How quickly opposite thinkers provided alternatives you didn't see before? How easy it was to eliminate dangers by understanding what was protected by the foreign recommendations?

TO SUM UP

Team Think offers an almost sure-fire route to elegant solutions: the solutions you and your company need. When you use Team Think regularly, you'll notice that your speed and efficiency increase rapidly. How else can you go faster and get such exciting results—include all the essential ingredients and get to cut things out?

American business needs "15-cent solutions to million-dollar problems." Perhaps combining vertical and horizontal thinkers is the way.

12 COMMUNICODING ON THE RUN

The work will teach you how to do it.

—ESTONIAN PROVERB

You're rushing from place to place, doing one task after another. You're under a mountain of pressure. Your world is fast-paced, you're always in a hurry. Delay is unacceptable.

What to do, then, when hit by the unexpected? When what you get bears no relation to what you asked for? When the solution you receive is not the one you need? When you can't sell your idea no matter what you say? When you're working on a project on deadline and getting nowhere fast?

You've read this book and somewhere in the back recesses of your brain you dimly perceive that you could be in the throes of a thinking style dilemma. You've learned how you're supposed to handle such situations. On paper, it sounded easy to do. But under these conditions?

The situation calls for Communicoding on the Run. This chapter wraps up the techniques you've learned in this book into a neat little bundle of Communicoding Cue Cards: a barebones reference guide to help you turn the tide. These indispensable aids sum up the key steps in decoding, encoding, recoding, and Team Think. Keep them in your pocket, purse, or briefcase so they'll be at your fingertips just when and where you need them to get you through a crisis or avert one.

Communicoding Cue Cards also are useful for quick daily review. Look them over each morning to keep your new learnings in the forefront of your mind and on the tip of your tongue when you suspect you may be dealing with a foreign thinker. You'll soon find that you've committed the steps to memory and are up and running at full speed.

DECODING: DEALING WITH AN UNEXPECTED RESPONSE

Imagine: You ask a colleague to research information vital to a report you're working on. What you receive is totally different from what you expected. The information is already a day late, and you're due in London in three days to present your findings. Your frustration level is zooming. You needed what you asked for when you asked for it! The fight over the acceptability of the unacceptable is under way.

Time to pull out your Decode Cue Card!

The *front* of the card is your concise combat manual. It tells you how to clear away the gunsmoke and regain your composure enough to make it possible to decode. The *back* of the card is designed for noncombat use—when you're ready to decode or want to avoid the need to decode in the first place.

DECODE CUE CARD

DECODE . . . Unexpected responses

RECOVER: During battle

What's happening:

- You're unable to decode.
- Interferences at work: Rush to Judgment, Thinking Style Snobbery, or Negative Write-off.

What to do:

- Get away for a few minutes.
- Say to yourself: "There's method in his/her madness."
- Chill out. If cooled down, see RESTART. If not, arrange meeting for later, then see RESTART.

(FRONT)

RESTART: After the fact

What's happening:
- You got an off-base response.
- You're ready to decode to find the logic in it.

What to do:
- Ask: "Clearly, you think you gave me what I wanted, but I don't see it. Can you explain how this fits my request?"
- Verify your understanding.

PREVIEW: Before the fact

What's happening:
- You suspect you're dealing with a foreign thinker.
- You want your request completed with no surprises.

What to do:
- Make your request.
- Ask: "What do you think your end result will look like?"

(BACK)

USING THE DECODE CUE CARD TO RECOVER DURING BATTLE

RECOVER (on this and all the other Communicoding Cue Cards) refers to situations in which you're deep in dispute and unready to put Communicoding into action. You begin to recognize that this "No-you-didn't-yes-I-did" scene is time-wasting and counterproductive. How do you recover?

What's happening:
In decoding, the battle is triggered by your receiving a response that to you is illogical. The argument is over whether or not the other party satisfied your request. Either you've been shooting holes in the other party's response, or you've already written him or her off, or you've been continually repeating and explaining why the response didn't meet your request. At some point you realize that this could be a foreign response rather than an unsatisfactory one.

What to do:
First remove yourself from the skirmish. Excuse yourself for a few minutes—get a drink of water, go to the rest room. When you're alone, recite the decode slogan: "There's method in his/her madness." This will cue you to reset your brain so you can be surprised by the other party's brightness. Then go back to the other party and begin to decode. (See RESTART.)

If you're not ready to do this now, WAIT! Chill out: cool down for the day and defuse your feelings. If you proceed to decode too quickly, you risk making matters worse.

USING THE DECODE CUE CARD TO RESTART

RESTART, on all Communicoding Cue Cards, reminds you how to start a Communicoding process after you've cooled down. You can also use these cues to start the process immediately, if you've kept your reactions under control or defused your feelings on the spot.

What's happening:

You're ready to decode—to talk to the other party and discover the logic behind his or her response to your request.

What to do:

Begin with the prompt, "Clearly, you think you gave me what I wanted, but I don't see it. Can you explain what result you anticipated?" A statement like this is disarming and gives the other party an opportunity to put his or her thinking on the table. Then, verify your understanding. Remember, you're trying to crack a code. Your goal is to uncover the other party's logic. Make sure you've really done it.

USING THE DECODE CUE CARD TO PREVIEW

PREVIEW, on all Communicoding Cue Cards, tells you how to avoid disappointing surprises and thinking style clashes by exposing your thinking and the other party's in advance.

What's happening:

You suspect that you're working with a foreign thinker. You want to increase the odds of getting what you want. Or, if you're willing to be influenced, you want to solicit the other party's input now rather than after the fact.

What to do:

When you make your request, ask the other party to describe the end result he or she envisions—what a satisfactory response would look like. Asking this question allows you, in turn, to make clear what result you're looking for. You may need to refine your request to cue the other party more precisely. Or you may redesign your request, taking the other party's thinking into consideration.

DECODING: PRACTICE MAKES A PRO

The need to decode arises at times when you least expect it and often when you're under the most pressure. At such moments, it's difficult for your brain to register the possibility that the disappointing response may be the result of foreign thought. But, given time and practice, you'll find that it becomes easier to decode. More and more, you'll find yourself able to bypass the front of the Decode Cue Card and turn immediately to the back. More and more, you'll find yourself avoiding battles and dealing dispassionately with foreign thought.

Going through the decoding process lowers your resistance to foreign responses. The more often you can push aside your emotional reactions and decipher the logic of unexpected responses, the more often you'll be pleasantly surprised at the outcome. After a while you'll find yourself intrigued by a foreign response, curious to see how it possibly *does* do the trick.

ENCODING: CONFRONTING A SOLUTION YOU DON'T LIKE

Imagine: You have a problem that requires immediate attention. You've assigned it to a staff person you believe you can count on. He comes back and tells you how he handled the situation. You can't believe your ears. His solution bears no relation to what you expected him to do. Didn't he appreciate the severity of the problem? Was he deliberately trying to make you look bad?

But hold on—could this unsatisfying solution be the result of foreign thought rather than sabotage? Might it be more useful than you realize? How can you get your brain on the right track and find value in the unexpected solution?

Often you receive unsatisfactory solutions to problems that needed to be solved yesterday, not tomorrow. You're tempted to wonder why the other party is doing this to you. When you're under the gun, it's only natural to train your fire on the party who seems to have put you there. Pushing aside your mistrust is difficult, especially when the heat's on.

The Encode Cue Card can help you cool down.

ENCODE CUE CARD

ENCODE . . . Unsatisfying solutions

RECOVER: During battle

What's happening:
- You're unable to encode.
- Interferences at work: Jumping to What's Missing, Investigating the Motive, or Adding Priorities.

What to do:
- Get away for a few minutes.
- Say to yourself: "He/she has done his/her homework."
- Chill out. If cooled down, see RESTART. If not, wait a few hours or a day, then see RESTART.

(FRONT)

RESTART: After the fact

What's happening:
- You've received an unsatisfying solution.
- You're ready to encode to find the gain.

What to do:
- Say: "I think I'm missing something. How does this solution meet my priorities?"
- Get an example of how the solution would work.

PREVIEW: Before the fact

What's happening:
- You suspect you're dealing with a foreign thinker.
- You want to make sure your priorities are met.

What to do:
- Explicitly state your priorities.
- Ask: "How do you think this can be done? Can you explain the thinking behind your game plan?"

(BACK)

USING THE ENCODE CUE CARD TO RECOVER DURING BATTLE

What's happening:

You're in the middle of an "I'm right, you're wrong—no, I'm right, you're wrong" dispute. You entrusted someone with a problem—someone whose input you value. The solution you received took you totally by surprise. You're hung up on what's missing from the solution rather than what's there. Or you're adding priorities you hadn't made explicit. Or you're suspecting some misbegotten motive on the other party's part. Or all of the above. Could you be dealing with a foreign thinker? How do you RECOVER, stop the battle, and find out?

What to do:

It's imperative to get away for a moment. Do anything—to get a glass of water, go and pick up your messages. Find a quiet place to think, and take out your Encode Cue Card.

Reset your brain with the encode slogan: "This party has done his (or her) homework." The slogan jogs your brain into readiness to accept the central principle of encoding: that the solution does satisfy the priorities you've established.

Now go back and let the other party know you're ready to listen. You want to know how the solution meets your priorities.

But hold on! You've just been telling the other party everything that's wrong with the solution. Can you suddenly reverse yourself? If you feel ready to do so, see RESTART. If not, wait until you're cooled off.

USING THE ENCODE CUE CARD TO RESTART

What's happening:

You've received a solution that seems contrary to what you wanted. Either you've recovered your cool and are ready to encode, or you were able to avoid a flareup by keeping your reactions under control. You're open to the possibility that the solution is smarter than it appears.

What to do:

The key question, "How does your solution meet my priorities?" allows you to tap into the other party's mental processes. It enables you to determine whether you are, in fact, dealing with a foreign thinker. Restrain the impulse to rule out a foreign solution without a fair hearing. Remember, the value is in what's there, not in what's missing. It will be helpful to ask for an example of the way the solution might work.

USING THE ENCODE CUE CARD TO PREVIEW

What to do:

If you're looking for a particular type of solution, discuss not only *what* you want done but *how* you want it done. Ask the rationale behind the other party's game plan, since it may be foreign to you. Be sure to explicitly state your priorities rather than merely imply what you want accomplished. Don't assume that what's obvious to you is obvious to the other party.

You may decide, after PREVIEWing, that you still want the problem solved your way. Or you may see that the other party has an equally good or better way. You may decide to incorporate parts of both solutions. In any case, PREVIEWing will help you crystallize and refine your priorities so that you, as well as the other party, are clear about your expectations.

ENCODING: PRACTICE UNCOVERS NEW ROUTES

Encoding becomes easier with practice. When you're geared to see how the foreign solution meets your priorities, more often than not you'll discover that you don't have to go back to the drawing board. Encoding lowers your resistance to foreign solutions. In fact, you may start purposely assigning problems to opposite thinkers just to see what unusual angles they'll come up with!

RECODING: GAINING INFLUENCE WHEN IT COUNTS

Imagine: Your boss has given you a plum assignment. Rumor has it that the person who handles this one, and does it well, is headed for the top. Now it's your day in court—you and the boss are going to review your recommendation. You've done your homework so well that you're not even nervous. You're anticipating the words of praise you've clearly earned.

Twenty minutes later, you think you must have walked into the wrong office. The boss is ripping your findings to shreds. No matter how you restate and explain what you were trying to accomplish, he doesn't get it. You're going round and round, repeating the same points to no effect.

On instant replay number three, you suddenly realize that your boss may be a foreign thinker. How do you find out, and what can you do about it? Is there any way to turn this nightmare around?

The hardest part of recoding is accepting the fact that you've actually harmed the other party's agenda—what he or she wants done. Every fiber in your being is straining to prove how valuable, rather than how harmful, your suggestion is. The Recode Cue Card will get your head in gear.

RECODE CUE CARD

RECODE . . . Unrecognized contributions

RECOVER: During battle

What's happening:
- You're unable to recode.
- Interferences at work: Advocating Your Own Agenda, Reluctance to Disappoint, or Disrespecting the Foreign Agenda.

What to do:
- Get away for a few minutes. or find a way to drop the subject for the time being.
- Say to yourself: "Influence requires being influenced."
- Chill out: If cooled down, see RESTART. If not, wait until you're ready to hear what you've harmed.

(FRONT)

RESTART: After the fact

What's happening:
- Your idea has been rejected.
- You're ready to recode. You want to know how you've harmed the other party's agenda.

What to do:
- Ask: "How does my idea interfere with what you want?"
- Reshape your solution to protect what the other party wants and doesn't foresee.

PREVIEW: Before the fact

What's happening:
- You suspect you're dealing with a foreign thinker.
- You want to ensure that your idea will impress.

What to do:
- Ask: "What do you see as the critical issues?"
- Fit your suggestion to the other party's agenda.

(BACK)

USING THE RECODE CUE CARD TO RECOVER DURING BATTLE

What's happening:

You're so shocked at the other party's negative reaction to your idea that you hardly know what to say. You're spending too much time and effort pushing your agenda and little, if any, discovering the other party's agenda. If you're making any effort to follow the foreign agenda, it's only to pacify the other party. But it's not working. Stopping the battle and winning the war seem impossible.

What to do:

You need time to think. Ideally, try to get away for a few minutes. But this could be tricky, since the need to recode (as in our hypothetical example) generally arises when you're dealing with superiors. The best thing to do may be to find a way to drop the subject for the time being. For example, you could say, "Look, my idea has obviously disturbed you. Let me think about it and get back to you."

Then, chill out. Take a deep breath and say to yourself: "Influence requires being influenced." These words will remind you of the surprising fact about recoding: your suggestion actually threatens the other party's agenda. Thus *you* are the one who has to be influenced. Once reminded of this essential fact, you can let the other party show you the harm you've unwittingly caused. If ready to do so, see RESTART. If not, wait.

USING THE RECODE CUE CARD TO RESTART

What's happening:

You've managed to get hold of yourself or to restrain your natural inclination to defend yourself. You're ready to recode—to reapproach the other party and find out how you've harmed the foreign agenda and how you can protect it.

What to do:

Go back, look the other party straight in the eye, and say, "Clearly, I've missed the mark. Can you tell me how my idea interferes with what you want?" Once you understand what the other party wants to protect, you can reshape your idea to protect it—and also to protect against dangers he or she didn't foresee. Being able to safeguard the other party's agenda will demonstrate your value. This step-by-step Recode Checklist will remind you how.

RECODE CHECKLIST

Step 1	Did you ask how you harmed the other party's agenda?
Step 2	Do you agree on the harm you've done?
Step 3	Did you acknowledge your agreement to the other party?
Step 4	Did you look for any harm the other party may not have anticipated?
Step 5	Did you reshape your suggestion to protect what you've harmed and the dangers the other party didn't foresee?
Step 6	Did you verify with the other party the protection your reshaped suggestion has added?

USING THE RECODE CUE CARD TO PREVIEW

What's happening:

You'd naturally prefer to avoid having your suggestion rejected in the first place. You'd like to be instantly influential. You need to PREVIEW what's critical to the other party so you can frame your presentation accordingly.

What to do:

Try to determine the other party's thinking style. What's the foreign thinker's agenda (priority + critical directive)? How can you take this agenda into consideration in formulating your suggestion?

If the other party is assigning a task to you, try to get that party to spell out his or her agenda in advance. Remember, because the agenda is obvious to the foreigner, he or she probably won't think to be explicit unless you request it. Use the information to shape your suggestion. Then verify the protection you've added.

RECODING: PRACTICE PROMOTES YOU TO THE INNER CIRCLE

Recoding requires tremendous self-discipline. Your ideas have been summarily dismissed. You've worked hard on them, and you know they have value. It's hard to switch gears and focus on the harm they cause rather than the benefit they offer.

However, you'll find that each time you force yourself to do this—each time you reshape your ideas to protect the foreign agenda—your credibility will build. Instead of being seen as an immovable object, you'll establish a reputation as a quick study—someone who can listen to what's needed and *produce*.

TEAM THINK: MAXIMIZING BRAINPOWER

Imagine: Your department is making a presentation to senior management in two weeks. You are in charge of planning what will be presented. Your manager wants your ideas in three days. You try first one thing, then another. You're going around in circles. The tension is building. You know you're on the wrong track. Suddenly you remember Team Think. You certainly seem to be stuck! Should you seek a new slant from a foreign thinker?

No, your brain tells you. You can handle this. Just keep at it—you're bound to get somewhere. Bringing someone else up to speed—especially someone who thinks differently than you—will waste too much valuable time.

Then again, is it worth a try? The deadline is looming. Your Team Think Cue Card can help you find a way out of this blind alley.

USING THE TEAM THINK CUE CARD TO RECOVER DURING BATTLE WITH YOURSELF

What's happening:

Before you can start decoding, encoding, or recoding, you have to stop the battle with another party. Before you can start to Team Think, the battle you have to stop is with yourself.

You're stuck on an individual or departmental project. You're trying to solve the problem on your own or with like thinkers. You've made at least three distinct attempts or tried to solve the problem at least three different ways and have made no progress. Or you keep using the same methods over and over without success. Either you're trying to use acquired abilities that don't come easily to you, or you're trying to use your natural abilities to solve a problem that requires opposite abilities. Yet you won't admit to yourself that you need foreign help.

You need to rescue yourself from your internal battle. When you're fighting the idea of utilizing foreign input, you have to reverse the mental set that you can DO IT ALL. You must make yourself admit that foreign thinking is necessary.

What to do:

The Team Think slogan, "Two heads are better than one," will reset your brain so it's receptive to what a foreign thinker can provide. It will remind you of the central principle of Team Think: that opposite thinkers, together, can get further faster than alone.

Once your brain is in gear, find an opposite thinker—someone who knows the type of problem you're dealing with and may be able to give you a hand—and say something like this: "I'm working on a problem

TEAM THINK CUE CARD

TEAM THINK . . . When you're stuck

RECOVER: During battle

What's happening:
- You're unable to Team Think.
- Interferences at work: Believing Motion is Movement, Reluctance to Cry "Uncle," or "People Impede My Progress."

What to do:
- Say to yourself: "Two heads are better than one."
- Chill out: Ready yourself to receive something you've missed. When ready, find an opposite thinker and see RESTART.

(FRONT)

RESTART: After the fact

What's happening:
- You're stuck—having difficulty completing a task.
- You're ready to Team Think—to utilize what an opposite thinker foresees.

What to do:
- Ask: "What am I missing?"
- Write down what the foreign thinking provides and protects.
- Add and subtract, blending what's critical to both.

PREVIEW: Before the fact

What's happening:
- You're working with a foreign thinker.
- You want to ensure that the project benefits from both vertical and horizontal foresight.

What to do:
- Determine what each thinker can best provide.
- Elicit dangers and opportunities each thinker can foresee.
- Check end result for blend of vertical and horizontal thought.

(BACK)

and I'm stuck. I think you may be able to provide a different angle. Can you take a look at what I've been doing and give me your thoughts?"

Now that you've set the stage for Team Think, see RESTART.

USING THE TEAM THINK CUE CARD TO RESTART

What's happening:

You're stuck. Either you've put aside your interferences or you've promptly recognized your need for foreign input. It's time to Team Think—to look at your dilemma from a foreign perspective. You've enlisted an opposite thinker to supply ideas on what you've been missing.

What to do:

Look for what the other party's ideas provide and protect. In this situation, what does this party's critical directive tell him or her to do? Hearing the foreign thinker's ideas will trigger additional suggestions and modifications in your thinking. Go back and forth, blending and refining each other's contributions. As the Team Think solution reaches increasingly sophisticated levels, continue clarifying, adding, and subtracting until it becomes apparent how to most efficiently integrate both views to ensure that what's critical to each thinking style is protected.

USING THE TEAM THINK CUE CARD TO PREVIEW

When you use Team Think, you're virtually guaranteed better results than you can get working with one thinking style alone. So why wait until you're stuck? Think ahead! Plan in advance to get the best of both worlds—to integrate vertical and horizontal contributions for maximum efficiency.

What's happening:

You're anticipating the need for both vertical and horizontal input. You know there will be value in getting a clear road map of both kinds of issues. You want to save time and minimize effort by getting as many questions answered up front as possible. You want to avoid glitches and come up with a solution that all will recognize as a bull's-eye.

What to do:

In the planning phase, anticipate what each thinker in your group or on your committee can best provide. Be sure that what's obvious to the vertical thinkers is made obvious to the horizontals and vice versa.

Teaming Up: The Best of Both Worlds

Goal: Maximizing brainpower . . . blending vertical and horizontal contributions.
How to read this chart: The first column lists five key questions to be answered for any project. The next two columns tell what vertical and horizontal input typically provides. The fourth column summarizes the result of simply combining vertical and horizontal input. The last column shows the Team Think result, when the two contributions are blended for maximum efficiency.

Work at hand	*V provides*	*H provides*	*Combination*	*Blending for maximum efficiency*
What's the problem?	Clear view of most pressing problem	Clear view of underlying problem	Delineation of most pressing and underlying problems	Identification of most critical problem
What are our priorities?	Priorities based on current payoff	Priorities based on future payoffs	Priorities based on both current and future payoffs	Priorities based on most relevant payoffs
What can be done?	Workable alternatives that eliminate steps	Workable alternatives that add impact	Workable alternative that excludes steps and includes impact	The most doable solution
How can it be done?	Way to eliminate immediate danger	Way to eliminate long-term danger	Way to eliminate short- and long-term danger	Safest and fastest route
What can we learn from the result?	Shortcuts to removing problems	Shortcuts to preventing problems	Shortcuts to removing and preventing problems	Methods for earlier detection and prevention of problems

Both parts of the vertical and horizontal agendas—the priority and the two critical directives—are needed to get a complete picture. The last step is to integrate the vertically driven and horizontally driven solutions into a final, improved end product. The end product should incorporate those critical elements of both recommendations in the most efficient way.

Our chart, "Teaming Up: The Best of Both Worlds," can help direct the process and also can serve as a final checklist of the end product.

TEAM THINK: PRACTICE PROMOTES PARTICIPATION

It's hard to overcome the notion that you can do everything equally well—that getting foreign help reflects negatively on your competence or will slow you down. Going through the Team Think process lowers your resistance to collaborative ventures. The results you achieve will be your best incentive. The more you partake of Team Think, especially when the stakes are high, the more you'll want to repeat the experience. In fact, when working alone after having successfully experienced Team Think, you'll find yourself wondering what simpler, speedier, or superior solutions you would have been able to develop with foreign thinkers. Whether stuck or not, you'll increasingly find yourself looking for every opportunity to seek out opposite thinking.

OUR FINAL WORD

We debated about different ways to end this book, to leave you with the most lasting impression. We sifted through dozens of testimonials and anecdotes from satisfied clients. Then, while we were in the midst of writing *Communicoding,* one of our clients told us something that, to us, said it all.

This man, who is in his mid-fifties, is a founding partner of a specialized international consulting firm. After using Communicoding for a short time, he declared that he now understood why he was still working so hard while a peer ran his businesses from the Bahamas: "My friend somehow learned long ago to respect and benefit from opposite thinking. He utilizes the differences he sees in others extremely well. He's not smarter or more diligent than I am—just more able to see the smartness of others."

We've given you the tools to use Communicoding wherever and whenever the need arises. As the saying goes, a book is no book at all unless, when you come to the last page, it goes on within you. That is our hope for you and your experience with Communicoding.

Selected Bibliography

Ken Auletta. *Greed and Glory on Wall Street: The Fall of the House of Lehman.* New York: Warner Books, 1986.

Beryl Lieff Benderly. *The Myth of Two Minds: What Gender Means and Doesn't Mean.* New York: Doubleday, 1987.

Alan Brownsword. *It Takes All Types.* San Anselmo, California: Baytree Publications Co., 1987.

David Campbell, Ph.D. *Take the Road to Creativity and Get Off Your Dead End.* Allen, Texas: Argus Communications, 1977.

Frank V. Cespedes, Stephen X. Doyle, and Robert J. Freedman. "Teamwork for Today's Selling." Harvard Business Review, March–April 1989, pp. 44–58.

Cho Chikun. *The Magic of Go.* Tokyo: The Ishi Press, Inc., 1988.

Robert C. Christopher. *The Japanese Mind: The Goliath Explained.* New York: Linden Press/Simon & Schuster, 1983.

Donald K. Clifford, Jr. and Richard E. Cavanagh. *The Winning Performance: How America's High-Growth and Mid-Size Companies Succeed.* New York: Bantam Books, 1988.

Allan Cox. *The Cox Report on the American Corporation.* New York: Delacorte Press, 1972.

Terrence Deal and Allan A. Kennedy. *Corporate Culture.* New York: Addison-Wesley, 1982.

Edward de Bono. *de Bono's Thinking Course.* New York: Facts on File Publications, 1985.

Edward de Bono. *Lateral Thinking.* New York: Harper & Row, 1970.

Edward de Bono. *New Think.* New York: Avon Books, 1968.

Peter F. Drucker. *Drucker, The Executive.* London: Pan Books, 1967.

Riane Eisler. *The Chalice & the Blade.* San Francisco: Harper & Row, 1987.

Joseph J. Fucini and Suzy Fucini. *Entrepreneurs: The Men and Women behind Famous Brand Names and How They Made It.* Boston: G. K. Hall & Co., 1985.

W. Timothy Gallwey. *The Inner Game of Tennis.* New York: Random House, 1974.

Charles Garfield. *Peak Performers.* New York: William Morrow and Company, 1986.

Ben Heirs with Peter Farrell. *The Professional Decision Thinker.* New York: Dodd, Mead & Company, 1987.

Ben Heirs and Gordon Pehrson. *The Mind of the Organization.* New York: Harper & Row, 1977.

Morton Hunt. *The Universe Within: A New Science Explores the Human Mind.* New York: Simon & Schuster, 1982.

David Keirsey and Marilyn Bates. *Please Understand Me.* Del Mar, California: Prometheus Nemesis, 1978.

Harold Koontz and Cyril O'Donnell. *Management: A Systems and Contingency Analysis of Managerial Functions.* New York: McGraw-Hill, 1976.

Andrew Kupfer. "Bob Allen Rattles the Cages at AT&T." Fortune, June 19, 1989, pp. 58–61.

Kenneth Labich. "The Seven Keys to Business Leadership." Fortune, October 24, 1988, pp. 58–66.

Harry Levinson and Stuart Rosenthal. *CEO: Corporate Leadership in Action.* New York: Basic Books, Inc., 1984.

Dudley Lynch. *Your High-Performance Business Brain.* Englewood Cliffs, New Jersey: Prentice-Hall, 1984.

Regis McKenna. *The Regis Touch.* Reading, Massachusetts: Addison-Wesley Publishing, 1985.

Ira Magaziner and Mark Patinkin. *The Silent War: Inside the Global Business Battles.* New York: Random House, 1989.

Ian I. Mitroff. *Break-Away Thinking.* New York: John Wiley & Sons, 1988.

Isabel Briggs Myers and Mary H. McCaulley. *Manual: A Guide to the Development and Use of the Myers-Briggs Type Indicator.* Palo Alto, California: Consulting Psychologists Press, Inc., 1985.

P. Ranganath Nayak, Ph.D. and John M. Ketteringhan, Ph.D. *Break-throughs! How the Vision and Drive of Innovators in Sixteen Companies Created Commercial Break-throughs that Swept the World.* New York: Rawson Assoc., 1986.

Roger Von Oech, Ph.D. *A Whack on the Side of the Head.* New York: Warner Books, 1983.

Charles Panati. *Extraordinary Origins of Everyday Things.* New York: Harper & Row, 1987.

Thomas J. Peters and Robert H. Watterman, Jr. *In Search of Excellence.* New York: Harper & Row, 1982.

Michael E. Porter. *Competitive Advantage.* New York: The Free Press, 1985.

Michael J. Prietula and Herbert A. Simon. "The Experts in Your Midst." Harvard Business Review, January–February 1989, pp. 120–124.

Sally P. Springer and Georg Deutsch. *Left Brain, Right Brain.* New York: W. H. Freeman and Company, 1985.

Robert J. Sternberg. *Beyond IQ.* New York: Cambridge University Press, 1985.

Robert J. Sternberg. *The Triarchic Mind: A New Theory of Human Intelligence.* New York: Viking, 1988.

Robert Wright. *Three Scientists and Their Gods: Looking for Meaning in an Age of Information.* New York: Times Books, 1988.